Tolley's
Tax Practice Management

First Edition

by

Sarah Deeks LLB FCA

Tolley Publishing

Published by
Tolley
2 Addiscombe Road
Croydon
Surrey
CR9 5AF
020 8686 9141

Typeset in Great Britain by
Action Publishing Technology, Gloucester

Printed and bound in Great Britain
by
Redwood Books Ltd

ISBN 0 75450 470 0

Preface

This is the first edition of *Tolley's Tax Practice Management*. It offers comprehensive guidance on all aspects of the operation and management of a tax practice. It is of particular relevance for those setting up a firm for the first time or who run a tax department. The book includes numerous checklists and resources for use by practitioners but it is not intended to be a tax compliance manual. Rather it is designed to complement such manuals by considering the client care and management issues.

Comments and suggestions for improvements in future editions are always welcome.

TOLLEY PUBLISHING

Author's note

The aim of this book is not to teach experienced tax practitioners what they already know. Rather it collects in one place all the topics that tax practices should consider in their day-to-day operations. It is designed to provide training to newly qualified staff, guidance to those considering a career change and inspiration for the jaded.

The suggestions in this book are not intended to be prescriptive because the implementation of procedures in any firm depends on its clients, work and size. The book is designed to provide a framework within which a tax practice can operate. For the majority of the subjects covered there is always more than one way of achieving the same goal. I have tried to strike a balance between best practice, legal and ethical requirements and risk management on the one hand, whilst maximising profit and minimising stress and unproductive bureaucracy on the other.

I wish that I had been given this book at the start of my professional career – it would have saved me a lot of time and effort, and provided me with information that it took me years to learn.

I would like to thank Martin Bell BA for his support and advice throughout the project.

Sarah Deeks LLB FCA

Contents

Chapter 1

Introduction: Getting Started

A holistic approach

1.1 *Tax Practice Management*, as its name suggests, is about the management of a tax practice. This book tailors good management techniques specifically to the needs of tax practitioners.

Running a successful tax practice involves more than delivering an excellent tax service. It requires a combination of client care, good communication skills, strategic thought, marketing, quality control and ethical behaviour. All of these are vital to the success of any business and tax practice is no exception. Part I of the book considers the client issues. The tax service itself is considered in Part II. The context in which the service is offered, namely the office environment and the structure and regulation of the firm, is dealt with in Parts III and IV.

1.2 Each subject covered in the book is connected with the others and a weakness in one area can cause problems throughout the practice. For example, poor communication with clients about their tax affairs may lead to a lack of appreciation of the nature and quality of work the firm undertakes. This may in turn cause fee resistance and lead to complaints. It will prevent clients recommending other work or requesting additional services. The inability to retain clients or recover fees will make it difficult for the firm to reward its partners and staff well, pay for the latest technology or good training. This may cause demotivation, leading to a lack of attention to detail and client care.

How to use this book

1.3 *Tax Practice Management* can be used on many different levels. It is relevant to sole practitioners, partners and staff working in the tax field and in particular to those who are:

- thinking about setting up a tax practice for the first time;
- joining a tax practice as a partner or manager;
- already running a tax practice but who want to run it more efficiently or to re-evaluate certain aspects of themselves or the firm;

- looking for career progression, for example as head of the tax department;
- interested in keeping up with the latest ideas;
- retiring from practice and setting up as a tax consultant;
- students interested in tax or general practice;
- administration staff employed by tax practices.

1.4 The book also has a wider application. Parts of it can be used to provide value-added strategic and business advice to clients operating in other professions and service industries. Before getting involved in the day-to-day detail of running a tax practice it is important to formulate a practice strategy.

Formulating a strategy

1.5 Devising a strategy for a tax practice involves asking searching questions. The level at which this needs to be done depends on whether you are already running a tax practice or just setting out.

Starting a new practice

1.6 If you are thinking about setting up a tax practice for the first time you need to be sure that you are temperamentally suited to running your own practice. Answer the following questions.

- Can you set your own goals and follow them?
- Can you work on your own and get a job done?
- Do you like to solve problems?
- Do you like to work with people?
- Are you a good communicator?
- Do you have professionalism, honesty and integrity?
- Can you cope with change?
- Are you financially motivated?

If you cannot answer 'yes' to at least half of the questions, you should probably think again. Assuming you can, ask yourself the following detailed questions about the tax practice you envisage running.

- What sort of clients do I want?
- Where will I get the clients from?
- What type of tax work do I want to do?

- What tax skills do I have, for example, compliance, planning, consultancy?
- Do I have the necessary qualifications and experience?
- What are my personal strengths and weaknesses, for example, diplomacy, communication, decision-making?
- Who are my competitors?
- How do I want to work, alone or with others?
- How much of the time do I want to work?
- Is it the right time to set up a tax practice?
- How much money do I want to make?
- Will the practice be profitable?
- Do I have sufficient savings or financial resources to set up the practice?
- Do I have any specific aims or philosophy?
- Do my family support me?
- Is it my idea of a perfect job?

Finally, see whether your answers to the following questions are compatible with running a tax practice.

- What do you see yourself doing next year, in five years and in ten years?
- What do you like doing best/least at work?
- What do you like doing best/least at home?

There are no right or wrong answers. However, if you want to be retired in two years' time, or you are someone who likes to start new projects but gets bored after a short period, tax practice may not be for you.

1.7 If you have got this far and you still want to set up a tax practice, you should now decide how to get started. This will vary according to the opportunities that present themselves and your personality. Some people will test the water by starting part time or on a small scale and then if they like it expand the practice. Others will jump in feet first.

1.8 Tax practices do not always see themselves as businesses but they should and, like any new business venture, formulating a practice plan is essential. The plan should consider short and long-term goals and set out ways to achieve them. The plan will help to clarify your ideas and minimise the risk of making costly mistakes. *Tolley's Tax Practice Management* takes you through each subject in a logical order. In particular you will need to consider the following issues.

- Attracting, keeping and dealing with clients (see Chapters 2, 4 and 5).
- How much to charge them (see Chapter 3).
- The type of work you will undertake (see Chapters 7 to 10).
- How many employees you will need (see Chapter 12).
- Where to set up an office (see Chapter 14).
- What equipment you will need (see Chapters 13 and 14).
- Risk management and insurance (see Chapter 16).
- Whether to set up a practice from scratch or to buy an existing practice (see Chapter 17).
- Whether to operate as a sole trader or have partners (see Chapter 17).
- Financing and accounting issues (see Chapter 18).
- Your reward (see Chapter 19).
- Notifying all the relevant agencies including professional bodies, Financial Services registration and the Inland Revenue (see Chapter 20).

Evaluating an existing practice

1.9 If you already have a tax practice the questions you need to ask should be more evaluative to assess the firm's strengths and weaknesses. The issues set out below will help you to focus on the important issues. Each partner and key member of staff should rate the following points on a scale of 1 to 5 (1 means that you are completely happy, 5 means that you are very unhappy). How satisfied are you with the following aspects of your work?

1. Client relationships (see Part I).
2. Tax authorities, regulation and legislation changes (see Part II and Chapter 20).
3. Fees, reward, remuneration and risk (see Chapters 3, 12, 16, 18 and 19).
4. Relationships with colleagues (staff and partners) (see Chapters 12, 17 and 19).
5. The public perception of the firm (see Chapter 5).
6. Competition from other tax providers and structural changes in the tax world such as mergers and new technology (see Chapters 5, 13 and 17).
7. The interaction with other aspects of life (family, social, physical) (see Chapters 12 and 19).

8. Your personal development and career progression (see Chapters 12, 17 and 22).
9. The quality of the work produced by the firm (see Part II and Chapter 15).
10. The work environment (see Chapter 14).

1.10 The answers to the questions can be analysed on an individual level and for the whole practice. An individual score of more than 30 indicates that the person is unhappy with their work. They may need to consider whether they are suited to tax practice. An isolated 4 or 5 highlights a particular problem requiring attention. Reference should then be made to the relevant sections of the book indicated above.

1.11 Where several people in the practice answer the questions and more than 25 per cent of the scores are above 30, this may be indicative of firm-wide problems. Average scores for individual questions above 3 should also be investigated.

1.12 The results of the exercise will help the firm to focus on the areas which require change and consequently to draw up a strategic plan for the practice. The plan should involve action but above all it should be interesting and innovative. It should challenge the practice to ask 'how are you going to keep clients coming back for more and staff and partners motivated?'.

Keeping tax in perspective

1.13 Finally, a word of warning about taking tax too seriously. It is easy to lose perspective about a subject which you are closely involved with day to day and it can assume an undue importance. As a tax practitioner tax is inevitably more important in your life than for your clients. As far as they are concerned tax should be just one relatively minor aspect of life. If you remember this it will help you to provide clients with advice that they will listen to and accept.

Part I – Clients

Chapter 2

New Clients

2.1 A prospective new client is always exciting but before agreeing to act the practice should ask whether the client is right for the firm and whether the firm is appropriate for the client. Too many advisors do not turn away work; they think that any work is good work. If the tax practice has a new business strategy it will know the type and size of client it wants. Saying 'yes' or 'no' to the work is then easy.

This chapter considers the issues involved with acting for a new client, including:

- winning new work;
- assessing risk;
- taking on new clients;
- engagement letters;
- developing the client relationship.

Winning new clients

2.2 New clients come from many sources. They are most likely to be recommended to the firm by another client or professional acquaintance. A few will contact the firm in response to a specific marketing initiative (see Chapter 5). Some new clients will never have had a previous advisor; others will already be represented by another practice.

Regardless of why the prospective client has contacted the firm or their background, it is essential to make their first impressions count. They should feel welcome and at ease. Staff should be trained to ensure that a prospective new client is referred to the appropriate person within the firm. Enthusiasm for them and their business combined with a first-class service from the outset are vital to securing the new work.

2.3 If, having spoken to the prospective client or lead, the firm decides that an initial meeting is appropriate, this should be arranged. Maps, travel instructions and an introductory brochure should be sent so that the prospective client knows how to find the firm and something about what it can offer prior to the meeting. Alternatively, the client could be referred to the firm's website for details. For further details about brochures and marketing materials see 5.22.

2.4 The initial meeting is important and may be highly valuable to both parties. The meeting is not only an opportunity to sell the practice to the client and obtain essential information but to find out what services the client wants, to identify areas of immediate concern and set an agenda for the work to be undertaken. It is customary to offer clients an initial meeting free of charge but care must be taken to allow for the cost of free meetings in the firm's charging structure.

2.5 The practice will need to decide which partner or manager is best to conduct the initial meeting based on the initial perception of the client's needs. Two people may need to be present depending on the complexity of the case. Some partners are better than others at obtaining new work and winning over clients for the firm.

2.6 Before agreeing to act for any new client, the practitioner should talk to them about their plans, ambitions and their past. If they are changing firms, the advisor should try to find out why, as well as to understand their future expectations and how the practice matches up to their requirements. The advisor should try to get a feel for the person. Are they easy to deal with? Is there an immediate rapport? Most importantly, the practitioner should trust their instinct and not act if they have any doubts. It is far easier to decline to act at this stage than later.

A first meeting agenda to help the firm focus on the essential issues is included in Appendix 2:1.

Risk assessment

2.7 Before accepting an appointment the firm should assess the risk associated with working for the client. The outcome may affect whether the firm accepts the engagement. It will also provide useful information to set appropriate fee rates and allocate suitable staff (see 3.13 and 12.35).

2.8 High risk clients include those which:

- are owned or controlled by a more significant company;
- have outside shareholders;
- are part of a complex group;
- operate in problem industries (for example, the construction industry, banking or insurance);
- have high profits and large tax liabilities;

- have complex remuneration packages and share schemes;
- have complicated trusts;
- have overseas transactions;
- have dominant, aggressive or disreputable owners or directors;
- have directors with numerous other directorships or businesses not all of which are dealt with by the firm;
- are high profile or controversial;
- have a history of litigation;
- are commercially significant for the firm.

2.9 If the overall risk assessment is high a more detailed review should be undertaken. Even if the risk is assessed as medium a further review of the risk areas should be considered. If the fee is low and the risk is high the client is probably not worth taking on unless there are other exceptional factors.

Taking on new clients

2.10 In accepting a tax appointment it is essential that the firm should behave with honesty and integrity. In particular, the firm should assess whether there are any independence or conflict of interest issues and whether the firm has the skills and resources to perform the work the client requires. Advisors should refer to their appropriate professional body for further details. For more details on ethics see 20.2.

2.11 If the firm is interested in acting for the client the following procedures will need to be undertaken after the initial meeting to minimise the risk of the relationship going wrong.

- Write to the previous advisor (see 2.15).
- Send a letter to the client thanking him or her for the meeting and advising them what will happen next.
- Obtain credit references from an agency.
- For corporate clients obtain a company search.
- Discreetly discuss the client with any mutual acquaintances, for example, bankers or solicitors. It is, however, vital to preserve client confidentiality.

2.12 In partnerships, the agreement of more than one partner should be obtained to the appointment, particularly if the risk assessment is high.

2.13 If the client has been recommended to the firm by another client or professional contact be sure to thank them as quickly as possible.

2.14 *New Clients*

Make it clear that similar recommendations are always welcome.

If the new client has had no previous advisor

2.14 If the new client has had no previous advisor all necessary information will have to be obtained directly from the client. The firm should advise the client at the first opportunity of the extent to which the lack of documentation limits the advice they can give or otherwise inhibits their work.

Taking clients from other tax practitioners

2.15 It will often be the case that the client will have had a previous advisor. The client should be made aware at the initial meeting that it will be necessary for the firm to contact the previous advisor. The client should be requested to advise the outgoing firm of the change of appointment, settle any outstanding fees and authorise them to pass over all relevant information.

2.16 The new firm should then contact the outgoing advisors to ensure that there are no circumstances concerning the appointment that the firm should be made aware of. In making the contact, compliance with the etiquette rules of the advisor's professional body is essential.

2.17 The firm will not be able to act for the client until consent is received. If there is an 'emergency', for example, a vital deadline is about to expire, it may be acceptable to start work before consent is received. In this case the firm should telephone, fax or e-mail the outgoing advisor.

2.18 It is usual to request information from the previous advisor so that the new firm can act with minimum inconvenience to the client. In doing so the outgoing advisor's position should be respected and requests for information should be appropriate and reasonable. If the client already holds the information there is usually no need to request it from the advisor.

A specimen letter to an outgoing advisor is included in Appendix 2:2.

Problems arising from the previous appointment

2.19 If the outgoing advisor draws to the new firm's notice any matter concerning the appointment, it must be taken seriously. Problems may include tax irregularities or unpaid bills. Sometimes the client will refuse permission for the old advisors to disclose relevant information.

2.20 In such circumstances it is likely that the new firm will decline to act. The commercial risk of accepting the work may be too great.

However, the existence of problems does not necessarily prohibit the firm from acting provided that:

- the client makes full disclosure of the relevant matter to the new firm and supplies it with the necessary information to resolve matters as soon as possible;
- the firm advises the client of the action necessary to correct the problem and the cost in tax, penalties, interest and fees;
- the firm warns the client of the civil and criminal consequences of not correcting the matter.

Action required after receiving consent from the previous advisors

2.21 After the consent from the previous advisors has been received it is important to start work on the new client's affairs quickly so that the relationship gets off to a constructive start. It is vital to communicate clearly in the early stages of the relationship. This may help to restore the client's confidence in professional advisors if it has been damaged in the past.

2.22 The following procedures will need to be undertaken after receiving the outgoing advisor's consent, if the firm has decided to act for the client:

- allocate appropriate staff and departments to handle the case;
- issue an engagement letter as soon as possible and before commencing work (see 2.24);
- submit the Form 64-8 to the Inland Revenue;
- send a letter of authority signed by the client to his or her stockbrokers, bankers etc. authorising them to disclose information direct to the firm;
- deal with any immediate work requirements;
- set up client files (permanent, current and correspondence);
- set up practice management, work in progress and billing records;
- set up tax records on the computer system;
- inform all partners and staff of the new appointment to avoid conflicts of interest and to celebrate the new work.

Joint appointments

2.23 Sometimes a taxpayer will use two firms of tax advisors. For example, a capital gains tax, VAT or investigation specialist may be engaged in addition to the advisor dealing with more routine matters.

2.24 *New Clients*

The specialist will often be recommended by the principal firm. If they are not, then whilst the original advisor's consent to the appointment is not necessarily required if the scope of the specialist engagement is beyond that offered by the existing firm, it is professionally courteous for the specialist to notify the existing firm of the work that they will be undertaking. This ensures that all parties are aware of who is doing what work and where the responsibilities lie.

Engagement letters

2.24 Once the firm has decided to act it is good practice to send the client an engagement letter. It may prove to be a useful defence in the event of a claim being made against the firm.

Engagement letters have two main purposes. First, they are issued to inform clients of the basis of charging fees in relation to professional tax work, and secondly, to limit the firm's liability in relation to that work. Many clients have the mistaken belief that if they appoint a tax advisor they are no longer responsible for their tax affairs.

2.25 Engagement letters are also required for the purposes of investment business. The provision of these services can be combined with the tax engagement letter where the investment advice is an integral part of the tax service (see 20.16). This may enable the firm to send clients a shorter investment business engagement letter than would otherwise be the case. Where the firm is not authorised under the *Financial Services Act 1986*, the engagement letter should make it clear that the firm is not eligible to carry out investment business activities.

2.26 The engagement terms can be included in a separate document with a covering letter for ease of updating. The client must sign the letter and return a copy of it to the firm. The firm should not start work until the signed letter has been returned. The letter should be filed on the tax permanent file or on a central master file of engagement letters. In the latter case it is recommended that a copy also be placed on the permanent file. The firm should keep a master list of all clients recording when engagement letters are issued, updated and returned. A member of staff should review the list periodically and chase up any outstanding letters.

2.27 Separate engagement letters should be sent to each client to whom a service is provided, including a husband and wife, a company and its directors and a partnership and its partners (see 2.33). It is also unlikely that all the issues relating to a client's personal affairs can be successfully incorporated in a corporate engagement letter, particularly with regard to investment business. For groups of companies one engagement letter to the parent company may suffice, provided that the letter refers to all the companies covered by the letter and the parent company has the authority to bind all the members of the group.

2.28 Engagement letters should be clear, simple and unambiguous. They should:

- identify the terms of the engagement;
- define the tasks to be undertaken and the duties of the advisor;
- detail those services which are excluded;
- define the client's responsibilities;
- specify the limitations on the work to be undertaken;
- refer to the quality of the service and the complaints procedure;
- detail the fee arrangements;
- cover investment business.

2.29 The letter should cover the entire range of services which the client is likely to require including VAT and PAYE.

2.30 It is important that clients understand engagement letters. They should be written in plain English but all the relevant details need to be included to protect the advisor. If an advisor is aware from the information they have obtained about the client that he or she does not respond well to letters or may have difficulty in understanding them, it may be appropriate to summarise the contents verbally to ensure that the client knows what they are signing.

2.31 Engagement letters should be regularly reviewed for changes in law and practice, for example, corporate self-assessment, and updated as necessary. Some firms have a policy of sending new letters with the tax return each year. If the firm believes that the client will respond badly to an updated engagement letter sent by post they should present it to the client in a meeting.

2.32 Some firms include limits on the firm's liability in their engagement letters. For example, the extent of the liability may be specified as a multiple of the fee charged. The legality and efficacy of such clauses could, however, be challenged as an unfair contract term. 'Hold harmless' clauses should also be considered.

2.33 A specimen personal tax engagement letter is included in Appendix 2:3. Practitioners should also refer to Tax 14/97 'Engagement Letters for Tax Practitioners' published by the Tax Faculty of the Institute of Chartered Accountants in England and Wales. Members of other institutes should refer to their professional body for guidance.

See 6.29 for details about disengagement letters.

Developing the client relationship

2.34 Possessing a detailed knowledge about a client's affairs and the personality of its key personnel makes it easier to act for them, to sell them appropriate services and to communicate in the most appropriate way (see also Chapters 4 and 5). This information is best obtained at the outset of the engagement. It should be recorded on a new client information sheet. A specimen new client form is included in Appendix 2:4.

Aspects of a client's personality to consider when accepting an appointment include the following.

Character and reputation

2.35 It will do a tax practice no good to be associated with clients who are disreputable. This might include clients:

- with a criminal record;
- who are excessively litigious;
- who are subject to consumer complaints;
- where there is a high degree of media interest;
- where there is a succession of companies and liquidations (so-called phoenix companies);
- who are generally believed to be involved in sharp practice.

Personal situation

2.36 Advisors should take into account a client's personal situation. For some clients, submitting their tax return or listening to tax advice may not be the most important thing in their life. Understanding this will assist the firm to give appropriate advice and to present it in an acceptable way. The advisor should consider whether clients:

- have trouble reading, writing or with numbers;
- have alcohol, drug or gambling addictions;
- are sick;
- suffer from depression or mental illness;
- have stresses in their life caused by being a single parent or looking after sick or elderly relatives.

2.37 Tax advisors should respect a client's view of the world and take into consideration their culture, race and religion. This may, for example, affect the type of investment they are prepared to undertake. They should also bear in mind a client's age. Some older people still find discussing their financial affairs on a par with other traditionally taboo subjects such as sex, politics or religion.

Positive or negative

2.38 An advisor should try to understand whether a client is primarily a positive or negative person since this will help the firm to provide tax advice that they will listen to. Positive people radiate energy and good humour and they are easy going. They generally take advice when it is presented in a positive way. For example, they will complete their tax returns because instinctively they feel it is right to do so.

2.39 Negative people can be draining and hard work. They deal with their tax return because they fear what will happen if the Inland Revenue catches up with them. They respond better to threats and warnings.

Risk taker or cautious

2.40 Advisors should know their clients' attitude to risk. This will depend on whether the client has a positive or negative outlook and whether they are an optimist or pessimist. Understanding this is vital to offering good advice. It may, for example, affect whether a client who is considering investing in a company wants to take shares or loans. It is of particular relevance when offering investment business advice (see 20.31).

Fears

2.41 Advisors should understand and empathise with their clients' fears. Many people find dealing with their tax and financial affairs extremely stressful and are fearful of numbers and authority (both accountants and the Inland Revenue).

Communication

2.42 Does the client respond better to letters, telephone calls, e-mail or by meeting regularly? Understanding this will improve communication and cut out wasteful and ineffective correspondence. Noting which method of communication clients prefer on the new client form is as important as noting the tax office. Communicating with clients in a way that they find easiest increases the chance of a successful relationship.

2.43 Practitioners can find out how clients prefer to communicate by asking them outright in an initial meeting. They can also observe how the client usually communicates with the firm. Monitoring the language clients use can also give useful indications. Clients generally fall into one of the following three categories.

- There are those who are visually orientated – they are happy to correspond by letter, fax or e-mail as they absorb information visually. They may use phrases like '*looks* good to me', '*focus* on', '*appears* to me', 'in *view* of' and '*see* you soon'.
- Some clients take in information aurally. They will respond better to telephone calls. They usually telephone and rarely write. They may use phrases such as '*sounds* good', '*speak* to you soon', '*discuss* it with you' and '*tell* you'.
- Some clients respond better to situations where they participate. These clients prefer meetings and like to take notes. They may use the following phrases: 'get a *feel* for', 'get a *hold* of', 'get to *grips* with' and '*handle* my tax'.

Quick review

2.44

- Procedures should be in place so that all new clients are treated well and efficiently from the outset.
- For larger appointments, the partner may wish to visit the centre of operations to obtain a better feel for the client before agreeing to the appointment.
- Before taking on new work assess the risk of acting for that client. Doing so may prevent bad publicity and future problems.
- Make sure that new clients understand the role of a tax advisor and the extent to which the relationship is governed by professional ethics.
- Engagement letters are vital for limiting the firm's liability. Firms should ensure that their procedures guarantee that all clients receive them, including company directors and partners for whom personal tax services are provided.
- Separate engagement letters should be issued for one-off assignments, for example, tax investigations, share valuations and corporate finance work.
- The *Contracts (Rights of Third Parties) Act 1999* applies to contracts entered into on or after 11 May 2000. It gives clearer rights to third parties to enforce contract terms which purport to confer a benefit on them. As a result engagement terms should be reviewed carefully to ensure that rights are not given unintentionally to third parties. The best way to do this is to state in the firm's engagement letter that no person who is not a party to the contract shall have any right to enforce any part of it. Appropriate disclaimers should continue to be given in letters and reports where appropriate.
- Understanding more about clients than simply their tax affairs can

improve client relations and help advisors to develop a rapport with them.

- Thank those introducing work to the firm. They are often a vital source of new clients and a tax practice's best marketing tool.

Appendix 2:1

First Meeting Agenda

Client name   Date

Completed by

1. Ascertain as much as possible about the client. Consider the following.

- Do they seem easy to deal with and open?
- Are they reluctant to discuss certain issues?
- Have they had several previous advisors?
- Why do they want to change?
- Is there a history of failed ventures?
- Are they interested in your opinion or only their own?
- Are they respectful?
- Do they expect you to achieve the impossible?
- Are they ambitious?
- Do they know what they want in the future?

2. Ascertain the client's immediate requirements for:

- income tax;
- corporation tax;
- PAYE;
- VAT;
- other.

Establish the stage of completion of any work currently in hand and the date that the firm will be required to act from. Advise the client of any immediate problems.

3. Find out what future work the client requires for:

- inheritance tax;
- trusts;
- general tax planning;
- capital gains tax planning;
- financial services;
- other consultancy advice.

4. What does the client want from the relationship? What problems do they have? What issues are they concerned about?
5. Discuss fees and charges. Give the client a menu card, brochures or leaflets as appropriate.
6. Complete the new client form (see Appendix 2:4). Make an assessment of risk (see 2.7).
7. Ascertain details of previous advisors. Advise the client of the procedure for changing advisors (see 2.15) and discuss the engagement letter.
8. Complete any relevant forms including 64-8 etc.
9. Complete authority for banks, building societies and brokers.
10. Find out who recommended the client to the firm.
11. Verbally summarise what the firm and the client have agreed to do following the meeting.

Specimen Letter to the Outgoing Advisor for a Self-Employed Individual

Dear Sir/Madam

Mr M C Brown (Trading as MCB)

We have been approached by Mr Brown to act as his tax and financial advisors.

We should be grateful if you would provide us with all the information necessary for us to decide whether or not we may properly accept this appointment.

Assuming that you possess no information which would lead us to decline the appointment we should be grateful if you would supply us with the following information which you have created or hold as agent for Mr Brown.

1. A copy of the last accounts.
2. The trial balance [at the last year end] together with copies of lead schedules, bank, sales ledger, purchase ledger and [other] reconciliations.
3. Details of any adjustments made to the accounting records that are not apparent from the accounts themselves or the accounting records.
4. Details of private use adjustments and estimates.
5. A copy of the last tax computation and capital allowances claim.
6. A copy of the last tax return submitted together with accompanying schedules and disclosures.
7. A copy of the last tax calculation working sheet.
8. A copy of the latest taxpayer statement of account.
9. Details of any correspondence with the Inland Revenue in the last twelve months.
10. Details of any losses.
11. Details of any claims or elections currently in force.

12. All relevant capital gains tax histories.
13. Details of any inheritance tax lifetime gifts.
14. Details of pension relief due and claimed for the last six years.
15. PAYE or VAT records.
16. Any of Mr Brown's original records or vouchers.
17. Any other information relevant to a smooth transition of Mr Brown's affairs.

Thank you for your assistance in this matter. If it is more convenient for us to collect this information please contact us.

Yours faithfully

A Firm

Specimen Engagement Letter – Personal Tax (Not Self-Employed)

The letter will require amendment as appropriate for partnerships, Lloyd's Underwriters and trust cases. A different letter will be required for corporate clients.

Dear Client

Engagement terms

You have asked the firm to act as your taxation advisors and we have accepted the appointment. The purpose of this letter is to set out the basis on which we will work for you and our respective responsibilities with regard to your tax and financial affairs.

1. Tax returns

- We will prepare your personal/partnership/trust tax return commencing with the return for the year ended 5 April .... In undertaking work on your affairs we may use both qualified and unqualified personnel. They will be allocated to you based on their experience and your needs as assessed by the partners. The work of all staff is subject to review and our quality control procedures.
- We will complete your tax return from the information that you and third parties such as your stockbroker and bank supply to us. We will send you a checklist each April to assist you in collating the necessary information.
- We will send you the return for review, approval and signature and we will forward it to the Inland Revenue on your behalf. [Include details of submission by ELS if applicable.]
- We will take all reasonable care that the information you supply is accurately reflected on the return.
- You remain responsible for making a correct return, for the completeness of the information contained on the return and for full disclosure of all relevant information. Penalties can be charged by the Inland Revenue for failure to make full or correct disclosure.
- We will advise you of the extent of your tax liabilities or refunds and when the tax should be paid.

- The Inland Revenue has the power to charge interest whenever tax is paid late.
- We will prepare tax computations based on your accounts and submit these to the Inland Revenue.
- We will advise you about possible claims and elections and assist you to make them where appropriate.
- In agreeing to the terms of this letter, you recognise that we will comply with the ethical guidance laid down by [professional body], in particular relating to the correction of errors found on your return or related documents.

2. Records

- If you are not self-employed or renting property you will be required to keep records relevant to your tax return for twenty-two months from the end of the tax year.
- If you are self-employed or rent out a property then you will be required to keep all records relevant to your tax return for five years ten months from the end of the tax year.
- If a return is submitted late the requirement to keep records is extended.
- It is your responsibility to keep all original records safely for the relevant periods.
- Whilst certain documents on our files of working papers may legally belong to you, we only undertake to retain our files for ... years after which time they will be destroyed. If you wish the files to be retained for a longer period, please advise us.
- We reserve the right to disclose our files to our regulatory body and [external reviewer] to maintain the quality of work within the firm.

3. Tax payments

- You are responsible for making two interim tax payments on account of your tax liabilities each year. Each payment is usually 50 per cent of the previous year's total tax liability. The interim payments are due on 31 January and 31 July. A final tax payment may be due on 31 January following the year of assessment if your total tax liabilities exceed the interim payments.
- Interest is charged on tax paid late and surcharges may be levied. You are responsible for ensuring that the interim and final tax payments are made by the relevant dates.
- We will advise you of the amounts due on the interim and final tax payments.
- If your tax liabilities fell below £500 in the previous tax year and in

various other circumstances, no interim payments are required.

4. Filing dates

- Automatic penalties will be levied if your tax return is submitted after 31 January each year. We cannot be held liable for any such penalties if the information required to complete your return is supplied to us after [31 October] following the end of the tax year or if you do not respond to questions or enquiries to our complete satisfaction within thirty days.
- If your tax return is submitted to the Inland Revenue by 30 September following the end of the tax year, then the Inland Revenue will calculate your tax due. Tax returns submitted after this date will require self-assessment calculations. If you are employed it may be possible to have any tax underpayments coded in your tax code. To take advantage of this your return must be submitted by 30 September. If you require your return to be submitted by 30 September we will require the information to complete your return no later than [15 July].

5. Enquiries

- The Inland Revenue has the power to enquire into a return within 12 months of the 31 January filing date. This is extended if the return is submitted late. The enquiry can either be because your return has been selected randomly or because the Inland Revenue is concerned about part or all of the information disclosed on the return. You will not be told the reason for their enquiry.
- The enquiry may result in you having to produce information in support of the entries on your return or accounts. Failure to supply the information can give rise to penalties.
- We will deal with any enquiry made into your return by the Inland Revenue. This will constitute a separate supply of services and will be charged for separately. We will require your full cooperation in the event of an enquiry since the degree of cooperation provided is a significant factor in determining the outcome.
- If no enquiry is raised into your return within the time limit, then the Inland Revenue will not be able to open an enquiry at a later date. However, the Inland Revenue still has the power to make a discovery assessment after the time limit has expired if they believe that you have been fraudulent, negligent or if you have failed to disclose all the relevant information.

6. Tax planning

- Upon instruction we will be pleased to review your income tax position and to help you to plan your affairs in an efficient way.
- We will be pleased to discuss proposed transactions with you and

advise on the most tax-efficient way in which they could be structured and the tax consequences of alternative courses of action.

- We shall be pleased to review your capital assets and advise on tax planning matters including the use of lifetime gifts and trusts.

7. Other taxation matters

- Upon instruction we will be pleased to offer advice on other tax matters as they become appropriate to your circumstances including employment, self-employed matters, VAT, PAYE, National Insurance, companies and corporate tax, capital gains tax, inheritance tax and wills, stamp duty and investments.

8. General business advice

- We will be happy to offer advice on any matter within the limits of our knowledge upon request. We will advise you of any limitations that may apply. We will take all reasonable care to ensure that such advice is accurate but our opinion will be limited to the information you supply to us. If we are unable to offer advice we will be happy to suggest others who may be able to help.

9. Financial services, commissions and client monies

- [See 20.16.]

10. Applicable law

- This agreement shall be governed by and construed in accordance with English law. The English courts shall have exclusive jurisdiction in relation to any claim, dispute or difference concerning this agreement and any matter arising from it. Each party irrevocably waives any right it may have to object to an action being brought in those courts.

11. Limitation of liability

- We undertake to exercise due care in the performance of our work and to perform it in accordance with applicable professional standards. You agree to hold harmless and to indemnify us against any misrepresentation (intentional or unintentional) supplied to us by any means in connection with this agreement.

12. Help us to provide you with the best service

- We aim to provide you with a fully satisfactory service. If at any time you are dissatisfied with the service you are receiving please contact your engagement partner as soon as possible. He or she will look into the complaint and do everything reasonable to put the matter right. If you remain unhappy after discussing the matter with them please contact [name — another partner]. He or she will look into any complaint promptly and endeavour to resolve the position.

If you are still dissatisfied you could discuss the matter with [professional body].

13. Fees

- Our fees are computed on the basis of the time spent on your affairs by the partners and staff and depend on the levels of skill and responsibility involved [or in accordance with our menu of charges]. A list of currently applicable rates is available on request. Fees will be subject to disbursements and VAT.
- We will invoice you at appropriate intervals during the course of the year. Payment is due within [14 days] of the invoice date.
- If you cease to use our services we will invoice you for any costs incurred between the date of the last invoice and the termination of our contract.

14. Agreement of terms

- This document will remain in effect until altered, cancelled or replaced by mutual agreement.
- If you are satisfied with the terms please confirm your agreement by signing below. If you have any questions please contact us.

Yours sincerely

A Firm

I agree to the terms set out in your letter of [ ].

Signed........................ Date.......................

Appendix 2:4

New Client Form

Completed by Date

Set up

Action	Yes/No	File Reference	Date/Initials
File set up			
Client management record set up			
Computer records set up			
Time ledger set up			
Initial letter to client			
Letter to outgoing advisor			
Engagement letter sent			
Engagement letter returned			
64-8 sent			

Client details

Name

Trading name

Usual contact

Position

Home address

Business/registered address

Home phone number

Business phone number

Mobile phone

FAX/DX number

Preferred means of communication

Personal information necessary to a full understanding of the client's needs

Source of introduction

Services required

Self-employed/partnership accounts	Y/N
Partnership returns	Y/N
Company accounts/audit	Y/N
Corporation tax returns	Y/N
Personal tax returns — self	Y/N
Personal tax returns — family	Y/N
Trust tax returns	Y/N
PAYE	Y/N
VAT	Y/N
NIC	Y/N
Tax planning	Y/N
Financial services	Y/N
Other	Y/N

Unusual transactions

Risk assessment	High/medium/low
Fee quoted	
Identification seen	

Previous advisors

Name	Address
Contact	Reasons for change
Contact made/date	Agreement given/date

Other advisors

Solicitor's name	Address
Contact	Telephone numbers
Banker's name	Address
Contact	Telephone numbers
Stockbroker's name	Address
Contact	Telephone numbers
IFA's Name	Address
Contact	Telephone numbers
Other advisor's name	Address
Contact	Telephone numbers

Ethical

Is the firm independent?

Does the firm have the skills to act?

Does the firm have the resources/staff to act?

Other considerations?

Tax/VAT offices

Tax district

Reference number

64-8 submitted/date

VAT office

Reference number

PAYE district

Reference number

Personal tax clients only

Date of birth

National Insurance number

Spouse's name/details

Children's names/date of birth

Grandchildren's details

Other key relations' details

Date of marriage

Country of domicile (origin/choice)

Residence/ordinary residence (date came to UK)

Spouse's domicile

Spouse's residence/ordinary residence

Details of wills

Sources of income

Employment/salary

Directorships

Benefits in kind

Deductions e.g. subscriptions

State pension/benefits

Other pensions

Bank accounts (balance)

Building society accounts (balance)

Shares/unit trusts (valuation)

ISAs/TESSAs/PEPs (valuation)

Other investments (valuation)

Rental income (gross/net income)

Trusts

Appendix 2:4

Businesses

Nature of business (sole trader/partnership/company)	History of business
Relevant laws/regulations	Ownership/share structure
Date started	Accounts year-end
Accounts details	VAT registration details

Outgoings

Pensions (contributions)	Covenants/gift aid (donations)
Mortgages (monthly payment)	Loans (monthly payment)
Other debts	Other outgoings e.g. EIS

Capital assets

	Date acquired	Cost
Principal private residence		
Let property		
Other property		
Overseas assets		
Collections		
Antiques/works of art		
Other		

Inheritance tax

Lifetime transfers

Estimated worth

Life assurance

Corporate tax clients only

Company number

Is the company a close company?

Group arrangements in force

VAT arrangements in force

Chapter 3

Fees

3.1 Fees are one of the most contentious areas of tax practice because they are so difficult to set and recover. Firms frequently think that other practitioners earn more than they do and clients often believe they can get a lower price elsewhere. This chapter considers some of the issues involved including charging methods and setting fees. Commercial considerations are, however, not the only concern. Tax practices must also avoid a number of legal and ethical pitfalls. These are considered at the end of the chapter.

Preliminary considerations

3.2 A tax advisor's relationship with his or her client is a commercial one and fees are central to the arrangement. Before starting any work for a client the tax practitioner should consider whether:

- the fee has been agreed by the client, usually by reference to the engagement letter;
- the work is in line with the service provided in previous years;
- the benefit to the client of undertaking the work is justified by the cost;
- the client can afford to pay the fee;
- the client has no other unpaid fees with the firm.

3.3 Too often tax practitioners are embarrassed by fees and undersell their services as a result. Supplying tax services is a two-way process. In return for a good service the client undertakes to pay the advisor's fees. If they dispute the fees or fail to pay them the mutual trust inherent in the relationship has failed and the firm should consider terminating the engagement (see 6.17).

3.4 Being upfront about costs will avoid potential problems. For instance, if there is an overrun on estimated fees tell the client at the first opportunity and involve the client in a decision as to whether to continue with the work or curtail it. Agree the additional costs with the client in writing.

3.5 It is good practice for the tax practitioner to work out a budget for all tax cases whatever the basis of charge and even if the budget is only used internally. The budget can be used to:

- monitor the performance of staff on the job;
- justify the fee;
- compare costs with previous years and with similar cases;
- provide valuable information for working out fixed fee quotes.

Formal quotations

3.6 For both commercial and ethical reasons the fee or the basis of charge should be agreed with the client in writing at the start of the engagement. This can be done either in the letter of engagement or by providing the client with an annual quotation. Fixed fee quotes can be produced in a standard format during the initial meeting.

When the work is complete the fee should be calculated in accordance with the agreement. Members of professional bodies should ensure that they comply with the requirements of their institute with regard to the fee calculation, quotation and notification. In the event of a fee dispute the absence of an engagement letter or other written agreement as to the basis on which fees will be charged may render them irrecoverable in whole or in part. For further information about engagement letters see 2.24.

Charging methods

3.7 Charging fees by reference to an hourly rate is no longer as popular as it once was. Firms should consider charging fixed fees or adopting value billing.

Charging by the hour

3.8 Most tax practices still use this tried and trusted method, which for many is seen as the most 'professional' of the three options; however, clients do not like it because they do not necessarily know how much the work will cost them. Firms should endeavour to provide an estimate of the likely cost to clients and fees for non-recurring work should generally be agreed with the client in advance.

3.9 Fees should be calculated on a fair and reasonable basis taking into account:

- the seniority and professional expertise of those working on the case;
- the time expended;

- the degree of risk and responsibility which the work entails; and
- the priority and importance of the work.

Fixed fees

3.10 Fixed fee quotes are most suitable for routine compliance work. Clients like them because they know how much the work will cost them. Care should be taken to specify exactly what work is and is not covered by the quotation. Additional work should be billed separately and the client kept informed of these costs as they are incurred. Firms should have a 'menu' of their charges to give to clients.

3.11 In fixed fee cases the costs need to be budgeted carefully. For example, a budget for personal tax compliance work should include the cost of:

- chasing the client more than once for information to complete the return;
- dealing with queries arising from the information supplied by the client;
- chasing the client to return the form;
- completing checklists and checking the return;
- internal review procedures;
- submission of the form to the Revenue;
- monitoring the progress of the return in the firm;
- a contingency factor for unforeseen complications.

Value billing

3.12 This refers to the concept of billing the value of the work to the client rather than by reference to an hourly rate or fixed fee. Such an arrangement will only usually apply to tax planning and non-recurring work. In most circumstances value billing should be ethically acceptable provided that the basis of calculating the fee is agreed with the client in advance. Where the work involves an objective professional opinion, value billing, percentage or contingent fees may harm the advisor's objectivity and should only be used after careful consideration.

Setting fees and charge-out rates

3.13 Setting an appropriate charge for clients involves a consideration of the following factors:

- the firm, its size, location, overhead costs, image and expertise;
- the client profile, industry risk, complexity of its operations and the amount that they can afford to pay;
- the work to be undertaken and its risk, priority and importance;
- the time to be expended on the work;
- the skills, seniority and expertise of the staff and partners undertaking the work;
- the amount of working capital it ties up;
- the amount that the market will accept for the service being offered and the impact of competition.

3.14 Practices should consider using different charge-out rates for each fee earner for different types of work assessed according to its risk or complexity. Differing rates can also be used for clients to reflect their risk or importance to the firm. For example, a firm might use three charge-out rates to coincide with its risk assessment. The highest rate would apply to high risk, complex work. The next band would be charged to for the majority of clients assessed as medium or low risk. The lowest rate would be a preferential rate for low risk clients who cannot afford to pay high fees.

3.15 The firm will only be able to determine an appropriate charge for its services if it has prepared a budget for the practice. It needs to understand the relationship between its staff costs, overheads and partner reward, and the total chargeable hours the practice generates having allowed for holidays, sickness, training and administration. The staff and partner mix will also need to be considered.

3.16 Traditionally charge-out rates for tax practices have been set at 2.5 or 3 times the staff cost. Smaller practices may work to much lower mark-ups. In a simple example ignoring employer's National Insurance and staff benefits, if a tax manager is paid £40,000 and expects to generate 1,300 chargeable hours a year, a charge-out rate of between £77 and £92 per hour should be applied to his or her work. Such a rate should be reviewed in the light of local competition and what is considered to be an acceptable market rate. Those setting up a firm or consultancy for the first time can also use the same exercise. In this case expenses and overheads should also be taken into account as well as the desired profit.

3.17 Where a sole practitioner acts as a tax consultant for a small number of clients and is paid a fixed fee or retainer, a theoretical rate per hour should be calculated and the work undertaken to that budget. Not doing this may result in underselling and low profitability.

3.18 Fixed fees for tax compliance work can comprise a basic charge plus a fixed amount for each entry on the return. Premium rates should be applied to self-employments, rentals and capital gains. Firms will have to establish a formula which works for them.

3.19 Tax practitioners are often reluctant to discuss the rates that they charge for work. The Institute of Chartered Accountants in England and Wales run an inter-firm comparison for its members on an anonymous basis which can provide useful information.

3.20 Most tax practices use different charge-out rates for different grades of staff. If this is the case, partners and managers must be careful to record all their time for on-the-job instruction, supervision, training and review. The lower rate for junior staff is lower to allow for all these costs.

3.21 A firm may be using too high a charge-out rate if it regularly writes off a high percentage of work in progress or if it receives constant fee complaints. The rate is likely to be too low if it never receives fee complaints. Having a few complaints indicates that the rate is probably set in the right area.

3.22 Tax practices usually set different charge-out rates for managers and partners. This policy should be considered carefully. If the manager is as experienced and qualified as the partner it would seem appropriate to use the same charge-out rate. Not doing so could result in the firm not earning as much from its tax work as it could do.

3.23 Care should also be taken when using hourly rates for tax compliance work. Individual staff and partners work at differing rates. It can result in an efficient manager or partner charging a client lower fees than a less efficient one. The head of the tax department should review the fees billed by each manager or partner for consistency across the client base.

3.24 Once the firm has set its charge-out rates, increasing them by more than inflation can prove difficult and is likely to meet client resistance. However, where a firm has difficulty recovering fees or where it is simply not profitable enough, drastic action may be called for. If a firm doubles its fees and loses half its clients in doing so, it will still have the same fee income but it will have more time to service clients. Firms that have undertaken such an exercise rarely lose half their clients and the firm usually ends up being more profitable. There are obviously many reasons why a firm may not want to take this course of action but, where fees and profitability are in issue, it should be considered.

Recovering fees

3.25 Whatever fee structure a firm adopts, it still has to convert time spent on tax work into bills and then into cash. Recovering fees not only involves good time recording systems for work in progress but careful billing. The following tips may help.

- Delegate billing to the staff. They are less likely to round the bill down or take a view that the work is only 'worth' a certain amount. Partners must still approve all fees charged.
- Round all bills up to the nearest £5, £10 or even £25 and never down. This may only amount to 2 per cent to 3 per cent of the value of the bills but this can have a significant impact on profits.
- Quote higher fees for the initial work to recover the set-up costs. Often the first work undertaken by the firm is high value, involving an objective review and follow-up advice for which clients are happy to pay. If a client complains about the fees at this stage, or does not want to use the firm because the quote is too high, at least a potential problem client has been identified early on.

For further information about debt recovery see 18.18.

Selling fees to clients

3.26 Part of the reason why clients find tax services expensive is psychological. Practitioners can also use psychology to sell their fees. Clients generally do not like the idea of paying tax and therefore do not like the associated fees. They often spend just as much a year on other essentials (contact lenses, osteopathy, dentists etc.). Some clients (but not all) respond well to an emphasis on the 'preventative' aspects of a professional tax service in avoiding costly mistakes and pitfalls.

3.27 Convincing other clients that your fees are affordable involves finding out what your clients like to spend their money on (their Achilles heel) and then comparing your fees with that expenditure.

3.28 Some clients respond well to free or cheap offers. These do not have to be costly or tacky. Offer to do a free lifestyle review. Compare their income and expenses and make recommendations about how they can improve their entire financial position, not just save tax (see 10.17). Undertaking this exercise will enable the firm to ascertain how much spare money the client has and whether they can afford or need additional services. The review should provide a good opportunity to sell more services. Do not be afraid to tell clients what they are getting for their money and always tell them how much tax the exercise has saved them or the benefits of the work. Remember the basics. Clients rarely complain about fees if they have had a prompt, efficient and courteous service.

3.29 Approach the issue of fees with clients as follows.

- Discuss fees and payment methods in the first meeting.
- Find out how much the client expects to pay. This will prevent underquoting.
- Ascertain what services the client wants now and what services they may want in the future. Will they only ever be a client who wants the basic service?
- Have a menu card of other services for clients to take away and discuss the cost of these.
- Offer payment by instalments. A monthly fee may be more affordable.
- Offer payment by a variety of means including credit card and standing order.
- If the client can afford the firm's services agree a fee. Make it very clear what it does and does not include and the basis on which the fee is agreed. Send bills regularly so that the costs do not mount up.
- Send detailed bills so that clients know what services they are paying for. Invoice as soon as possible after doing the work so that clients do not 'forget' what work has been done. Consider sending invoices for routine tax compliance work with the tax return.
- Word bills so that clients do not query them. Avoid the phrase 'sundry advice'. Clients generally believe that the most expensive work is that which produces the finished product i.e. a tax return.

Risk fees

3.30 It may be possible to take on a few clients on the basis of a 'partnership'. Invest non-chargeable time and effort in some carefully selected clients in the hope that they will grow and produce larger fees in the future. Both parties must be committed to the relationship. It is risky because the client may stay small and might not produce the anticipated fees for several years but only few clients need to be successful for this strategy to work. It will work best with self-employed clients or owner-managed companies in the early days of their business.

Clients who cannot afford high fees

3.31 Tax advisors will sometimes face a dilemma where clients cannot afford high fees but need professional advice. This may apply to those with multiple sources of income, single parents, the elderly or disabled. Does the practice accept a percentage of *pro bono* work or does it only undertake commercial work? The answer will depend on the philosophy of the firm. Work charged at low fees must still be performed to the same professional standards.

3.32 There are situations when it may make commercial sense to act for clients who cannot afford to pay high fees because:

- the practice recovers good fees from other clients and can afford some lower paying ones;
- the client may introduce new clients who can afford full fees;
- the firm may have acted for the client for a long time and be happy with the relationship because the client makes few demands and is low risk;
- the practice is in a small community and the client is well known or influential.

Legal and ethical considerations

3.33 Fees can give rise to a whole raft of ethical and legal considerations, some of which are considered in the following paragraphs. Practitioners should also refer to their professional bodies for guidance.

Fee manipulation

3.34 Practitioners are sometimes tempted to adjust the allocation of fees to the advantage of the client when working on several projects for one client or for connected clients. A classic example is where the firm acts as tax agent for an owner-managed company and for the key director (and probably his family). The director may place pressure on the firm to bill the company for the work so that the company can obtain a corporation tax deduction and the VAT can be recovered.

Be under no illusions about such a course of action. Potentially it constitutes tax evasion, is fraudulent and likely to be a criminal offence. In the Revenue's *Employer Compliance Manual* at paragraph ECM 11032, the issue of accountancy fees paid by directors and senior staff is highlighted for discussion in PAYE compliance visits. As a result it is increasingly likely that the Revenue will scrutinise professional fees. It treats fraud by professional advisors with the utmost seriousness. Criminal prosecutions resulting in jail sentences are not unknown.

When tax practitioners charge fees for several projects to the same client or to connected clients, care must be taken to ensure that the allocation of the fees is commercially justifiable and that it reflects the benefit of the work to those clients.

Nominal fees

3.35 Generally nominal fees should also be avoided. Firms may consider that it is good tax planning to charge the director (in the situation above) a nominal fee for their tax return and merge the other costs into the company. This may be contrary to the firm's engagement letter, which may state that fees will be charged on the basis of the time expended. There is a fine line between charging no fee and a purely nominal fee. A fixed fee clearly stated in the engagement letter might be a preferable option.

Charging fees for unqualified staff

3.36 It is important to stipulate in the letter of engagement that the firm may use unqualified staff in carrying out its tax work. The qualifications of staff (or lack of them) should also be highlighted when introductions are made to tax department personnel. For example, the firm's tax manager could be introduced as follows: 'this is the firm's tax manager Anna Black. She has no formal tax or accountancy qualifications but she has had over fifteen years' experience in tax practice'. This recommendation follows the case of *Pearless de Rougemont v Pilbrow [1999] 3 All ER 355.*

In this case, Mr Pilbrow telephoned a firm of solicitors and requested an appointment with a solicitor. The receptionist arranged for him to see an unqualified member of staff who handled his affairs throughout. Subsequently Mr Pilbrow discovered that she was not a solicitor and refused to pay the firm's bill. In the Court of Appeal it was held that Mr Pilbrow was not obliged to pay any part of the bill because the firm had not provided the services which he had requested, namely the services of a qualified solicitor. The Court held that it was irrelevant that the member of staff had handled the matter as competently as a solicitor would have done. It also emphasised that the decision was equally applicable to other professions and laid down guidelines for similar cases.

Guidelines

3.37 In cases similar to that above, the client should be referred to:

- a qualified person;
- an unqualified person with an explanation that they are unqualified;
- someone who is aware of the client's requirements and can take appropriate action to ensure that an appropriately qualified person deals with them.

Delegation, although routine in professional firms, should always be based on client consent. Suitable engagement letters should be issued. It should be noted that no engagement letter was sent in *Pearless de Rougemont v Pilbrow.*

Investigations

3.38 Care should be taken to ascertain which professional fees are allowable for tax and which are not. Tax and accountancy fees for ongoing professional work are usually allowable for Schedule D purposes. In Tax Bulletin 37, the Revenue indicated that where fees are incurred in dealing with an Inland Revenue investigation, they will be allowable if the investigation:

- gives rise to no adjustments; or
- there is an adjustment to the profits for the year of enquiry only arising as a result of conduct which is neither fraudulent nor negligent.

In all other situations the fees relating to that work must be disallowed.

Fees and offset against tax repayments

3.39 All tax repayments sent directly to tax practitioners should be paid into a client account and kept separate from the firm's funds until such time as a bill is approved by the client. Each professional body has its own rules with regard to the handling of client funds which must be observed (see 20.27).

3.40 In order to avoid problems money must not be withdrawn from a client bank account for payment towards fees unless the following general conditions are satisfied.

- The precise amount of the fee has been agreed by the client (or court or arbitrator) and the fees have been accurately calculated in accordance with the formula agreed by the client in writing as part of the engagement letter or at some other point in the engagement.
- Thirty days have elapsed since the client received a detailed invoice specifying the work done and the cost and the client has not questioned the amount charged. It is good etiquette to stipulate on the invoice that the client's agreement will be deemed to have been received after the thirty-day period has elapsed.

Fee disputes

3.41 If a client questions the amount charged for the services the tax practice should be prepared to justify its charge by reference to its time and budget records and to provide the client with such explanations as they reasonably require without further charge. The firm should have a complaints procedure and the details should be included in its engagement letter. A review of the charge by the senior or managing partner often helps to restore client confidence as will the issuing of a credit note if the amount charged is found to be excessive. Knowledge of the client's psychology is vital in understanding why the fee is being questioned.

3.42 Following the Woolf proposals with regard to civil claims, the courts are to be regarded as a last resort. Disputants are encouraged to resolve their differences. Arbitration under the *Arbitration Act* is one way of doing this. The Institute of Chartered Accountants in England and Wales offers an arbitration service to its members involved in fee disputes. The cost is fixed in relation to the disputed amount. If the fees are upheld to within 5 per cent the client pays the costs. If the fees are reduced by more than 15 per cent the member pays.

Fees and lien over records

3.43 Generally, when a client relationship terminates due to a fee dispute, arrangements should be made for the fees to be settled before information is released to the new tax advisors (see 6.27). The practice may also consider exercising a lien over certain books and papers. Liens are very difficult to establish. Legal opinion is such that unless the right of lien is a specific contractual provision (presumably in the letter of engagement) it is generally not a good idea to adopt such a course of action. Instead steps should be taken to resolve the dispute as quickly and amicably as possible using arbitration if necessary.

Lowballing

3.44 This refers to the practice of undercutting another tax practice by quoting a lower fee to obtain work. For some firms it is cost effective to offer a discounted or free compliance service for the first year in order to obtain new clients. This may be a cheaper way to obtain new work than purchasing a practice or block of fees. Quoting low fees is not improper provided that the client is aware of what is covered by the fee, their responsibilities and the basis on which the fee will be calculated in future years. The firm should also ensure that its professional standards, ethics and the quality of work are unaffected by the reduced fee.

Free meetings

3.45 Some tax practices offer free initial meetings to discuss the work to be undertaken and the level of fees to be charged. This is professionally acceptable. Care should be taken from a commercial point of view to monitor how much practice time is expended in conducting such meetings and the success rate of clients joining the firm. The firm should recover the costs by including them in administration overheads and reflecting the cost in the hourly charge-out rate or fee.

3.46 *Fees*

Advertisements

3.46 It is important not to mislead taxpayers about the basis of a firm's fees in advertisements. Practitioners who are members of professional bodies must comply with the rules of their institute with regard to advertisements. Information about fees is generally inappropriate in adverts due to the limited space. It is also unprofessional to make fee comparisons with other tax practices.

Financial services

3.47 Care must be taken when offering tax advice not to fall foul of the *Financial Services Act*. Fees charged for investment business services provided by authorised tax practices are subject to the *Investment Business Regulations*. Suitable engagement letters must be in place for all investment business and corporate finance work. For further information see 20.7.

Quick review

3.48

- The fee charged for tax work must be commensurate with the benefit to the client.
- Advisors should be upfront with clients about fee issues.
- Fee rates should be thought about carefully before they are set.
- Firms should consider setting a minimum fee below which it is not worth opening a new client file.
- Liens over clients' records cannot be exercised if it means that a client cannot comply with their statutory obligations.
- Firms should incorporate the legal and ethical fee issues in their tax manual.
- In most situations relationships with clients are commercial. Clients who do not pay bills or who regularly question fees are not worth having as clients.
- Understanding something of a client's psychology can help to convince clients that a firm's fees are reasonable.
- If clients complain about fees, do not take it personally. Remember that it is only business.
- Tell clients what the firm does for the fee. For instance, when preparing a personal tax return the firm probably:

— meets the client;
— liaises with the Inland Revenue;
— provides telephone support;
— reminds the client to send the information;
— checks the information;
— asks for what is missing;
— prepares computations;
— advises of tax liabilities, interest and penalties;
— prepares elections;
— gives advice;
— checks the return for reasonableness;
— sends in the return;
— checks statements of account;

after which the completion of the return itself is probably free.

Chapter 4

Communicating with Clients

4.1 Good client communication is the key to running a tax practice. A firm can provide creative tax planning but, if it cannot communicate that advice to clients in a way that they will understand and accept, it will have failed. Effective communication is also essential to creating and maintaining good client relationships and it will save the practice time and money. It involves:

- being clear and succinct about the subject;
- asking straightforward questions;
- avoiding surprises;
- being easy to work with;
- keeping clients involved;
- ensuring that the message has been understood;
- understanding any feedback.

This chapter covers a wide range of communication issues including:

- writing letters and reports;
- phoning, e-mail and faxes;
- meetings, including room layout and body language;
- presentation skills;
- neuro-linguistic programming and advanced communication.

Does the practice have communication problems?

4.2 Many tax practices do not perceive that they have a communication problem. Consider the following questions. Most tax practitioners can answer 'yes' to some of them. If so they may need to examine the way in which they communicate with their clients.

- Do you frequently have to chase clients to get them to send you their tax return information?

- Do you have clients who do not send you their tax return information until December?
- Do your clients sometimes claim not to understand your letters or instructions even if they seem straightforward to you?
- Do you undertake tax planning exercises which clients do not act upon or follow through even though they originally seemed interested in the ideas?
- Do you provide advice that is often ignored?
- Do your clients claim that you are not sufficiently pro-active?

Communication technology is changing rapidly. To remain efficient and competitive a tax practice needs to be fully conversant with all methods of communication and to try to remain one step ahead of its competition.

Writing

4.3 Tax practitioners prefer to communicate by letter so that they have evidence if there is a complaint. Most firms use a series of standard letters to communicate with clients.

Standard letters

4.4 Letters, particularly standard letters, are often considered the cheapest way to communicate. Clients do not understand why firms send so many letters because they fail to appreciate the need for file notes or the frustration of telephone calls when no one is in. Standard letters also ensure that all the points are covered including risk warnings. They help firms to delegate tax compliance work to more junior staff whilst retaining control over it and this keeps costs down. However, if a letter is ineffective, in the long run it is an expensive form of communication.

Many clients do not respond to letters from their tax advisor because this is not a means of communication with which they feel comfortable. This is because many people have difficulty reading more than two short paragraphs. Standard letters, by their very nature, tend to be long unless they are well tailored. A long letter will be off-putting. A badly structured letter without sub-headings is likely to prove too difficult for all but the most able clients. Remember that anything to do with tax and finances is unfamiliar territory to most clients and, regardless of how many times a client has dealt with their tax return in the past, they only have one return to do each year, not several hundred.

4.5 *Communicating with Clients*

Alternatives to letters

4.5 Some clients are happy communicating by letter but for others a little more thought is needed. Consider the following.

- For technologically-minded clients send them the letter by e-mail or fax. A short header asking them to read the attachment personalises the communication.
- If the client only communicates by telephone do not send the letter and instead go through the points on the telephone. Use the letter as a file note by adding details of the date and time of the call.
- If a client prefers meetings use the letter as a file note but be aware that frequent meetings will be more expensive.
- If it is essential to send clients who prefer to communicate by telephone a letter, telephone them first, warn them that they are about to receive a letter and what it says. This removes some of the surprise and fear inherent in opening the envelope.

See 4.43 and 2.43 for ways to tell clients' preferred means of communication.

Tips for effective letter writing

4.6 It is often necessary to send letters, particularly where they accompany tax returns or documents requiring signature and when providing advice. The following points will make a firm's letters more user friendly.

Contents

- Begin and end positively.
- Tailor letters to clients' specific needs. Remember that all clients are individuals.
- Keep in mind the main point of the letter and avoid waffle.
- Start with the big picture and then move on to the detail.
- Make sure the letter includes all the information in a logical order.
- Write long and complicated letters early in the day. Communication skills deteriorate with tiredness.
- Communicate the important information clearly, for example, the tax due and the payment dates.
- Learn to communicate complicated ideas simply. For example, when discussing the payment of a dividend from a family company, tell the client 'for every £1 you take out it costs you an extra 25p in tax if

you are a higher rate tax payer'. When comparing bonuses and dividends tell the client 'a bonus will cost approximately 10 per cent more than a dividend in most circumstances but there are reasons why a dividend may not be a good idea'.

- If you are unsure how reader friendly something is try it out on your clerical or administration staff. If they cannot understand it the chances are that your client will find it difficult too.
- Be careful when referring to dates. Clients do not always understand references to tax years, for example to the 'current tax year'. Refer to tax years and accounting periods by stating the specific dates.
- Keep it concise and simple.

Layout

- Use headings, sub-headings, bullet points and bold type for emphasis.
- Use a simple typeface that is easily read.
- Break up the text of letters by using graphics, tables and charts. For example, add a table of tax payments and due dates.
- Ensure that all letters are dated in case they have to be used in evidence or to resolve disputes.
- Use titles and names correctly. Clients get upset if such things are wrong and it may undermine their confidence in the rest of the letter.
- Ensure that client references are correct. If writing to the Inland Revenue, the wrong reference can delay the letter arriving in the right place and attachments may become lost. Lack of accuracy will waste time and money.
- Be careful with the firm's references, particularly where they contain file references. The letter may be filed in the wrong place as a result.

Language

- Avoid jargon and abbreviations, for example, CGT, IHT.
- Use simple language and avoid long multi-clause sentences.
- Write as you speak and avoid formal stilted language such as 'pertaining to', 'at this moment in time', or 'I am inclined to conclude'.
- Most word processing packages show the reading age of the document. Aim to keep this as low as possible.
- Avoid the passive voice, for example, 'your tax return was submitted ...' and use the active instead – 'I submitted your tax return ...'.

The passive voice disclaims responsibility, is unfriendly and impersonal. The only situation when it should be used is if there had been a mistake and the firm is trying to distance itself from the error.

- Keep the average sentence length to no more than 25 words.
- Avoid negative words, for example, 'poor argument' and 'mistaken belief' and try to use positive language wherever possible.
- Avoid spelling mistakes, poor grammar and punctuation. Remember that the spelling checker will not always find them.

Response

- The use of coloured stickers or handwritten post-it notes can highlight issues, the need for a signature and personalise the communication.
- Where a reply is needed include a stamped addressed or reply paid envelope. Busy people cannot easily find stamps or envelopes and providing them is the best way to get a quick response.
- Use tear-off slips or copy letters with space for a reply to make responding to the letter as easy as possible.

Providing advice

4.7 Advisory letters and reports must of necessity be more formal than other tax letters. They are often high-risk documents and may be read by more people than just the client. Care is needed over their structure and contents in addition to the above points.

- The purpose of the letter and the main conclusions should be summarised in the opening paragraph.
- The main body of the letter should contain the detailed findings, legislation, cases and calculations.
- The conclusion can be a series of action points.
- If there is no clear-cut answer say so and present the options.
- Letters should state the assumptions on which they are based, disclaimers and where necessary contain restrictions about who they are to be shown to.
- Use numbered paragraphs and pages.
- Make the letter as short and concise as possible.

Telephoning

4.8 The telephone is one of a tax practice's principal means of communication; and yet often tax practice staff have no training in how to communicate effectively on the telephone. Communicating by telephone can be quicker and more cost effective than a meeting but a poor telephone manner can result in lost opportunities. This is particularly true in the case of mobile phones used out of the office. Firms should lay down guidelines for their use covering who is to use them, when and where. The remainder of this section considers general points for good telephone communication.

Making calls

4.9

- Write a brief agenda if the call is complicated. This means that important points are not overlooked. The notes will also serve as a record of the call if the response is noted. Ensure that the minute is dated.
- Ask whether it is a convenient time to speak. If it is not call back.
- Indicate what the call is about. This pre-warns the client and helps the advisor to manage the call. For example, 'I would like to discuss some issues arising from the preparation of your tax return' or 'you asked me to call you about selling your rental property'.
- Take care with pronouncing names.
- Try to repeat the main point two or three times. Include the main issue when summing up. Try to ensure that the other person has understood the key message.
- Try to smile even if it is about something serious. It will be reflected in your tone of voice and will invite a more positive response. Be enthusiastic: it's infectious. Using gestures also improves a telephone call. Avoid a contrived telephone manner.
- Speak slowly and try to keep pace with the other person; try not to do all the talking. Avoid jumping to conclusions.
- Remember that it is easy to confuse similar numbers, for example, 50 and 15.
- Always be polite and friendly. It is hard to overuse 'please' and 'thank you'. There is no excuse for rudeness. Take care not to be patronising or angry.
- If you are making no headway on a particular problem, end the call and offer to ring back later. Alternatively, suggest a meeting or respond by letter.
- Close the call positively.

Failing to get through

4.10

- Repeatedly failing to speak to a person on the telephone can be a frustrating experience and may be more costly than writing a letter.
- If the client is always 'in a meeting' ask for specific details of when they will be free and say when you will ring back. When you do ring back say that the call is expected.

Returning calls

4.11 Aim to return telephone calls promptly. If you say you will return a call do so within a reasonable time period. If you cannot reply within a day, have a member of staff call the client to let them know when you will be able to speak to them.

Taking calls

4.12

- Answer promptly; ideally in less than four rings.
- Identify yourself fully, for example, 'Good morning, Tony Green speaking' or 'Tony Green, tax department speaking'. Project the right image – bright and helpful.
- Decide quickly whether the call should be passed on to someone else, for example, if the query is too technical.
- If it is inconvenient to take the call, say so and tell the caller when you will have more time to talk to them.
- Listen carefully, take notes and sound organised. Acknowledge what the client is saying by making affirmative noises or saying 'yes'.
- Be polite even with problem clients. The telephone can make people sound more abrupt than they are.
- If you need to leave the telephone to get information call the client back. Pauses on the telephone can seem long. Keep up a dialogue such as 'I have the file now and I'm looking it up for you' or 'I am just waiting for the computer to open the record'.
- Keep tax tables and important files close to hand.
- Put the telephone down last. It avoids the client thinking that they have been cut off too quickly.
- Make notes as soon as possible after the call so that you do not forget what was said.

Chargeable time

4.13 If the call is other than purely administrative, time the call and the time it takes to make notes carefully. It is easy to underestimate the time phone calls take. Having a clock in a prominent position on your desk may help.

Receiving messages

4.14 It should be the responsibility of someone in the office to check the firm's answerphone and allocate the messages. Voice-mail should also be checked promptly. Try to deal with incoming messages within a day. If not have someone else return the call. Update voice-mail messages regularly. During holidays or absences from the office leave details of a named colleague for clients to speak to instead.

When installing a voice-mail system consider the clients' reaction. Many people want a 'live' person to speak to. In the future this may denote a premium, client-friendly service.

Leaving messages

4.15 Know how to leave clear concise messages on answerphones and voice-mail.

- At the beginning of the message leave your name, telephone number and the date and time of your call.
- Speak slowly and, if you are calling a third party who does not know you, spell any difficult words.
- Keep messages brief and professional.
- Let the person know when would be a suitable time to return the call or who to speak to in the event of your absence.
- End the call with your name and number.
- If you have to leave a long message consider faxing it or e-mailing it if the recipient has these facilities.

Deflecting calls

4.16 Every professional practice needs to deflect calls because the person requested is in a meeting or too busy to respond. Members of staff should be trained in how to do this effectively. They should be clear about when the advisor will be available and they should offer an alternative person. Many calls are about routine administration matters which can be dealt with by a capable assistant but getting clients to accept this can often be difficult.

Electronic communication

4.17 Electronic communication is now essential to managing an effective tax practice. Those firms who are not exploiting the latest technology will find themselves at a significant disadvantage.

E-mail

4.18 E-mail has revolutionised client communication. It is a hybrid form of communication that works well for many people because it combines the informality, speed and efficiency of a telephone call with the ability to give a considered reply and to keep a permanent written record. The marginal cost of a simple e-mail is virtually nil. The benefits of using e-mail for client communication include the following.

- It is an easy and convenient means of information gathering for tax returns and for passing on and receiving instructions.
- It avoids wasteful telephone conversations and the problems of engaged lines.
- Clients can answer e-mails in their own time without feeling the pressure of a telephone call.
- It can be used to send data back and forth via attached spreadsheets and other documents. These can then be worked on and incorporated into calculations and returns.
- Attachment letters can be sent electronically. This is quicker and cheaper than post.
- It speeds up communication for clients who are abroad.
- Partners and staff working away from the office can communicate with clients via laptops.
- It enables the electronic submission of returns and forms to the Inland Revenue and other regulatory bodies although ELS is currently operated via a private network.
- Incoming e-mails can be replied to intelligently based on a key word or name. This can be useful during holidays or for dealing with routine requests.

4.19 The informality and speed of electronic communication can cause problems for tax practices. Off-the-cuff advice may be given without sufficient control being exercised over it and it can cause lax spelling and grammar. This has to be weighed against the speed and effectiveness of e-mail as a means of communication. The practice must ensure that e-mails are subject to the same system of review as any other letter. Where a letter is sent as an attachment it should be reviewed in the usual way before sending. Otherwise it can be routed via the internal network to the reviewer and then on to the recipient. Confidentiality should also be considered when e-mailing financial information to a client without prior warning.

4.20 Members of the Institute of Chartered Accountants in England and Wales should ensure that, for both statutory and ethical reasons, the information required on the firm's letterhead is also stated in precisely the same way on e-mails (and faxes) sent to both clients and third parties. This includes details of partners and, in the case of a limited company, the place of registration, the registered address and the registration number.

4.21 The practice should set out guidelines for the sending of e-mails including the following.

- Who is allowed to send e-mails to clients and third parties.
- What subjects they can cover without review, for example, administration and information.
- The need to print out file copies of e-mails.
- The review process.
- Ensuring that clients are charged appropriately.
- Guidance on personal e-mails.
- The time period within which e-mails should be answered.
- When e-mails can be deleted.
- A procedure for checking in-boxes during absence or holidays.
- Procedures for monitoring unanswered e-mails, for example, by leaving them in the out-box or a designated folder.
- Internal e-mails.
- Procedures for monitoring unsolicited e-mails for viruses.
- Netiquette.

4.22 Using the correct etiquette for e-mails is important.

- Send only essential messages.
- Be careful to address them correctly. Confidentiality may be an issue.
- Keep them short.
- Do not attach large files unless you know that clients can open them.
- Be careful about lists of other clients' names being shown when sending standard e-mails. This may breach confidentiality.
- Use meaningful subject titles and do not leave the subject box blank.
- Do not use block capitals – it is the equivalent of shouting.

- Take immediate action against obscene or racist material.

Faxing

4.23 In spite of the proliferation of e-mail not everyone has it yet and faxes will still be around for a few more years. Faxes can either be freestanding or run via a computer. Faxing is a good means of communication where:

- it is necessary to communicate quickly;
- signatures are required;
- the client lives abroad;
- it is important that the client has written advice;
- there are non-computer-generated documents to send.

Use header sheets to ensure that the fax reaches the intended recipient. If there is a risk that another person may intercept confidential information telephone the client first. Consider the time of day when faxing to a client's home, particularly if they live abroad.

Video conferencing

4.24 Setting up meetings with several people present can be very expensive, particularly so where some of the participants are abroad. Video conferencing and conference calls offer a cheaper alternative. Video cameras and the necessary technology are now cheap and simple. Video technology can also be used not just for meetings but to collaborate on specific tasks and to review and work on the same document.

4.25 Video conferencing has advantages over conference calls in that body language and facial expressions can be seen. When setting up a video conference telephone all the participants in advance to clarify the issues to be discussed. Set as short an agenda as possible. Circulate any documents by post or electronically before the call and take into account time differences.

Meetings

4.26 Many different skills are called for to conduct effective client meetings, not just detailed tax knowledge. Ensure that there are breaks in long meetings to help concentration. Clients will generally only remember about 50 per cent of the information that is conveyed to them and predominantly the information which is provided first and is specific to them rather than general. Those with some tax knowledge may retain more than those with none. The retention rate can be improved by warning clients in advance about the subject under discussion and thereby giving them time to think about it in advance of the meeting.

Listing

4.27 It is important to develop good listening skills. Some techniques to consider include the following.

- Learn to ask open questions to encourage clients to talk about themselves, for example, 'tell me about your business'.
- Avoid questions where the answer is just 'yes' or 'no'.
- Empathise with them. Talk little and encourage the client to open up with nods.
- Consider the situation from the client's point of view.
- Listen attentively. Hear what is actually said. If you are not sure ask for clarification.
- Trust what is said until it is disproved.
- Learn to ask the same question in several different ways to see if the answer is the same.
- Try not to interrupt or finish the speaker's sentences.
- Learn to live with silences and do not rush to fill them.
- Avoid prejudice and preconception.

The Inland Revenue use this approach when interviewing clients.

Planning and note-taking

4.28 Meetings will be conducted most effectively when questions have been prepared in advance. Have a list of questions or an agenda. Take all the necessary resources into the meeting including tax tables, brochures and aide-memoires.

4.29 Make notes throughout the meeting and write them up as soon as possible. Have an action list of follow-up points. Ensure that the notes would withstand scrutiny in the event of a dispute or claim. Written and visual shorthand are fine for personal note-taking but not where they have to be read and used by others (see also 15.18).

Body language

4.30 The use and appreciation of unconscious gestures and signals can improve the effectiveness of face-to-face client communication. It can also:

- avoid potential problems, such as clients who lie;
- help negotiations with the Inland Revenue;
- help the practice to sell tax planning advice to clients;

- assist fee negotiations;
- confirm 'gut' reactions about how a meeting is progressing.

It must be used carefully and in conjunction with other evidence. It takes a great deal of practice to be confident about people's reactions and even then there may be other explanations for the gestures.

4.31 Positive gestures include:

- body and feet are facing the front;
- arms and legs are slightly apart, open and relaxed;
- eye contact or a direct gaze is maintained;
- the palms of the hands are open;
- smiling;
- the head is level or slightly tilted to one side;
- hand to chin gestures;
- raised eyebrows indicating interest;
- mirroring gestures.

To create a relaxed atmosphere with a client copy their positive gestures. Mirroring gestures used in return indicate a developing rapport.

4.32 When advising a couple or attending a meeting where more than one partner or director is present, watch carefully to see which person copies the other's gestures. Be alert to direct the presentation to the passive partner even if they seem less vocal. If their actions are the ones that are copied they are likely to be the key decision-maker.

4.33 Negative gestures include:

- body and feet are turned away;
- looking slightly down, maybe with the head slightly tilted back;
- crossed arms;
- partially crossed arms;
- using a folder, pen or other object as a barrier;
- sucking pens and glasses indicates a lack of confidence;
- tightly crossed legs;
- gripping the arms of the chair;
- hand to face boredom gestures;
- hand to neck gestures and knitted eyebrows indicate uncertainty and doubt;

- pointing the body and leaning forwards indicates aggression;
- hands on the hips;
- the mouth is turned down;
- picking imaginary dust or fluff from clothes;
- constant watch or clock watching.

Negative body language may also be exhibited by:

- someone who is nervous – the signs may disappear as they become more relaxed;
- a smoker who is not permitted to smoke in a meeting.

4.34 It is important for tax advisors to identify deceit or lying gestures. Remember the three wise monkeys; the classic signs are hand to eye, mouth or ear gestures. Children use them very openly. In adults it is subtle. The gestures happen only when the client is speaking, not the other way round. Sometimes they are disguised by turning them into a cough or scratch, earlobe pulling and ear bending. Other hand to face or neck gestures can also indicate deceit, including hand to nose (usually the subtlest of the gestures), hand to neck and collar pulling. These gestures are often combined with evasive looks, in particular looking up or down. Watching eye movements can also give an indication about whether information is made up or remembered.

Seating arrangements

4.35 Learn to control meetings by understanding where to sit. Whether the meeting is a one-to-one client interview or a meeting with several partners or directors, the success of the meeting can depend on the seating arrangements.

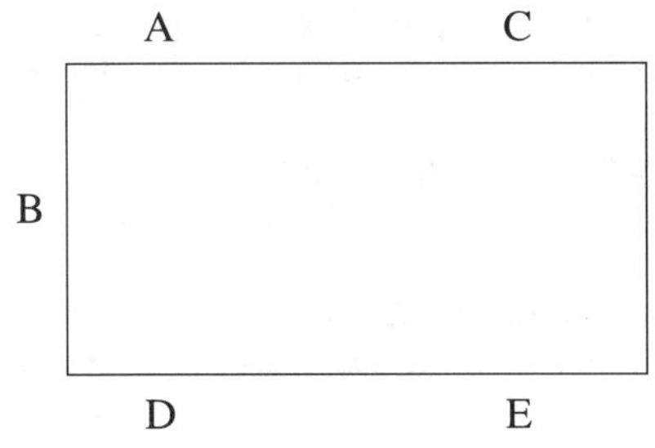

In the above diagram 'A' is the advisor. He or she should expect to have the following reaction from clients seated individually in positions B to E. Where all the places are filled, the advisor will have most influence over the meeting by sitting at position B, provided that his or her back is not to the door.

- The corner position (A to B) is a friendly, one-to-one position. It is the most effective seating arrangement for winning over a new client in the initial meeting or selling additional services to existing clients.
- The cooperative position (A to C) is also a good position for presenting a case and having it accepted. It works well when two people are working on an issue or problem together. However, the position may make one of the parties feel uncomfortable and they may feel as if their territory is being invaded.
- The competitive position (A to D) creates a defensive atmosphere. The desk may literally be a barrier to good client relations. It can lead to entrenched positions. It should also be avoided in Inland Revenue interviews. In large meetings the person sitting here will be competing with A for influence.
- The independent position (A to E) indicates a lack of interest or hostility and is not conducive to effective communication. In a meeting where all the places are filled watch out for the person sitting here.

4.36 In a meeting with several people present it is hard to make them all feel included, particularly if one person asks most of the questions. The best technique is to look at the questioner when they ask the question and when starting the reply. Then look to the other participants but conclude the answer back at the questioner.

For further information on office layout see 14.10.

Personal presentation

4.37 Presenting the right image can enhance client communication. Advisors must present an approachable and successful image before they even speak. We live in an increasingly visual world and clients make split-second judgements based on appearance. If the image conflicts with the advice it will be much harder to get clients to accept it.

4.38 Dress to fit in with the firm's clients. A more formal look will be necessary for a city practice rather than a rural one. Tax practices tend to be conventional, so unless it specialises in the entertainment industry err on the conservative side. Some firms have a formal dress code. This may be questionable under human rights legislation. Others are adopting more relaxed dress to present a more approachable image to clients.

Wherever the practice is located it is important to wear clean, pressed clothes and smart shoes and to have neat hair and understated jewellery. Individual taste can be reflected in ties and scarves.

4.39 It can be useful to study the effect of different coloured clothing on individual clients. For example, wearing blue looks trustworthy.

This quality may be important for some clients but for others it may appear too predictable. Beige is good for conciliation. Grey is neutral and balanced if a little bland but a grey suit worn with a red tie or blouse gives a more powerful image.

Presentation

4.40 Many tax practitioners are asked to make presentations ranging from in-house training to public courses and budget meetings. Presenting is a nerve-wracking experience even for experienced lecturers. Whilst a detailed discussion of presentation techniques is beyond the scope of this work the following tips may help.

- Demonstrate a detailed knowledge of the subject.
- Use interesting examples and anecdotes.
- Be positive and enthusiastic even if the subject matter is dry.
- Maintain eye contact with the audience and talk to them, not at them.
- Keep to the point.
- Speak slowly and clearly. Do not be afraid to pause.
- Emphasise and repeat the main points.
- Make complicated ideas as simple as possible.
- Be wary of presenting strong opinions.
- Avoid offending the audience.
- Take questions but keep the answers short.
- Do not let one member of the audience hijack the presentation.
- Take a training course in presentation skills.
- Learn how to use PowerPoint and incorporate graphics and pictures wherever possible.
- Know how to use all the audio visual aids. Check the equipment thoroughly before starting.
- Incorporate tax-related jokes. They are excellent icebreakers. The Chartered Institute of Tax website has a good selection.
- Close with a clear summary.
- Do not overrun or rush off at the end.

A good presentation will also involve other communication skills including writing, body language, personal presentation and room layout.

Advanced communication techniques

4.41 Tax advisors operate in an increasingly competitive business world and need to take on board new communication techniques. Many of these are now taught in schools and colleges. A consideration of these issues is inevitably open to the criticism that it creates stereotypes, but an appreciation of these areas can help client communication, particularly if there are difficulties.

Gender

4.42 In the days when there were no female tax advisors and few female clients, gender was not a problem. Good communication skills need to take into account gender as well as other knowledge about clients. Generally, female clients:

- do not always ask for help or advice but expect it to be offered;
- appreciate follow-up telephone calls;
- fear asking questions or seeking clarification in case they are wrong;
- will need to be asked questions to draw them out – if a tax advisor talks a lot they will listen and may volunteer very little;
- have different life goals from men;
- are not necessarily after a definite solution to a problem but want to understand all the possibilities open to them.

Regarding male clients:

- if they want help they will specifically ask for it;
- they may resent unsolicited advice;
- successful communications are brief, succinct, direct and well timed;
- the use of 'could you' and not 'would you' is likely to elicit a more positive response.

Neuro-linguistic programming

4.43 Neuro-linguistic programming offers techniques that can be used to improve client communication, such as using what clients say as an indicator of their personality and preferences.

- A reactive person may take a long time to act on advice and responds well to phrases such as 'let's think about it' and 'shall we pause to reflect'. A pro-active person is motivated by expressions such as 'it's time to act' or 'let's get on with it'.
- Some clients' standards are internalised; they do not need supervision. Others can only function by reference to external standards.

They need affirmation that what they are doing is right. They may ask an advisor what they would do in a certain circumstance and can have difficulty making decisions.

- Some people like to be given options and respond well to suggestions that expand their choices. When asked 'how did you get into your line of work?' they will often say *why* they do what they do. In contrast, procedures people like one definite idea. In answer to the same question they will describe *how* they got there.
- Generalists see the big picture and may omit information. Other people are good at the detail. Note how information is provided. Is it lots of detailed steps or just the significant issues?
- Some people notice what is the same about things and others what is different. Mis-matchers will look for discrepancies and may get involved in arguments but they enjoy change and will be attracted to new or different suggestions. Some clients fall in the middle. They like evolving situations and may use comparative words such as 'better' or 'more'. They respond best to language that describes something as 'improved' and 'advanced'.

Cultural

4.44 If the practice regularly deals with clients from other countries it is important to learn about unacceptable social gestures and phrases and the national business etiquette. Consider learning relevant languages or allocate staff to clients accordingly. A few general tips to assist effective communication include the following.

- Americans communicate via sound bites and exchange. They prefer strong visuals.
- Australians are usually forceful and direct and say what they mean.
- Japanese and other Asians find it easier than Europeans to keep silent. The Japanese will rarely be confrontational but they may appear ambiguous and confusing. They expect business to be conducted formally. They may only shake hands when better acquainted. They will usually present a business card at an initial introduction and expect one to be offered in return.
- Head shaking meaning 'no' can mean 'yes' in India.
- Northern Europeans talk less than Southern Europeans but Southern Europeans use more physical gestures which may be lost on the telephone.
- In China finger pointing is considered rude.

Quick review

4.45

- Selling tax services is like selling any other service or product; it requires effective communication.
- Do not let the telephone become a time-waster.
- All the factors that go to make good letters and reports apply equally to e-mails.
- Match the medium to the message.
- Before holding meetings with clients find out whether it is really necessary and decide what it will achieve.
- Positive body language starts with a firm, non-dominant handshake.
- The impact people make on each other depends 55 per cent on looks, 38 per cent on speech and only 7 per cent on what is actually said i.e. the tax advice (Professor Albert Mehrabian, *Silent Messages*).
- The key to a successful meeting is to know what you want, what the client wants and to find a way to achieve it.
- When making a presentation aim to educate, entertain and explain.
- When making conference calls always state your name before speaking.
- Neuro-linguistic programming can also be used to develop a rapport with clients (see 2.43) and to target marketing (see Chapter 5).

Chapter 5

Marketing

5.1 In this chapter we look at various ways of generating work for the tax practice. After a period of time most firms will find what works best for them but it is still important to keep an open mind about all the possibilities. In the early days of a practice or after a major event such as a merger, firms should experiment with a range of options. Marketing should be an ongoing process even in the smallest firm and not simply something that happens once a year.

For many tax practitioners the word 'marketing' still has a brash, unprofessional image but marketing encompasses more than persuading new clients to use the firm; it also includes:

- client care;
- image and design;
- soft-sell marketing;
- using the Internet;
- public relations;
- internal marketing.

Client care

Selling more services to existing clients

5.2 A firm's existing clients are a perfect marketing target; they simply need to be nurtured. The firm knows a great deal about their needs and desires from the information it has gathered about them and it simply needs to use this information to offer them new services. The firm needs to get the relationship with the client off to the right start by telling them about the full range of the firm's services in the initial meeting.

5.3 Tax practitioners often get caught in an established pattern of service. The firm offers the client nothing new and the client does not request additional services. Clients' affairs should be reviewed at least annually to appraise the level and type of service they receive. The scope for additional tax planning or other services should be identified and offered to the client. Generating work in this way has a very low administration cost. Clients almost always appreciate the offer of more services even if they do not take it up, thus increasing client loyalty and satisfaction.

5.4 The following points should be considered when selling more services to existing clients.

- Have services to sell. For example, pre-year-end tax planning, inheritance tax services, PAYE/VAT health checks, remuneration package reviews and debt management reviews (see Chapter 10).
- Expand the firm's services beyond just tax. Consider IT consultancy, business coaching, training and outsourcing (see Chapter 10).
- Offer profitable clients occasional free or more detailed reviews, particularly on financial planning. Use the opportunity to sell further services (see Chapter 10).
- Provide an excellent and timely client service. Return telephone calls promptly and meet deadlines.
- Do not sound or appear to be too busy to undertake more work.
- Ensure that clients think that the firm is pro-active and use the word wherever possible.
- Show a genuine understanding of and interest in the client's business.
- Develop a good rapport with clients (see 5.6).
- Keep employees motivated to provide the best service. Consider staff bonuses or awards for good customer care (see 12.25).
- Forge closer links with clients. For example, offer to share the cost of marketing and public relations personnel. Rent or loan spare meeting rooms to clients who do not have meeting facilities.
- Take clients' comments and criticisms seriously. Consider the issue from their point of view and treat it as positive feedback.

Client relationship management

5.5 Satisfied clients will not only buy more services themselves but are an excellent advocate for the firm. To get clients to recommend work they need to receive more than an efficient and competent tax service. They have to feel like they are treated with compassion and sensitivity and that instead of their tax and financial affairs being a burden they actually feel good about them.

5.6 Considering the following issues will help the practitioner to develop a rapport with his or her clients, which in turn can lead to recommendations.

- Make clients feel welcome from the outset (see 2.2).
- View things from the client's perspective. Are the firm's letters easy to understand? Try to keep things simple and clear (see 4.3).
- Ask whether the firm's clients are receiving the kind of service you would want to receive.
- Think about the essence of what clients want to know. If the firm is sending a client a tax return, the most vital piece of information they can tell them is how much tax they owe and when it is due to be paid.
- Avoid saying negative things. There is always a positive and a negative way to say the same thing. A positive statement is always more attention grabbing because it is unexpected. For example, instead of saying 'if you do not pay your tax on time you will be charged interest' say 'I know you will want to avoid an interest charge. The way to do this is to pay your tax by 31 January'.
- Be honest and be careful not to promise more than the firm can deliver. Do not tell a client that a full enquiry will be straightforward when it will not. This will only raise their hopes and they will feel let down. Do not promise to work to impossible time scales.
- Remember that clients rarely communicate good news but often assume that they have.
- Fear of the tax system and a feeling of being out of their depth often causes negative remarks by clients. This can result in 'nit picking'. For example, a client may criticise spelling mistakes because they feel comfortable operating at this level.
- Advisors should bear in mind that the real issue bothering a client is probably not the one they are raising. Good listening skills, time and open questions will allow clients to express their real concerns and to get the most out of the relationship.
- Accept that most clients will never understand the tax system. Try to explain things as simply as possible and be prepared to discuss it with them until they develop a sufficient understanding.
- Bear in mind the relevant aspects of a client's personality (see 2.35).
- Clients often consult their tax advisor when they are involved in significant life events, for example, bereavement, marriage, divorce, the birth of children, retirement and business adjustment. All of these events rank high in the stress league tables. Tax advisors should try not to exacerbate a client's stress.
- Use advanced communication techniques. For example, adopt sympathetic body language (see 4.30) and consider whether there are gender issues (see 4.42).
- Operate from a conducive office environment (see 14.10).

Getting too close to clients

5.7 Some practitioners have a natural rapport with their clients and this can cause its own difficulties. If an advisor comes across as sympathetic or if they operate more informally, for example, by meeting at the client's home, the client may expect a closer involvement and can become dependent on them. This will not suit all advisors and providing this level of advice can be time consuming and cause fee problems. If too many clients become dependent on one advisor this can lead to compassion fatigue. Take care to strike a balance.

Ask existing clients to recommend work

5.8 This method of generating new work has a low cost to the firm both in outlay and administration and it is usually gimmick free. The following methods should be used to encourage clients to recommend the practice to their friends and acquaintances.

- Tell clients that the firm is looking for more work. It may sound obvious but often clients are not aware of this. It is not too early to mention this in the initial meeting.
- If a client is pleased about a particular piece of work remind them that the practice is always looking for referrals.
- Ensure that clients are aware of the full range of services on offer by having clear, informative brochures and marketing materials.
- Forge links with employers. They may be able to offer your tax return services to employees, particularly where their employees regularly work abroad or where foreign nationals come to the UK to work.
- Be a positive and upbeat firm and use a positive slogan on stationery and marketing materials, for example, 'recommended by our clients'.
- Consider commissioning an independent client survey to highlight the firm's good points and identify areas for improvement. This may help to target other marketing initiatives.

Conducting a survey

5.9 A client survey can be conducted in-house but it is more usual to commission an agency to conduct it on behalf of the firm. Practitioners should be aware that to get the best from a client survey the following points should be borne in mind.

- Survey the right mix of clients (some satisfied and less satisfied ones).
- Keep it simple, short and limited to a few key questions.

- Avoid questions which influence answers.
- Avoid long scales of satisfaction, for example, one to ten.
- Ensure that the sample size and response rate produces a statistically valid result and that the sample size is large enough.

5.10 Subjects to include in a survey include:

- the range of services;
- quality, for example, speed of service or whether the firm is pro-active;
- topical issues, for example, IR35;
- fees;
- marketing initiatives, for example, a new Internet site.

Marketing

5.11 It is important to identify what the practice is trying to achieve through any marketing initiative. Usually it is to:

- retain existing clients;
- get new work from existing clients;
- get work from new clients;
- sell additional services to new clients.

5.12 Not all partners and staff will be good at marketing or converting prospective clients but the whole firm should be committed to excellent client care. In larger firms a marketing manager or partner should be appointed. Those partners who have good client conversion rates should be used to win new business for the whole firm by attending new client meetings, presentations and marketing events. Care must be taken to ensure that they are supported by the rest of the firm in undertaking day-to-day client work.

5.13 A significant part of marketing and customer care involves good administration and clerical work. A member of staff should be appointed to undertake this work.

Developing and monitoring a simple marketing plan

5.14 Each year the firm should draw up a marketing plan and set marketing targets. These are best done on a firm-wide basis rather than partner by partner. Such a policy recognises that not all partners are good at marketing but compensate for it by being good at other tasks. The plan should cover:

- the firm's objectives (client services, new clients and profit);
- client services offered (current and future);
- competitors;
- prospective leads and contacts;
- initiatives.

Its marketing targets should include:

- the number of new clients;
- the value of new tax work;
- industry sectors, for example, dentists and farmers;
- the type of work, for example, trusts and remuneration packages;
- the number of leads (generated within the firm);
- the number of enquiries (external).

5.15 It is important to monitor the source of new work. This will enable the firm to be more focused in its marketing and client initiatives in the future. It may take several years to build up reliable data, but even after one year helpful trends may emerge. A spreadsheet or database will be the most useful tool for monitoring this. Useful information to monitor may include:

- the client making the referral;
- other sources of recommendations, for example, banks, solicitors, staff;
- responses to adverts (and conversions);
- responses to direct mail (and conversions);
- responses to other marketing initiatives, for example, seminars, PR (and conversions);
- the reasons why the firm was chosen, for example, specialism, location, price;
- the most profitable new clients.

Image and design

5.16 Marketing does not just include supplying clients, contacts and prospective clients with materials and promotional goods and services, it also extends to the firm's image. Good, consistent design is important for:

- enabling the practice to be easily and consistently recognised by clients, other professionals and the public;

- promoting employee loyalty;
- conveying subtle messages about the practice.

5.17 It is worthwhile engaging a designer to create the practice image but before commissioning a design the practice should have a clear idea about what message it wants the design to give, for example:

- clean and clear;
- elegant;
- traditional;
- modern.

5.18 The practice should also consider the following.

- The wording of letterheads and documents. For example, members of the Institute of Chartered Accountants in England and Wales can use the phrase 'Chartered accountants and tax consultants' or 'Chartered accountants, business advisors and tax consultants'.
- The image given by the firm's e-mail address. It can be as original as the firm likes but it could be @accountant.com, @consultant.com or @advisor.com.
- The use of colour. The more colours that are involved the more expensive it will be.
- The type, quality, colour and availability of the paper.
- The typeface. It should be clear, consistent, easily read and not too small.
- The use of logos or graphics.

5.19 A designer can also assist with the design of a logo and website (see 5.46). It is worth testing out potential designs on staff and partners before finalising them. The design should be reviewed or updated every few years or in conjunction with partnership changes.

5.20 Once the design is agreed it should be included on all the firm's stationery, brochures, newsletters, advertisements, mailshots and documents without exception in order to reinforce the firm's identity.

Soft-sell marketing

5.21 This can encompass a range of materials, events and services. The materials or event should enhance the firm's image, convey a simple message and information about the firm. The practice should make it clear that the materials or event are pro-active and are free of charge. They are a 'bonus' for being a client of the firm. Marketing materials and events should engender a 'feel good' factor. This will be lost if the client thinks they are being charged.

Materials

5.22 Ideas for subtle marketing materials include the following.

- A good brochure about the tax practice. It should be brief and to the point, up to date and include an invitation to new clients to come for an initial meeting without obligation.
- Business cards. Ensure that all key staff have them and give them out freely.
- Newsletters (either written or e-mail) sent out at regular intervals.
- Bulletins or guides to tax topics, for example, corporate self-assessment, the construction industry, wills. These can be both printed and sent out newswire style by e-mail.
- Budget summaries.
- Tax data, for example, tax rate cards or mouse mats (these have a long life).
- Diaries and calendars incorporating key tax payment dates.
- Drinks coasters (these have a very high use rate and long life).
- Plastic carrier bags for returning and storing clients' records.
- Folders or files for clients to store their tax papers in.
- Pens, notepads, post-it notes, stress balls, stress testers, calculators and 'how to find the office' postcards, all bearing the firm's name, logo and telephone number in a prominent position.

5.23 Each tax practice will need to develop their own range of materials or commission them from an outside agency. All materials should:

- have a clear, clean image;
- include the firm's name/logo, phone number and slogan;
- be written in plain English;
- not try to convey too much information but provide a taste of what the firm can offer;
- avoid references to fees.

Newsletters and information sheets

5.24 These can be effective communication and marketing tools but they have to be used carefully. Not all clients like to receive them as they think it will result in higher fees. Check clients' attitude to them at the initial interview. Periodically give clients a list of all the firm's publications and information sheets and ask them to select the ones they would like. Make it clear to clients that they will not be charged for them. Alternatively include them on a website or send them out by e-mail.

5.25 Information sheets should be a taster to whet a client's appetite. Good subjects include: setting up in business, self-assessment (including enquiries), family matters, record keeping for the self-employed, ten tax planning tips, being a company director and inheritance tax and wills.

5.26 Many firms buy in newsletters and materials produced by specialist tax writers. These ensure accurate, clear articles but care must be taken to ensure that they are relevant to the firm's clients. If the newsletters are produced in-house take into account the good letter writing tips at 4.3 and ensure that they are light to read yet technically accurate.

5.27 To obtain maximum impact from newsletters they must be well timed. Good times to send them out are in the spring (post-Budget), in the autumn (to remind clients to complete their tax returns) and early in the New Year (to remind clients to pay their tax). Do not only send them to clients but also to general contacts, leads and prospective clients.

Events

5.28 Many firms like to hold marketing events. They should be a taster, light and brief. Some firms charge a nominal fee (£10) for seminars and Budget meetings as this encourages people to attend and covers the cost of refreshments. Late afternoon is usually the most suitable time to hold them.

5.29 Suggestions for subtle marketing events include the following.

- Seminars about topical tax subjects and changes, for example, IR35 and personal service companies. Alternatively, they could be held jointly with a solicitor and cover employment issues, wills and inheritance tax or stamp duty mitigation.
- Quarterly meetings with top clients to discuss business issues, for example, the Euro.
- Budget breakfasts.
- Regular phone calls to key clients. The advisor should have a topical subject pre-prepared to discuss.

- In-house lunches either one to one or in small groups. Include bankers and solicitors.
- Office open days. Prospective clients may feel less intimidated if there are other prospective clients there at the same time. Base it round a tax 'quiz' to see whether the prospective client needs the firm's services or do a basic healthcheck, for example, checking tax codings and personal allowances.

5.30 In planning events the firm needs to consider the following.

- The location. Provide clear instructions about how to find it and where to park.
- The subject. It must not be too technical and it must be relevant.
- The quality of the speaker. They should be able to use up-to-date presentation equipment competently.
- Keep it simple, keep it short and finish on time.
- Allow time for networking before and after the event.
- Ensure that the clients attending are properly introduced to the partners, staff and each other.
- Ensure that there is a good partner and staff to client ratio.
- Have plenty of brochures and handouts available.
- Give out marketing goodies such as pens (see 5.22).

5.31 It is essential that the partners and staff feed back relevant information to the marketing partner or manager so that appropriate follow-up calls can be made about areas where the client has expressed an interest.

Public relations

5.32 The reputation and integrity of a tax practice is an important asset. Public relations can be used to enhance that reputation both within the profession and externally and to mitigate damage to the firm in the event of adverse publicity surrounding a client. Firms may engage a consultant who will usually arrange his or her work to complement advertisements or other marketing events. (Refer to 14.53 when negotiating contracts.) Cultivating good public relations is not, however, just for large firms; small firms can also use it to their advantage.

5.33 Examples of positive public relations include issuing press releases to appropriate publications publicising:

- charity events that the practice is involved in;
- partners achieving public appointment or office in a tax-related body – this may be followed up by the magazine running a profile article;

- staff and student success, for example, in exams;
- practice achievements or awards;
- developments or new services offered by the practice;
- client success (with their consent);
- the results of client surveys about topical issues such as IR35.

Writing articles and media appearances can also be good public relations for some firms and more effective than advertising, as can being involved with tax-related bulletin boards and Internet chatgroups.

Writing and media appearances

5.34 Some tax practices aim their services at other professionals, for example, those who are experts in trusts, offshore tax planning, share valuations, international VAT etc. Writing articles, books, appearing in the media and on the professional lecture circuit can be invaluable in enhancing the firm's image and reputation as an 'expert' and getting the firm's name mentioned widely. The firm does, however, have to have trained staff who are happy to take on such a role. It certainly is not suitable for every practice.

5.35 Tax and accountancy publications are usually hungry for articles or stories. Before sending unsolicited pieces it is worth checking whether the subject is of interest to the editor and the required length of the article. Ask to see proofs prior to publication.

5.36 Local newspapers often run a tax column and some journals regularly take articles on topical tax issues and replies to readers' letters. This is a good way to start writing.

5.37 Journalists like tax specialists who offer a concise, strong opinion. Do not pretend to know about a subject. Care should be taken not to give off-the-cuff answers that are later regretted. The impact of any comments on the partnership as a whole should also be considered. It is a good idea to tape conversations or make notes so that the firm is not misquoted. Even tax and accountancy journalists are looking to make a good story from their interviews. Do not thank a journalist for a quote or ask to see proofs.

5.38 Sometimes tax practitioners are asked to appear on radio or television, particularly around Budget time or if there are controversial changes in legislation. Before appearing on either radio or television it is essential that the practitioner receives media training so that they appear as natural as possible. Video conferencing is good practice. When making such a presentation try to cover no more than three or four main points otherwise the audience may be confused. Remember to remain professional, calm and friendly; be honest and do not criticise others.

5.39 The format of many financial programmes is question and answer. Most practitioners are well trained in answering such questions, the only difference being that they usually come from clients. Presentation skills are covered in more detail at 4.40.

5.40 The firm should maintain a press cuttings and articles file. This can be made available in the firm's reception area. Good articles can be framed and hung in the firm's meeting rooms.

Hard-sell marketing

5.41 Advertising, direct mailing and events can all be used in conjunction with more subtle marketing techniques. The firm should ensure before spending any money on these initiatives that the expense will be justified by the new business generated.

5.42 Advisors should be careful to comply with the ethical rules of their professional body when conducting any marketing initiative (see 5.45).

Advertising

5.43 Advertising includes everything from high profile campaigns, advertisements in the *Yellow Pages* and the trade press to recruitment adverts. In each case the advertisement should be planned carefully to convey a positive message about the practice. Specialist advertising agencies should be used for larger campaigns.

5.44 The advertisement should be linked to a clear marketing objective, for example, to attract new clients operating in a specific industry to the firm, to highlight new tax issues or to promote new services (see 5.14). Large firms may have different agendas, for example, to keep their name in the public arena and to retain market share. Advertisements should give potential clients a good reason to use the firm. Remember that no campaign is guaranteed to get results.

Ethics

5.45 Tax practitioners who are members of a professional body must comply with its rules on advertising. For example, members of the Institute of Chartered Accountants in England and Wales may seek publicity and advertise in a manner that is consistent with the dignity of the profession. Care should be taken, however, when advertising to ensure that:

- the image projected is not inconsistent with that of a professional person bound to high ethical and technical standards;

- all advertisements comply with the law and the requirements of the British Code of Advertising Practice, the ITC and the Radio Authority code as to legality, decency, clarity, honesty and truthfulness;
- the greatest care is taken when mentioning fees or the basis of charge (see 3.46);
- although advertisements may contain justifiable factual statements, they do not make disparaging references or comparisons with the services of others;
- the practice does not make inappropriate claims with regard to its size, for example, a claim to be *the largest* tax practice in the region may be misleading and unclear as to whether this means in relation to partners, staff, turnover, clients or simply office space;
- the firm does not claim to be '*the best* tax practice' – such a claim is purely subjective.

The Internet

5.46 Tax practices should think about how they can use the Internet to sell and enhance their services. It is a relatively cheap medium and increasing numbers of people use it to find tax advisors. A firm can design its own website or it can include its name and details on another organisation's site.

5.47 If a firm is considering its own website it makes sense to engage a professional website designer. Useful tips for commissioning a site include the following.

- Keep the home page simple and the site fairly small.
- Check out other sites and see what works best about them.
- Avoid the overuse of graphics or moving images as this slows down the access time.
- Include useful data, hints, tax tips and advice (this could be taken from the firm's newsletters or other brochures).
- Keep the site up to date.
- Ensure that all links to other sites are worthwhile.
- Include an e-mail link to the firm for further information.
- Include full contact details.

Direct mail

5.48 This is a popular means of marketing amongst tax practices. A target list of businesses or individuals is obtained. This may come from a mailing list company or be built up by the firm internally from contacts and research. The more focused the list the higher the response rate is likely to be. Simply sending a mailshot to all FTSE 100 companies will not produce a good response. If the mailshot is small this may be able to be handled in-house using a mail-merge program. If it is large an outside agency may be required.

5.49 Before sending out a mailshot the firm should:

- ensure that the material is concise, well designed and appropriate (not more than one page);
- that it contains a message or topical information likely to appeal to the target group, for example, details about the National Minimum Wage could be sent to small owner-managed companies;
- that it is personally and correctly addressed to the proprietor or finance director.

5.50 After the mailshot has been sent out there should be a programme of follow-up telephone calls subject to the following constraints.

- Members of the Institute of Chartered Accountants in England and Wales may not send unsolicited promotional or technical material electronically or by fax. From 1 May 1999 it is an offence for anyone to send individuals direct marketing faxes.
- Care should be taken during the course of telephone conversations not to discuss audit, financial reporting or insolvency work unless it is at the specific request of the prospective client.
- The prospective client must not be harassed.

Cold calling

5.51 The conditions applicable to follow-up calls for mailshots should be followed for all cold calls. Use teleconsulting rather than telesales. Teleconsulting warms up leads by discussing personal and business needs and relationships from the outset and offers a more positive approach.

Letters of introduction and follow-up telephone calls may also be sent to other potential introduction sources, for example, solicitors, banks and other professionals.

Commissions

5.52 Practitioners who are members of the Institute of Chartered Accountants in England and Wales may not offer commissions, fees or rewards to third parties in return for introductions to potential new clients.

Sponsorship

5.53 This includes everything from sponsoring sporting and charity events to offering prizes for raffles at tax conferences and sponsoring tax lectures and training courses, both for students and qualified professionals. The firm should consider whether the expense is necessary and cost effective. If it is, make sure that the firm benefits from the PR by the firm's name and logo being displayed in a prominent position.

Networking

5.54 Tax practitioners should make full use of the many networking opportunities available to them. They may be an invaluable source of work. If there are several partners in a practice each one could take responsibility for a different organisation. Examples of possible contacts include the following.

- Tax practitioner bodies, Chartered Institute of Tax, the Tax Faculty of the Institute of Chartered Accountants in England and Wales, Association of Accounting Technicians.
- Local District Societies.
- Business and lunch clubs.
- Other clubs and bodies.
- Those working from communal premises such as artists' studios or 'alternative' medical practitioners.
- Solicitors, tax counsel, banks, estate agents, stockbrokers and independent financial advisors.
- Chambers of Commerce.
- Alumni contacts from previous practices and universities.

5.55 Often membership of relevant societies, clubs and organisations gives not only an opportunity for networking but also a chance to speak at a meeting. This provides an excellent opportunity for publicity. A good range of firm brochures, newsletters and materials should be distributed at such events and appropriate staff and partners should attend as guests.

Marketing organisations

5.56 New work can be obtained by belonging to a marketing group. Such organisations can carry out co-ordinated advertising campaigns for members and promote the practice outside its immediate locality and overseas. Some groups offer more than marketing and include training, manuals and systems. Some cover more than simply tax services and are run more formally than others. Some charge a subscription and others operate on a franchise basis. Examples include The UK200 Group and The Tax Team.

Events

5.57 Lavish entertaining is now a less popular form of marketing. There are more subtle ways of winning new business and busy professional people often do not have the time to attend long events. Nevertheless, clients and staff always appreciate the occasional 'jolly' and entertaining overseas clients or other clients used to conducting business in this way may be appropriate.

5.58 Tax-related marketing events are covered at 5.28. The most effective way to plan non-tax related events is to ask clients what they are actually interested in, for example:

- golfing days;
- wine tasting;
- parties;
- meals;
- trips to sporting events;
- day trips to France;
- theatre, opera or ballet tickets;
- weekend conferences.

5.59 Such events are about networking. It is important to have people there that clients will want to meet. Introductions should be made carefully. It is better to have a purpose to the event as this breaks the ice and gets everyone involved in the activity.

5.60 Be upfront and offer more than one ticket to existing clients. Ask them to bring along a business colleague or friend from outside their organisation who may be interested in using the practice for tax advice.

Internal marketing

5.61 Last but by no means least the firm should use the techniques outlined in this chapter to market internally to its own staff, partners and their relations and friends. A firm's personnel are some of its most important clients. They are the public face of the practice and they need to be well motivated and committed to the practice to offer clients a first-rate service. If they are they should prove excellent advocates capable of attracting new work for the firm.

5.62 There are many ways of keeping staff motivated, for example, staff newsletters, social events and facilities, team meetings and mentors, but the majority of staff are most highly motivated by financial reward. Offer bonuses to employees who make introductions or obtain new work; 10 per cent to 20 per cent of the first year's fee paid as a bonus is still a relatively inexpensive way to obtain work and engenders a lot of goodwill (see also 12.25).

Quick review

5.63

- Many tax practices know that they need to market their services proactively but they are often unsure what they should be doing. Policy Publications in association with the University of Luton published research in September 1999 showing that the top five sources of frequent or regular new business for accountancy practices were extra services to existing clients, closely followed by referrals from existing clients. Much further down the scale came referrals from other business units, specific marketing activities and contact through professional organisations.
- Tendering for tax work has become more common for large corporate and partnership tax work. Research has shown that, when putting together a tender document and presentation, including the senior partner and members of the tax team who will work on the case can pay dividends. Ensure that they are well trained in presentation techniques.
- Adopt good procedures when clients leave. They may come back to the firm at a later date or introduce other clients (see Chapter 6).
- When sending out marketing materials or products, send two of everything and ask the client to forward one to a friend or associate.
- It is not ethical to pay commissions to third parties but it is possible to have bonus schemes for staff providing excellent customer care and for bringing in new business.
- A report published in November 1999 concluded that lavish corporate entertaining was generally ineffective marketing for accountants.
- Instead of a client survey consider a focus group.
- Marketing tax services can be difficult because many people only change advisors for negative reasons. This makes new businesses and young clients who have never had a tax advisor worthwhile targets.

Chapter 6

Losing Clients

6.1 This chapter looks at the ending of the client relationship. In particular it considers:

- why clients leave;
- asking clients to leave;
- complaints;
- the handover procedure and disengagement letters.

Losing clients does not have to be a negative experience

6.2 This aspect of managing a tax practice is rarely written about. The conventional wisdom says that a tax practice will attract and keep clients through marketing and customer care; but should a practice hold on to its clients at any price?

From time to time clients will choose to leave the practice, sometimes amicably and sometimes not. There are also a number of situations when it may make sense for the firm to ask the client to leave. The appropriateness of the advisor/client relationship should always be kept under regular review.

6.3 If there is a lack of new work a firm may do anything to try to keep a client. This can be a dangerous course of action. The advisor/client relationship will become unbalanced and this may cause undue client pressure. Ultimately this can lead to poor client relations, complaints, stress and claims.

6.4 The manner in which the engagement is ended and the way that the transfer to another firm is handled can indicate a lot about a practice. Regardless of the circumstances the practice must behave professionally and courteously. It also makes commercial sense to be as pleasant as possible. Losing a client does not have to be a negative experience. It can be a positive move for both client and advisor. Variety and a regular change of clients can be stimulating. Advisors gain interesting new work and clients may benefit from a fresh opinion and a new approach.

Complaints

6.5 Often before a client leaves a tax practice they will have made a complaint. Many complaints arise not as a result of poor tax work or advice but because of delays in completing work, failure to answer telephone calls or correspondence and misunderstandings over instructions. Fee disputes are dealt with at 3.41.

6.6 Firms can avoid losing clients by the way they handle complaints. Being defensive or adversarial will usually fail whereas a genuine apology and rectification will often solve the problem. Try to deal with complaints in a meeting. Telephone calls can give rise to misunderstandings and impersonal letters may inflame an already delicate situation. Do not take the criticism personally. Treat complaints as positive feedback and try to see the matter from the client's point of view.

6.7 All complaints must be taken seriously. Failing to do so may not only result in lost clients but could give rise to a professional indemnity insurance claim. Most firms will want to understand the circumstances that gave rise to the complaint so that action can be taken to avoid similar problems in the future, for instance, by improving staff training or internal systems.

6.8 The various professional bodies have their own guidance on investigating complaints. For example, members of the Institute of Chartered Accountants in England and Wales must:

- advise clients of the right to complain in the letter of engagement (see 2.24), including the right ultimately to complain to the member's professional body;
- have a partner investigate the complaint;
- after investigation and if the firm decides that the complaint is justified, do everything possible to correct any errors, provide information to the client or a new advisor, apologise or reduce the fees.

6.9 Adoption of a formal complaints procedure is recommended, particularly for larger practices, so that staff and partners know how to behave in the event of a complaint. Such a policy should set out who will handle the complaint at each stage of the proceedings and what action will be taken if the complaint is justified or not. It is also recommended that a list of complaints be retained together with the action taken to remedy the problem.

Why do clients leave?

6.10 The firm should always ascertain and monitor why clients leave the practice so that if any trends emerge, remedial action can be taken if appropriate. The practice should try to be positive about the loss and to see it as part of a natural cycle of client gains and losses.

Reasons why clients leave

6.11 There are many reasons why clients change tax advisors including the following:

- they are unhappy with the service;
- there is a personality clash with staff or partners;
- the cost;
- a change of location (either the firm or the client);
- client growth or complex tax issues (for example, capital gains tax or VAT) indicating a need for a larger firm;
- their affairs are simpler and there is no longer a need for an advisor (for example, after retirement);
- alleged lack of pro-activity by the firm;
- 'the grass is greener elsewhere' syndrome;
- the client has had a strong recommendation to another firm.

Reducing negativity

6.12 No one likes being told that a client is unhappy with the firm or its work but a practice should be philosophical about the loss. It is worth remembering that all firms lose clients; if they did not no practice would ever get new work. Treat the change as a new opportunity and try not to take the loss personally. A firm can actively encourage this by adopting a positive handover procedure.

6.13 If the move to another firm is a positive experience for the client he or she may be a useful advocate for the firm, recommending work or even becoming a client again if the circumstances which led to the move in the first place change. If the move was amicable keeping in touch with the ex-client at Christmas (or other suitable occasions) and inviting them to seminars can be good marketing.

End of engagement questionnaire

6.14 Sending a brief questionnaire about the termination of the engagement to the departing client can demonstrate that the firm is keen to learn from any mistakes it may have made. The firm can also take into account the client's comments in the way that it provides its services in future. Such an approach shows respect for the client's view (even if the firm disagrees with it) and makes them feel valued. Before issuing such a questionnaire, the firm should be prepared for any potentially harsh comments and staff should have the support of the partners.

6.15 Suggested questions to include are as follows.

- Why are you leaving the firm?
- What could the practice have done to improve matters?
- Apart from the reason why you are leaving, were you happy with the service and/or cost?
- What did you particularly like/dislike about the firm?
- Would you recommend the firm to others? If not, why?
- Any other comments?

Monitoring lost clients

6.16 The firm should adopt a monitoring system for lost clients. At regular intervals the practice should review client losses (and gains) by reference to client type, fee and industry sector, together with the reason for the loss. This provides an opportunity for appropriate remedial action to be taken.

Asking clients to leave

6.17 A tax advisor/client relationship is both a professional and commercial one. Accordingly the relationship must work for both parties and on a number of levels. Sometimes it will be appropriate for the firm to ask a client to leave because it is not right for them or because the client can not afford the level of service that the firm wants to provide. Not every client will be right for every firm. The firm can offer a better service if it recognises when a relationship is not working. Passing on a client at the right time can avoid a relationship deteriorating, complaints and negligence claims. It can even earn respect from the client such that they recommend other work which is more appropriate for the practice.

6.18 Handling such an issue with a client is sensitive and it needs to be done carefully, preferably in a meeting conducted by the partner or senior manager. It should focus on why the move is in the client's best interest.

Sometimes the client will be relieved that the firm has tackled the issue before they have had to raise it themselves. This may particularly be the case where the client has been with the firm for a long time but needs a new firm because of substantial growth. Having successor firms to recommend can ease the transfer (see 6.23).

6.19 It is important to time such a request so as to cause minimum inconvenience to the client. Accordingly February and March, before the new tax year begins, is a good time for personal tax clients. The right time for corporate clients will depend on the nature, timing and extent of the work being undertaken.

Reasons to ask a client to leave

6.20 A decision may be reached that a client is not right for the firm due to a specific incident, as the relationship develops or as a result of a strategic review of the tax practice. Reasons to ask a client to leave include:

- they have become too big for the firm;
- they are too demanding;
- the client needs specialist help on a regular basis;
- the firm is focusing on specific clients, industries or types of work and the client does not fit the profile;
- the client cannot afford the firm's fees, frequently questions bills or delays payment;
- loss of key staff/partners;
- conflict of interest;
- personality clash;
- rudeness or aggressive behaviour (see problem clients);
- regular non-compliance with deadlines or irregularities (see problem clients).

Strategic review of the client base

6.21 From time to time it will pay a firm to undertake a thorough review of its clients to ascertain whether they are still appropriate for the firm or whether some have become 'dead wood'. The criteria to be used for such a review will depend on the firm, its philosophy and motivations. The firm may decide to focus only on clients with fees above a certain level or those who buy a range of services rather than just basic tax compliance.

6.22 Weeding out clients in this way can either be done by telling the client directly about the change or increasing fees to such a level that the client moves anyway. Care should be taken with the latter approach. Most clients prefer to be treated directly and honestly. Simply raising fees above the agreed level may only cause fee disputes and stress.

Recommending alternative firms

6.23 If a firm is going to ask a client to leave the firm it makes sense to have a range of firms to recommend as alternatives. The tax practice should cultivate links with much larger firms and specialised tax practices, for example, those offering offshore or overseas advice, VAT specialists etc. This can be done through local accountant/tax advisor groups, meetings at conferences, links with ex-employers or by a direct approach. The relationship may work both ways, with the larger firm referring on work which does not fit its profile to the smaller practice.

Care should be taken to effect an introduction only. The client should be left to arrange a meeting and make up his or her mind as to the suitability of the recommendation.

6.24 Sometimes the practice will not know a suitable firm to recommend, particularly if the client is moving to another part of the country. In this situation one of the professional bodies (or the local district society) should be able to provide a list of suitable practices in the area. Alternatively, consult one of the membership directories (some even include members' specialisms) or the websites of the professional bodies. If a client is leaving because he or she cannot afford professional fees but they still require advice consider referring them to TaxAid (see 21.7).

6.25 Care should be taken not to effect an introduction for known problem clients as this may harm the firm's reputation.

What to do about the client who does not want to leave

6.26 Sometimes a client will not want to leave the firm. They may be genuinely horrified and frightened at the idea of finding a new advisor. In this case a view will have to be taken as to whether it is counter-productive to insist on a change. The suggestion will, however, provide an opportunity to discuss the professional relationship and the reasons why the client is being asked to leave. The firm may need to allow time for the client to get used to the idea of a transfer. There may be no easy solution to such situations and it is likely that a degree of compromise will be required.

Handing over to other professionals

6.27 The various professional bodies each have their own detailed rules about relationships between professionals. These must be followed in effecting a transfer irrespective of whether the new advisor is a member of the same professional body. It is important to ensure that letters from other professionals are answered promptly and the relevant information passed on as quickly as possible. Delay only adds to the stress of the change. Once the case has been transferred everyone can move on. The reason for the change of appointment is a matter between the firm and the client. It is not a matter to be discussed with the Revenue or any third party.

Handover procedure

6.28 In general the following steps will need to be undertaken.

- The client advises the firm of the proposed change of appointment.
- The firm issues its termination questionnaire (see 6.14) and disengagement letter (if appropriate) (see 6.29).
- The new advisor writes the appropriate etiquette letter to the firm.
- The client settles any outstanding fees. (For details about lien over records see 3.43.)
- The firm seeks authorisation from the client to disclose the relevant information to the new advisor.
- The firm responds to the new advisor and supplies the necessary information.
- The transfer date and responsibility for dealing with any outstanding matters or work in hand are agreed between the existing and new tax practice.
- The Inland Revenue is notified of the change of appointment and the Form 64-8 completed and submitted.
- The firm amends its client database and transfers the ex-client's files to its storage facility.

Disengagement letters

6.29 It is good professional practice to send a client who is leaving the firm a letter confirming various matters in connection with the ending of the engagement. This prevents misunderstanding and confusion as to which advisor is responsible for what work. The letter should cover:

- the date that the transfer takes place;
- the date the client ceases to receive services from the firm;

- details of any outstanding work or issues;
- details of any forthcoming deadlines;
- details of the information transferred to the new advisor;
- sufficient information to enable the client to deal with their own affairs if they are not appointing another tax advisor – such information might include a copy of the last tax return, capital allowances claims, capital gains tax asset histories and inheritance tax transfers;
- confirmation that the Revenue has been notified of the change.

Problem clients

6.30 Many problems with clients come down to poor communication. This may give rise to unrealistic expectations or fee disputes. Occasionally clients are unnecessarily abusive, rude or aggressive. Sometimes ethical problems arise. The firm should have internal and external procedures to discuss these.

Irregularities

6.31 The ethical (and legal) reasons why a firm may no longer be able to act for a client include:

- failure to make full disclosure to the tax authorities;
- tax evasion;
- failure to correct known errors.

Where the firm becomes aware of such irregularities the client should be informed at once and preferably in writing. Meetings and discussions may also be necessary. This is the case whether or not the firm was involved with the matter concerned. The taxpayer should be told of:

- the action necessary to correct the problem;
- the cost in tax, penalties, interest and fees of correcting the problem;
- the civil and criminal consequences of not correcting the matter and the cost.

6.32 Tact and good communication skills will be called for. If the client refuses to co-operate the firm should resign and inform the client in writing. The Inland Revenue should be advised that the practice has ceased to act for the client.

6.33 The firm should have internal and external procedures to discuss ethical issues. If the matter is serious the practice should consider taking legal advice. See also 20.2 and following paragraphs.

The former client refuses permission to disclose information to the new advisor

6.34 If the former client refuses permission to disclose information to the new advisor, the firm cannot then disclose any details about the client to them. However, it can refer the new firm to correspondence sent by the practice to the client.

Unpaid and disputed fees

6.35 Fee disputes are a good reason to lose a client. A professional relationship is about mutual trust. Failure to pay fees properly rendered for work done is breach of that trust and the relationship is likely to be harmed. From a commercial point of view the practice is in the business of earning fees for tax work. It makes no sense to keep a client on the books who refuses to pay fees or who regularly questions them.

Rude and abusive clients

6.36 Who needs them? It matters little whether their hostility is directed to partners or staff. Trust your instincts and encourage them to leave at the first opportunity. One approach is to say that the firm does not seem to be right for them. Time it carefully to avoid unpaid fees and be diplomatic to minimise the risk of complaints and claims.

Clients who disappear

6.37 From time to time a client will fail to reply to letters but will not contact the firm to advise that he or she no longer requires them to act. In such cases tax return deadlines will often be missed. Firms should be aware that there may be good reasons why a taxpayer 'disappears'. Mental illness and personal trauma are possible examples. Alternatively, it may be because of a tax irregularity.

6.38 The firm should review such cases periodically and try to ascertain the reason for the disappearance. If the client is unwell, refusing to act for them may simply exacerbate their problems. In this case an attempt should be made to visit the taxpayer or liaise with his or her friends or family (taking care to avoid a breach of confidentiality) to establish the full facts of the case before resignation is considered.

6.39 In other cases the firm should resign. Before doing this the firm should send a letter by recorded delivery post to the taxpayer's last known address advising the client that the relationship has failed and asking them to contact the firm as soon as possible. If this elicits no response a letter of resignation should be sent and the Revenue advised that the firm is no longer acting. It goes without saying that the recovery of fees in such a situation is likely to prove problematic.

Quick review

6.40

- The appropriateness of the advisor/client relationship should be kept under regular review.
- There are sometimes good reasons for a firm to ask a client to leave.
- Losing a client does not have to be a negative experience.
- All firms lose clients.
- Not every client is right for every firm.
- When handling complaints it is worth remembering that 10 per cent of the client's complaint is because of something the firm has done; 90 per cent is probably caused by other factors in their lives.
- Firms should ascertain and monitor why clients leave.
- Cultivate successor firms to ease a transfer.
- Regardless of the circumstances, the transfer to another advisor should be handled professionally and courteously.

Part II – Tax

Chapter 7

Tax Compliance

7.1 Tax compliance involves assisting clients to meet their legal obligations to complete returns, registrations and notifications, accurately and on time in order to minimise the risk of penalties. Although much of the work consists of routine processing, it is nevertheless a vital and sometimes underestimated service which enables firms to understand their clients' needs, and thereby to offer them relevant tax planning services (see Chapter 8).

7.2 This chapter is about managing the firm's tax compliance work. It does not prescribe a specific system as would be the case in a tax compliance manual. Instead, it highlights the various policies and procedures that the practice needs to implement to ensure that it offers a consistent compliance service throughout the firm. Once decided these can be incorporated into the firm's tax manual.

This chapter considers the following issues:

- the need for standardised compliance systems;
- areas requiring policy decisions;
- procedures for completing returns, including standard documentation;
- managing the tax department;
- the contents of tax files.

Maintaining quality by monitoring the firm's tax compliance systems is dealt with in Chapter 11. Chapter 15 considers the related office procedures such as post and file management, notes and diaries.

The need for standardised compliance systems

7.3 Tax is not regulated work like auditing or investment business and therefore many firms, particularly smaller practices, do not see the necessity of having controls or consistent systems of work throughout the firm. Even if a firm accepts the need for compliance systems they may not see the need for these to be standardised throughout the firm. Furthermore, reaching a consensus within the firm as to the one right system can be difficult to achieve. Nevertheless there are many good reasons why standard tax compliance systems should be adopted for the firm's tax services.

- The work is likely to be carried out more efficiently and therefore profitably.
- The firm will be able to offer clients a consistent, quality service which is part of good client care (see the chapters in Part I).
- Files will be consistent and therefore easier to review, thereby simplifying quality control procedures (see Chapter 11).
- To minimise the risk of Revenue enquiries (see Chapter 9).
- To minimise the risk of something being overlooked which could lead to a professional indemnity insurance claim (see 16.22).
- Members of staff know where they stand and what is expected of them (see 12.34).
- It makes it easier to transfer cases between partners in the event of retirement or death (see 17.46).
- The Revenue has announced that if members of professional bodies consistently produce poor quality tax work, they will be reported to the professional body concerned.
- Standards are laid down for tax work by the professional bodies, breach of which may constitute a disciplinary offence. Guidance on how to handle tax work is laid down in 'Professional Conduct in Relation to Taxation' which is produced jointly by the main professional bodies. It sets out guidelines for firms to follow in their dealings with the Revenue and Customs and Excise (see 20.4).

Setting tax compliance policies

7.4 Firms need to agree a number of procedures when setting up or running a tax compliance department. Most of these are dealt with in other chapters (see 7.17).

7.5 As far as ethical policies are concerned, firms should consider basing them on the guidance in 'Professional Conduct in Relation to Taxation'. Three aspects requiring particular attention are:

- disclosure;
- errors;
- the true and fair view.

Disclosure

7.6 Practices need to adopt procedures governing the disclosure of information on tax returns. Disclosure issues are equally applicable to both companies and individuals.

7.7 For personal tax cases, the Revenue has until 30 January following the 31 January after the end of the tax year to open an enquiry into the return. If they do not the return is considered final unless a discovery assessment can be raised. Discovery assessments can be issued where there is a loss of tax arising from fraudulent or negligent conduct. They can also be issued where the Inspector could not have been reasonably expected to have identified the circumstances giving rise to the loss of tax before the end of the normal enquiry period (or before the conclusion of the enquiry) by using the information supplied in or with the return (or supplied at some other time).

This places the onus on taxpayers to disclose all relevant information in the additional information boxes of the return to enable the Inspector to have a full understanding of their affairs.

7.8 The information which should be disclosed includes:

- private use percentages;
- estimated figures;
- accounting policies, for example, the valuation of work in progress (see 7.16);
- contentious items of income or expenditure;
- information relating to capital gains;
- the reason for provisional figures;
- the reason for reducing tax payments on account.

7.9 Information should usually be disclosed in the additional information boxes rather than in a separate letter. This makes the return complete as it stands. If additional information is supplied separately it should be referred to on the return so that it forms an integral part of the return.

7.10 The submission of unincorporated accounts poses particular problems. The practice must decide whether it will submit accounts where these have been prepared for the client. Where they add little or nothing to the information on the return, the value of their submission is debatable. Where they do enhance the information on the return they should be submitted. Most accounts provide a more detailed breakdown than the information shown in the Standard Accounts Information (SAI) and may therefore give the Inspector a fuller understanding of the client's business. Accounts should also be submitted for highly specialised or complex businesses. They must be submitted for all businesses with a turnover in excess of £15 million.

7.11 Where accounts are submitted the fact that they are enclosed should be referred to in the additional information box so that they form an integral part of the return. Where returns are filed by ELS the accounts will have to be supplied separately and on paper. It is therefore important to ensure that they are not overlooked.

7.12 Where relevant, clearances and pre or post-transaction rulings should be sought from the Revenue to give the client as much certainty as is possible with regard to their affairs. Disclosure is highly relevant in this circumstance and failure to disclose all the relevant facts may render the clearance ineffective.

Errors

7.13 Firms should have procedures to notify the tax authorities of errors relating to their clients' affairs. It does not matter whether the mistake arises because of taxpayer or Revenue error, or whether it gives rise to overpaid tax, underpaid tax or an excessive repayment. In all cases the error should be corrected and, under self-assessment, the onus is on the taxpayer to do this. If the firm is involved, however innocently, in obtaining a tax advantage for a client by failing to draw the Revenue's attention to a mistake, they and their client could be prosecuted.

7.14 The practice should have procedures to deal with situations where it becomes aware of an error but the client refuses to disclose it to the tax authorities. It is likely that the firm will have to decline to act (see 6.31).

7.15 Firms should also ensure that their staff are aware of:

- the time limits for correcting errors;
- the possibility of claiming relief under the error and mistake provisions; and
- equitable liability.

The true and fair view

7.16 Tax practices must ensure that the accounts that they produce for all businesses show a true and fair view and have regard to the concept of materiality (*Finance Act 1998, s 42(1)*). This means that Accounting Standards must be considered when preparing the accounts of all entities. Whilst the disclosure requirements of the Accounting Standards are not relevant for unincorporated businesses, consideration should be given to disclosing the accounting policies used in preparing the accounts to prevent the Revenue raising later discovery assessments.

Other policies

7.17 Firms should also have policies and procedures for dealing with the following issues which are integral to a tax compliance service:

- new clients and changes of appointment (see 2.10);
- clients who leave the firm (see 6.27);
- claims and complaints (see 6.5 and 16.16);
- tax planning and the distinction between tax avoidance and evasion (see 8.2);
- enquiries (see Chapter 9);
- tax irregularities, discovery, civil and criminal sanctions and the power to seize documents (see 7.7, 9.36 and 15.44);
- signing out letters (see 11.5);
- file completion and quality control (see 11.8 and following paragraphs);
- staff appraisal and training (see 12.37);
- choice of tax software (see 13.11);
- computer back-up and security (see 13.26);
- libraries and reference resources (see 14.39);
- incoming and outgoing post (see 15.3 and 15.25);
- making and retaining notes of meetings and telephone calls (see 15.18);
- files and records (see 15.28 and 15.51);
- documents subject to legal professional privilege (see 15.44);
- ethical issues (see 20.2);
- money laundering (see 20.46);
- consultation arrangements with other professionals (see 21.2).

Procedures for completing tax returns

7.18 The introduction of personal and corporate self-assessment has brought with it the need for firms to have much tighter systems for preparing tax returns in order to minimise the risk of taxpayers incurring interest and penalties.

7.19 Handling tax cases under self-assessment requires the firm to have procedures with regard to:

- completing returns by the filing deadline (see 7.20 and 7.38);

- identifying taxpayers that need to file returns by 30 September in order to have their underpayments included in their tax codings (see 7.21);
- being 100 per cent accurate in completing returns and computing the tax liability (see 7.20, 7.22, 7.23 and Chapter 11);
- ensuring that clients understand their responsibilities to keep records (see 15.51) and pay their tax on time – this is best done by including the details in the engagement letter (see 2.24) and by using standard letters which ensure that nothing is overlooked (see 7.31);
- receiving statements of account for clients (see 7.26);
- minimising the risk of a return being subject to enquiry by critically reviewing it prior to submission and by making full and relevant disclosure (see 7.6 and 9.4);
- filing returns electronically (see 7.34);
- allocating suitably trained staff to each case. Specialist training will be required for those dealing with Lloyd's underwriters, MPs, ministers of religion, trusts etc. Clients assessed as high risk (see Appendix 11:1) should be allocated to a more experienced member of staff.

Completing tax returns

7.20 The main aspect of compliance work is the completion of tax returns. Undertaking the work in the following way should ensure that clients receive an efficient and cost-effective service, they are not irritated by unnecessary questions and quality control is maintained throughout the firm.

- At the beginning of each tax year write to the client reminding them of their obligation to complete a return, the filing deadlines, the penalties for failure to submit the return on time and any internal deadlines imposed by the firm. The previous year's return should be reviewed and general suggestions made about the information required to complete the form. Care should be taken not to be too specific about this information, otherwise the client may not think widely enough about their affairs and overlook a new source of income. (For a suggested letter see Appendix 7:1.) Some firms send clients an extract of the previous year's return. Care should be taken with this approach since an error in one year's return may simply be repeated each year.
- Pertinent facts gleaned from meetings held with the client during the year or whilst completing the client's return for the previous year should be carefully noted so that they are not asked for information already held by the firm.
- When clients send their tax return information to the firm they

should receive a prompt acknowledgement that it has been received safely. They should be advised of any missing information and when the return will be dealt with. (See 15.51 for further information about client records and for a pro-forma record logging-in sheet.)

- Tax returns will be completed most efficiently by only touching each piece of paper once. Therefore, unless the firm has no other work available, the return should not be started until the majority of the information has been received. The member of staff dealing with the case should work through the information in an efficient and logical way.
- If the tax department and the accounts/audit departments differ, the firm must have procedures to ensure that the accounts department produces all the information necessary to complete the return on time. This includes both accounts and computations. The extent to which the tax work is integrated with the firm's other work will depend on the nature and structure of the firm and the skills of its personnel.
- Before the return is sent to the client it should be critically reviewed to minimise the risk of a mistake or an enquiry (see 9.4).
- The return should contain adequate disclosure of all relevant details (see 7.6).
- Care must be taken when computing the tax even if the firm uses a computer program (see 7.23). Particular attention should be paid to amounts included in tax codings either for the year in question or future years (see 7.22) and to related back pension contributions and losses. All tax liabilities should be reconciled or subject to reasonableness checks. If the client is advised to pay the wrong amount of tax it not only has interest implications but it can damage the client's relationship with the firm. Consideration should be given to the benefit of sending clients a copy of their tax calculation working sheet.
- Details of the payments on account required for the following tax year should be computed. These should be discussed with the client and an application made to reduce the payment on account if it is likely to be too high because of a change in circumstances, falling profits or additional payments such as pensions. Care should be taken to ensure that the calculations are accurate. Where the tax payments on account are reduced, evidence of the basis of calculation should be retained. Clients should be warned about the risk of interest on underpaid tax.
- A file completion checklist should be used to ensure that no matters have been overlooked during the preparation of the return (see Appendix 7:3 for an example of a corporation tax completion checklist). Tax planning issues should be considered and any relevant matters drawn to the client's attention (see Chapter 8).

- The return should be sent to the client for approval. For a sample letter see Appendix 7:2. The client should be advised to check the return and where to sign it. They should be advised about the tax due, the payment date(s) and given details of the tax payments due for the following tax year. Warnings should be given about the risk of interest and penalties.
- Clients should not be sent incomplete returns to sign. If this happens, for example, close to the filing deadline, the client must always be sent a copy of the final return and schedules to approve before the return is submitted to the Revenue. A note should be made if the client confirms his or her final approval of the return by telephone.
- The client should be sent a copy of the return for retention either before or after signature. Some firms provide copy returns only on an 'as requested basis' where clients are known to be averse to receiving unnecessary paper or letters.
- The return should be submitted to the Revenue before the filing deadline. The firm will require controls to monitor which returns have been completed and submitted (see 7.38).

Submitting returns

7.21 There are two main issues involved with submitting returns to the Revenue.

- The firm must decide when to submit each client's return. If the return is prepared towards the end of the filing period there will be no choice about when to submit it. Where the return is prepared earlier in the cycle, the firm should consider whether submitting it early will give rise to an increased risk of an enquiry. This is the case even though the Revenue advise that the early submission of returns does not affect the risk.
- The firm should identify and give priority to submitting returns where there are repayments due or Schedule E underpayments which can be included in the taxpayer's notice of coding rather than being collected directly. In the latter case the return must be submitted before the 30 September filing date.

Coding notices

7.22 Completing returns accurately requires firms to have a policy with regard to notices of coding because these are not sent to agents. It is vital to make sure that clients are aware of this fact and consequently the need for them to forward the coding notices to the tax practice each time they are received in order to accommodate the following procedures.

- Enable the return to be completed correctly. Returns require the details of unpaid tax for earlier years included in the tax coding for the year in question as well as tax due for the year which is coded in a later tax year. Consideration should also be given to checking the coding position directly with the Revenue on each relevant case.
- Check their accuracy. Many contain errors and estimated underpayments.
- Advise the client of the implications for their net monthly income.
- Warn the client about likely under or overpayments at the end of the tax year.

Computing the tax liability

7.23 In most cases where a computerised tax compliance system is used, computing the tax liability is straightforward. Members of staff should nevertheless ensure that the resulting tax liability accords with their expectations. Undertaking basic reconciliations will minimise the risk of a clerical error occurring.

7.24 Manual returns pose particular problems. The firm will require additional quality control checks to ensure that the computations are accurate. In addition to reconciling the computation with the expected tax liability, tax staff should review each other's computations.

7.25 Where the return is submitted before 30 September, the practice should decide whether it will compute the taxpayer's liability or leave it to the Revenue. If the firm is using a computerised system, there seems little point in not calculating it, since the firm will need to do so in order to advise the client about his or her tax position.

Statements of account

7.26 Agents receive statements of account for their clients twice a year unless the client authorises the firm to receive them all on his or her behalf. In this case the firm will need to liaise with the client to ensure that they are aware of the tax liability and to ensure that it is paid by the due date.

7.27 Some tax practices do not check the entries on statements of account on the basis that they have already advised the client about their tax liabilities. Instead they leave it up to the client to query the amount requested if they are unsure about it. Most clients probably expect a higher degree of care than this and when the practice receives its bulk mailing of statements of account it should have procedures to review the statements for errors.

7.28 This does not involve checking all the entries on the taxpayer statement of account in every case. Most statements will show a nil liability and therefore can be assumed to be correct. Where a liability is shown this should be compared to the firm's tax calculation and if it agrees the client should be advised to settle the outstanding amount and warned of the interest (and surcharge) implications. If the liability does not agree more detailed checking may be required.

7.29 Where a credit is shown, the repayment should be claimed. This frequently involves a call to the Inland Revenue. If the client does not require the amount to be refunded (for example, if it is small), the overpayment should be deducted from the next half-yearly payment. Repayments under £10 will automatically be carried forward by the Revenue to offset against future tax liabilities.

7.30 If the statement contains an error, the firm should, with the client's consent, notify the Revenue so that it can be corrected (see 7.13).

Standard letters and forms

7.31 The most efficient tax practices will be those that develop a series of standard forms, documents, letters and checklists specifically tailored to the needs of their clients. (Examples of standard letters and documents are included in the Appendices.) Standard documents, available for use by all staff, ensures a consistent approach throughout the firm and minimises the risk of an issue being overlooked. Care must be taken not to use standard documentation blindly. If it is not appropriate staff should be encouraged to substitute an alternative approach and in any event all letters should be tailored to the specific needs of the client (see 4.3).

Corporation tax self-assessment (CTSA)

7.32 In most cases the procedures required to deal with CTSA cases are no different from personal self-assessment. However, CTSA requires firms to have procedures to identify all the associated companies of the client company. This is important for ensuring that quarterly payments on account are made where necessary and marginal relief, particularly between the starting and small company rate, is correctly calculated.

7.33 Procedures should also be in place to identify all dormant companies. They may not require a CT600 but this cannot be assumed. The Inland Revenue should be advised about a company's dormant status. If a return is issued to a dormant company the tax practice should check with the Revenue whether it is required before the form is completed.

Electronic Lodgement Service (ELS)

7.34 ELS has only been used by a minority of tax practices. With the introduction of Filing By Internet (FBI), the future of ELS looks uncertain. Once the teething problems have been overcome and agent filing is introduced, it is likely that Internet filing will become the norm. The controls for both systems are likely to be similar.

7.35 In order to submit returns by ELS the firm has to agree to transmit 50 returns a year and the software must be approved by the Revenue. Practices must also follow certain procedures.

- The client must provide written authorisation for the return to be submitted by ELS.
- A hard copy of the return signed by the client must be kept on file.

7.36 If the return is accepted no further action is required. If the return fails to be transmitted because of a format error or non-delivery it can be re-submitted. However, if there is an error a new form must be used.

It remains to be seen how many of these conditions will apply to FBI.

Managing the tax department

7.37 A fundamental part of managing the tax department is maintaining controls over the work done to ensure that deadlines are not missed.

Controls

7.38 Firms should maintain tax diary controls over the progress of their tax work. These should cover all compliance cases including personal, partnership, trust and corporation tax returns, accounts, PAYE and VAT work. A list of recommended controls is set out in Appendix 11:3 and at 7.57, 7.72, 7.77, 7.85 and 7.89.

7.39 There is no hard and fast way of maintaining such controls. Many computer systems include effective logs and report generators. It is, however, important to ensure that:

- all clients are included in the control;
- they are used consistently throughout the firm;
- duplicate controls are not maintained – this may result in unnecessary work in reconciling them;
- they are meaningful;
- they are not complicated to maintain;
- the reports can be generated easily;

- they are accessible to all personnel, partners and the head of the tax department;
- they are kept continually up to date;
- they are regularly reviewed by the head of the tax department or partners;
- action is taken as a result of the information shown, for example, clients are chased to send in their tax return information or to return forms for submission to the Revenue.

7.40 The firm's tax controls only exist as a management tool. There is no point in maintaining them if no one looks at them or takes action as a result. They must be regularly reviewed by the head of the tax department and used to manage peaks and troughs in the department's workload.

7.41 One way of using the controls effectively is in conjunction with a Monday morning meeting attended by all tax personnel. The meeting can be used to set an agenda and work targets for the coming week, to discuss any problems which arose during the previous week and to consider outstanding work and work in hand.

Provisional figures

7.42 Tax practices require controls over provisional entries on tax returns to ensure that:

- they are made for valid reasons (pressure of work is not one of them);
- correct disclosure of the reasons for the provisional entry is given in the additional information box on the return;
- the return discloses the date by which the correct information will be available;
- the return can be amended within the twelve-month time scale.

7.43 Failure to provide adequate explanation or disclosure can lead to the return being rejected and to the client incurring a late filing penalty. If the return is not corrected on time it could give rise to an enquiry.

Claims and elections

7.44 The firm will also require controls to monitor all claims and elections made outside the return in case there is a change in the law or client's circumstances which requires the claim to be reconsidered. Under self-assessment most claims are made on the tax return itself. This makes it more important to keep track of those made outside the return, such as principal private residence elections. The firm should do this by maintaining a centralised register either manually or on the computer system.

7.45 Staff should have access to published lists of standard claims and elections and time limits. These should be referred to when preparing tax returns and reviewing clients' files (see Appendix 7:3).

7.46 Where a return is late in being prepared particular consideration should be given to those claims or elections which may be out of time and to warning clients of the consequences of filing their returns late.

CTSA quarterly payments

7.47 Where the firm is involved in computing quarterly tax payments for clients, it will need to keep a log of the companies concerned so that nothing is overlooked. It should use a control, monitoring the payments and revisions to them as the year progresses so that clients can be advised to:

- make supplementary tax payments where necessary;
- be warned of the interest consequences of underpaying tax;
- reclaim any excess tax paid.

7.48 Being able to demonstrate that the payments are made appropriately is vital in avoiding penalties in the event of a large underpayment. For a quarterly payment log see Appendix 7:4.

Notifications and other forms

7.49 Tax practices will also be involved in helping clients to complete other forms. For example, notifying the Inland Revenue about the commencement of a self-employment (Form CWF1), or helping clients to VAT register (Forms VAT 1 and 2).

7.50 Staff should be trained in the procedural requirements for completing and submitting routine forms and must be familiar with the filing deadlines.

7.51 The firm must have control systems to ensure that forms with an imminent deadline are given priority over other less urgent work, and to chase up those forms which have not been returned. The best way to achieve this is by using the firm's post and diary systems (see 15.22).

Files

7.52 Files are considered generally at 15.28 and following paragraphs. Ways for firms to organise their tax files and working papers are suggested below.

Not all clients will require separate files for tax papers, correspondence and permanent information. Separate sections will often suffice.

7.53 Maintaining permanent information is essential to the proper management of a tax case. If it is not properly managed, over a period of years the relevant papers will become hard to find. The use of permanent files or sections also allows for efficient archiving and destruction of old papers and, in the long run, doing so will save a lot of time (for example, looking for the acquisition details of capital assets). Even if a permanent section has never been set up, it is never too late to start. Permanent information can also be kept on the computer.

7.54 A separate fee file or section should be set up including copy fee notes, work in progress reports and details of amounts written off. Statements or letters chasing late payment should also be filed here so that those working on the case can see which clients are slow or problem payers. This means that they can take appropriate action if they are asked to undertake extra work for the client or encounter problems with their tax records (see 3.25).

7.55 Tax working papers should be filed in separate tax years. There should also be separate sections for correspondence and accounts. Each partner and each family member should have a separate file or section.

7.56 A standard index for each section is a good idea and will produce more uniform files. This makes them easier to review and enables those unfamiliar with the case to locate key documents quickly.

7.57 The following paragraphs set out the information which should typically be found on tax files. The information listed can be used by firms to create a standard index for their tax files.

Personal tax — Schedule E taxpayers

Tax working papers

7.58 The file should contain the following.

- Completion sheet and review.
- Taxpayer statements of account. These should be ticked to indicate agreement with the firm's calculations and annotated with notes of discussions with the client and Revenue.
- Notices of coding.
- Copies of SA310s reducing payments on account. These should be supported by calculations, estimates and discussions with the client.
- Notice to file a return.

- Tax calculation working sheet. This should be reconciled by the person working on the case to ensure that the tax liability is logical.
- A hard copy or summary of the tax return together with a photocopy of the taxpayer's signature. Where the firm uses ELS the signed hard copy should be retained on file.
- Supporting schedules to the return cross-referenced where appropriate to the detailed working papers, original documents or copies of them. Original records should be retained or stored in accordance with the firm's policy (see 15.51).
- ELS control sheet if ELS is used.
- Notes of relevant telephone calls, meetings and discussions.
- Critical review and comparison of the entries with the previous year return and reasons for any differences (see Appendix 8:2).
- Disclosure made in the additional information box of the return (see 7.6).
- Planning exercises, reviews and advice. These may be filed on a separate file or section (see Chapter 8).
- Elections and claims.
- Confirmation of receipt of the return by the Revenue.
- Repairs or corrections to the return.
- Enquiries. A separate section or file may be required (see Chapter 9).
- Copies of key correspondence if the correspondence file is particularly large.

Correspondence file

7.59 Tax practices have differing views on where tax-related correspondence should be filed. In practice it does not matter where it is filed as long as it is easy to locate and a consistent approach is used throughout the firm.

7.60 The correspondence section for a typical year should contain the following letters.

- A letter sent at the beginning of the tax year requesting information to complete the return. Often this will be accompanied by an extract of the previous year's return or a checklist (see Appendix 7:1).
- Exchanges of correspondence with the client and third parties regarding the completion of the tax return and the information required.
- A letter sending the client their tax return for approval and signature. The letter should advise the client about the consequences of

submitting the return including the tax due, the due dates for paying the tax, the risk of interest or penalties and the risk of an enquiry (see Appendix 7:2).

- Comments on taxpayer statements of account or further advice about tax liabilities and reductions in payments on account.
- Planning or tax advice.
- A letter returning the papers to the client with retention instructions (see 15.56).

Permanent file

7.61 The file should contain:

- an up-to-date engagement letter (see 2.24);
- personal and background information about the client;
- details of connected files including trusts and companies (see also 15.36);
- the details of key advisors;
- new client form (see Appendix 2:4);
- a copy of the Form 64-8 and other authorities to third parties;
- a summary of any planning advice;
- employment/service contracts;
- pension payments, carry-forwards and carry-backs;
- elections and claims;
- capital gains tax histories and acquisitions;
- inheritance tax transfers;
- a summary of residence and domicile status;
- agreements, for example, rental;
- will;
- trust deeds.

Personal tax — Schedule D taxpayers (sole traders and partnerships)

7.62 Partnerships are required to complete a partnership return but, apart from this form, the tax and correspondence files required for Schedule D taxpayers will be very similar to those for Schedule E taxpayers, with the addition of the following extra information.

Accounts file

7.63 The file should contain the following.

- A completion and review sheet (see *Butterworths Tax Compliance Manual*).
- A copy of the final signed accounts. It is good practice for these to include a report signed by the firm and the client.
- Links from the accounts to the Standard Accounts Information (SAI) on the tax return. The easiest way to do this is to produce the accounts in such a way that the numbers transfer easily into the return and the client can easily see how they are derived.
- Schedule D computations and capital allowances claims.
- Other tax calculations, for example, with regard to changes of year- end or the catching up charge for professional partnerships previously on the cash basis.
- Details of the client's accounting records and systems or a photocopy of them if they are straightforward.
- A work programme detailing the work done to produce the accounts.
- A critical review to ensure that the accounts are meaningful and consistent with the previous year to minimise the risk of an enquiry (see Appendix 9:2).
- Details of the accounting policies. These may need to be disclosed to the Inland Revenue in the additional information boxes on the return, particularly for the valuation of work in progress (see 7.6).
- A trial balance cross-referenced to the supporting working papers.
- Reconciliations, for example, bank, sales, purchase ledger and wages.
- Adjustments to the client's records, for example, accruals, prepayments and stock.
- Details of estimates. These should be disclosed in the accounts or on the return.
- Details of private use adjustments. These should be disclosed in the accounts or on the return (see 7.16).
- An analysis of contentious items of expenditure, for example repairs and renewals.

Correspondence file

7.64 The file should contain:

- letters regarding the quality of the accounting records, problems with them and suggested improvements;
- information sent to the partner's personal accountant where the firm does not prepare the personal return.

Permanent file

7.65 The file should contain:

- partnership agreement and deeds of admission or retirement;
- copies of past accounts and accounting policies;
- fixed asset registers;
- details of hire purchase agreements;
- business asset acquisitions for taper relief claims;
- Industrial Buildings Allowances and Agricultural Buildings Allowances;
- initial notifications, for example, Form CWF1.

Rental income

7.66 In addition to the papers necessary for a personal tax file, rental income and expenditure cases will require some or all of the following documents.

Rental file

- File completion and review sheet.
- Rental accounts with links to the relevant pages on the tax return.
- Working papers to support the entries on the return or accounts.
- An analysis of items of expenditure, for example, of legal and professional costs.
- A critical review to ensure consistency of the accounts.
- Details of disallowable items.

Correspondence file

- Letters about tax liabilities arising on the sale of the property.

- Correspondence with FICO where the owner is abroad.
- Correspondence with letting or managing agents.

Permanent file

- Rental/tenancy agreements.
- Details of the letting agents.
- Details of freeholders and managing agents.
- Details of the acquisition of the property and the dates of letting for capital gains tax purposes.
- Losses.
- Loans or mortgages secured on the property.
- FICO non-resident landlord agreements.

Lloyd's underwriters

7.67 Lloyd's underwriters should be handled by appropriately experienced staff. 'Names' will require separate files relating to the completion of the Lloyd's section of the tax return in addition to a personal tax file. The Lloyd's file should be divided into separate Lloyd's years of account, for example, 1999 or 2000. It is important to ensure that when information is received it is filed on the correct section.

7.68 Lloyd's files will contain some or all of the following documents.

Lloyd's file

- Syndicate advices such as LL185Es, LL9s and LL200s.
- Correspondence with the managing agents.
- Information about profit distributions, investment income and capital gains.
- Investment income from Lloyd's Deposits, Special Reserve Funds etc.
- Details of loss claims.
- Transfers to and from the Special Reserve together with the relevant forms.
- Expenses such as accountancy fees.

Lloyd's permanent file

- Details of the managing agents and syndicates.
- Authorisations signed by the client for the firm to receive information from the agents.
- Details of stop loss policies including the policy excess and premiums paid.
- Details of estate protection plans.
- Solvency statements.
- Statements of means, means verification reports and supporting information.
- Assets in the Lloyd's Deposit, Special Reserve Fund and Personal Reserve Fund.
- Details of bank guarantees.

Trusts and estates

7.69 Trust cases are also specialist work. Even in a small firm one or two members of the tax department should be specially trained to deal with them. The department may need to liaise with other personnel in the firm for the following reasons.

- To ensure that a deceased taxpayer's personal return is completed to the date of death.
- Inheritance tax issues may arise, for example, regarding claims for business property relief.
- Specialist advice may be required regarding the valuation of private company shares.
- Estate work may offer marketing opportunities, for example, to offer beneficiaries personal tax services and investment advice.

7.70 It is vital that proper permanent files are maintained on trust and estate cases so that, if there is a change of personnel, all the relevant information is readily to hand. The use of a trust fact sheet is also recommended (see *Butterworths Tax Compliance Manual*). Background information will also be relevant in the event of a Revenue enquiry and to minimise the risk of important issues being overlooked.

7.71 Trust and estate cases will require some or all of the following working papers.

Trusts

- An engagement letter signed by the trustees.
- Copy of the trust deed and background notes about the nature of the trust.
- Planning advice regarding the setting up of the trust.
- Details of solicitors and financial advisors.
- Details of related trusts.
- Residence status.
- Details of the trustees, beneficiaries and the settlor.
- Investment powers.
- Standing instructions.
- A record of distributions made and related advice.
- Details of the financial advisors.
- The trust and estate tax return.
- Tax status and the tax rates applicable to income and gains.
- Trust accounts showing details of the distributions to the beneficiaries.
- Tax certificates for beneficiaries.
- Correspondence with the Revenue, beneficiaries, trustees and investment advisors.

Estates

- An engagement letter (the letter for the deceased taxpayer lapses on death).
- A copy of the will.
- Details of the beneficiaries and their tax districts.
- Certified copies of the death certificate.
- The IHT200 (or IHT202) Inland Revenue Account, correspondence and supporting documents.
- Deeds of variation or disclaimer.
- The grant of probate.
- Details of solicitors, executors, trustees, bankers and investment advisors.
- Letters of authority.

- Trust and estate tax return.
- Accounts.
- Tax certificates (R185Es) for the beneficiaries.
- Correspondence with the Revenue, beneficiaries and executors.
- Certificate of discharge from the Capital Taxes Office for the payment of the inheritance tax.

Controls

7.72 The trust department will require the controls set out in Appendix 11:3 to monitor the completion of the trust and estate return. In addition the firm will also require controls to monitor:

- the distribution of accounts and certificates;
- the time limit for deeds of variation;
- tax payments (including inheritance tax);
- ten-year charges (for discretionary trusts);
- the date on which a beneficiary attains a life interest;
- the date of absolute appointment;
- the date when the trust accumulation period ends.

Corporation tax

7.73 The compliance work undertaken for corporate clients may consist of the preparation and audit of accounting provisions as well as preparing the CT600 and tax computations. The extent to which these functions are divided between the tax department and other departments depends on the size and structure of the firm and client. The tax department may have to liaise with the firm's internal insolvency department or external insolvency practitioners.

7.74 The firm may also act for the directors or prepare P11Ds. The firm will need to ensure that staff dealing with personal tax or P11Ds are aware of all relevant corporate tax matters if they are not involved in completing the company's corporation tax return. Good liaison between team members will avoid important matters being overlooked or inconsistencies between returns which may trigger an enquiry. Particular items to watch out for include:

- dividends;
- share acquisitions or disposals;
- share schemes;

- benefits in kind;
- overdrawn directors' loan accounts.

7.75 If the client pays quarterly payments or is at risk of making quarterly payments the corporation tax work should be undertaken as soon as possible after the year-end to minimise interest charges (see 7.47).

7.76 The files and working papers necessary for the proper management of a corporation tax case include the following.

Tax working papers

- Completion checklist and review (see Appendix 7:3).
- CT600 signed by the client and cross-referenced to supporting entries on the return.
- Tax computations.
- Details of adjustments to the accounts.
- Analysis of key items of expenditure.
- Details of disallowed expenditure.
- Capital allowances claims.
- Details of group relief claims, overdrawn directors' loan accounts, controlled foreign companies, transfer pricing, double tax relief and shadow ACT. (Depending on the complexity of these issues separate files or sections may be required.)
- A copy of the signed accounts on which the return is based.
- Analytical review of the return and accounts for consistency and to ensure no issues are overlooked (see Appendix 9:2).
- Tax statements.
- Notice to file a return.
- Assessments for pre-CTSA years.
- Details of quarterly payments on account and supporting calculations (see Appendix 7:4).
- Warnings about the interest due on quarterly payments.
- CT61s for quarterly interest payments.
- Amendments to returns.
- Enquiries (a separate file may be needed).
- Notes of telephone conversations and meetings with clients.
- Planning and advice (a separate file or section may be needed).

Correspondence file

- A letter from the firm sending the client the return for approval and signature. Advice about the consequences of submitting the return such as the tax due, the due dates for paying the tax, the risk of interest or penalties or the risk of an enquiry.
- Comment on tax statements or further advice about tax liabilities.
- Advice about quarterly payments on account.
- Planning or tax advice.

Permanent file

The corporation tax permanent file should contain the following.

- An up-to-date engagement letter covering CTSA and quarterly payments (if applicable).
- Statutory information if not held elsewhere.
- Key personnel.
- Shareholdings and shareholder agreements.
- Background information about the client.
- The company's advisors.
- New client form.
- Form 64-8.
- Third party authorities.
- Accounting policies, for example, stock and work in progress.
- Group structure and arrangements in force.
- Associated companies.
- Losses.
- Summary of planning advice given.
- Elections and claims, for example, roll-over relief.
- Capital gains tax asset histories.
- Industrial Buildings Allowances or Agricultural Buildings Allowances.
- Agreements, for example, licences, royalties and loans.
- Gift aid payments and deeds of covenant.
- Clearances.
- Transfer pricing documents.

- Exchange differences.
- Share valuations.
- Pension fund details if not held elsewhere.
- Details of enquiries and their outcome.

Controls

7.77 The tax department should control its work by reference to a monthly list of companies due to:

- pay tax within the next three months;
- file returns within the next three months.

This time scale will ensure that tax payments are made and returns completed on time. The approach and procedures cannot be the same as those for personal tax because of the different filing dates.

The Revenue sends agents lists of returns due for filing and these should be used in conjunction with the firm's own systems to ensure that nothing is overlooked.

7.78 Details of the CT600 controls are set out in Appendix 11:3. Controls for quarterly tax payments are detailed in Appendix 7:4. The tax department will also need controls to monitor the preparation of accounts and CT61s.

VAT

7.79 Many tax practices undertake VAT work for clients. The compliance services offered may consist of:

- preparing returns (usually where the firm also provides bookkeeping services);
- checking returns prepared by clients;
- registration and deregistration;
- notifying changes in partnerships and groups;
- advising on appropriate accounting systems and the choice of VAT schemes (for example, retail, cash, accounting);
- attending assurance visits;
- pre-visit healthchecks;
- general advice.

7.80 Firms can provide valuable services to clients who prepare their own VAT returns by checking the composition of the return when completing the annual accounts. This means that the client can correct any errors they have made by amending the next return or making voluntary disclosure within the three-year time limit. Care must be taken, however, to ensure that the client will pay for this service. Bulletins notifying clients that prepare their own returns of key VAT changes can also be a cost-effective means of helping clients to avoid costly mistakes (see 5.24).

7.81 VAT is a highly complex tax, particularly with regard to overseas issues and property. Firms should cultivate links with specialists to help in complicated cases or in the event of an appeal to the VAT Tribunal (see 21.2 and 21.12).

7.82 Separate VAT files will be necessary for some clients. For others a separate section within the main tax file will be sufficient.

VAT file

7.83 The information on the file should include:

- copies of signed VAT returns;
- a summary of the VAT return cross-referenced to supporting working papers;
- the VAT account and reconciliations;
- adjustments to the returns, for example, fuel scale charges, private disallowances, partial exemption or retail schemes;
- adjustments to previous returns because of error or serious misdeclaration;
- intrastat and EC sales listings;
- healthchecks, reviews and planning;
- notes of meetings and discussions, including assurance visits by Customs and Excise.

Permanent file

7.84 The file should include:

- the registration certificate and copy of Forms VAT 1 and 2;
- an engagement letter covering the VAT services supplied;
- group VAT arrangements;
- changes in partnerships and groups;

- details of special schemes, for example, cash basis, annual accounting, retail schemes, Tour Operators' Margin Scheme;
- cars subject to private fuel scales;
- other industry-specific guidance, for example, auctioneers or second-hand schemes;
- property transactions;
- details of international transactions, imports and exports;
- summaries of VAT returns;
- details of assurance visits.

Controls

7.85 The firm must have controls to monitor the VAT returns that need to be prepared. This will assist the department in its day-to-day management and enable the head of the department to ensure that deadlines are met.

7.86 Registration, deregistration and other notifications (for example, of a serious misdeclaration) must take place within prescribed time limits. These are best monitored by means of diary notes (see 15.22).

PAYE

7.87 Many tax practices also offer PAYE services. This may include the operation of the entire payroll as a bureau. It will also usually include the preparation of Forms P35 and P11D. Other PAYE services offered may include:

- help with compliance visits;
- pre-visit healthchecks (for a checklist see Appendix 9:3);
- advice on status issues – this is particularly relevant with the introduction of IR35;
- National Insurance planning (including Class 1A contributions);
- remuneration packages;
- share schemes.

7.88 The working papers and permanent files of payroll clients should contain the following documents and information.

PAYE file

- P35, P14s, P11Ds, sub-contractors' returns and other end of year forms signed by the client.

- Summaries of the entries on the forms cross-referenced to supporting working papers.
- A reconciliation of the PAYE records and resulting adjustments.
- Class 1A National Insurance calculations.
- PAYE Settlement Agreements (PSAs).
- Salary and wages records and payslips.
- Client and Inland Revenue instructions.
- Details of bonuses and benefits.
- An assessment to ensure that pay rates comply with the National Minimum Wage.
- Sub-contractors' records.
- Coding notices.
- Details of leavers and joiners, P45s and P46s.
- Details of those working abroad.
- Information for statutory sick pay.
- Information for statutory maternity pay.
- Details of students employed.
- Student loan repayments.
- Working Family Tax Credit instructions.
- Returns of company cars.
- Records of expenses and benefits in kind.
- Payroll giving.
- Pension information.
- Notification/payment of the PAYE and National Insurance due.
- BACs transfers or other payments.

Permanent file

- A signed engagement letter. Particular care should be taken to ensure that it covers P11D work in sufficient detail to limit liability. It may also be prudent to ask the employer to sign a letter of full disclosure of all matters relating to P11Ds given the high penalties for their incorrect completion.
- Copies of standard employment contracts.
- Details of consultants (not subject to PAYE) and their contracts.
- Details of compliance visits and meetings with the Revenue.

- BACs.
- Standing instructions and changes to them.
- A note of whether the employer is a small employer entitled to pay its PAYE quarterly.

Controls

7.89 The firm will require a calendar or diary listing all the key dates for paying wages, PAYE and National Insurance and for submitting the end of year returns. This will ensure that nothing is late or overlooked. The diary should be used in conjunction with a control listing all the clients for whom the practice undertakes PAYE work. This will enable the head of the department to control and monitor the outstanding work on a day-to-day basis.

Appendix 7:1

Letter to a Client Requesting Information to Complete the Tax Return

Dear Client

Your tax return for the year ended 5 April 2000

I expect that you have recently received a notice to complete a tax return for the year ended 5 April 2000. The return must be completed and submitted to the Inland Revenue no later than 31 January 2001 but if possible I would like to submit it before 30 September 2000.

I attach a list of the information I will need from you to be able to complete the form. When you have it all available please let me know and we can arrange a convenient time and place to meet. The checklist is based on the details disclosed on last year's tax return but some aspects of your affairs may have changed. I will need details of any new sources of income or any changes you have made to your financial affairs in the period 6 April 1999 to 5 April 2000. I would also recommend that you go through all your bank and building society statements to ensure that there are no other sources of income that should be disclosed.

If you have any questions please call me. I look forward to arranging a meeting in due course.

Yours sincerely

A Partner

Checklist of likely information needed to complete your tax return for the year ended 5 April 2000

Please tick the box to indicate the information you have given to me.

The tax return or notice to file a return sent to you by the Inland Revenue.	
Any letters or tax calculations sent by the Inland Revenue since 6 April 1999.	
Payslips and Form P60 for your occupational pension.	
Details of the amounts received from your state pension for the year to 5 April 2000 and the amount you will receive for the year to 5 April 2001.	
Details of your self-employed consultancy income and expenses for the year ended 5 April 2000 and supporting invoices and receipts.	
Bank and building society statements for all accounts in your name.	
Details of the interest received on all your bank and building society accounts. I believe the relevant accounts to be .... However, you may also have opened other accounts that I don't know about.	
Vouchers showing the dividends received on all your shares and unit trusts. Last year these were	
Details of any shares/unit trusts sold. I will need to see contract notes, details of the date the shares sold were bought and their original cost.	
Details of the sale of your holiday flat.	
Any other relevant information.	

Appendix 7:2

Letter to a Client to Accompany the Tax Return

Dear Client

Your tax return for the year ended 5 April 2000

Thank you for letting me have the additional information to complete your tax return for 1999/2000. I now enclose the form for your approval and signature. Please would you check it carefully and if you are sure that it is complete and accurate please sign it on page 8 where I have indicated and return it to me. I can then submit the form for you. Please note that the return must be submitted by 31 January 2001 if you are to avoid a penalty. I also enclose a further copy of the return for your records.

The information shown on the form is as follows.

- The interest on your bank and building society accounts.
- Your employed income.
- Your self-employed income and expenses (see below).
- Details of the gifts from your father. These are not taxable but I have disclosed them on the return so that the Inspector has a full picture of your affairs and can see how you have supported yourself in spite of your low profits.

Tax liabilities

Your tax liabilities are as follows. I also enclose a calculation sheet to show you how the total liability for 1999/2000 is worked out.

Payment for 1999/2000	£592.64	Due 31.1.01
First payment on account for 2000/2001	£296.32	Due 31.1.01
Second payment on account for 2000/2001	£296.32	Due 31.7.01

This means that your total tax payment due on 31 January 2001 will be £888.96. The tax must be paid by 31 January 2001 regardless of whether you have heard from the Inland Revenue or not. If you have not received a statement of your tax liability by 20 January 2001 please contact me and I will advise you how to make payment. If you do not make payment on time you will be charged interest. If you pay the tax later than 28 February 2001 you will also be surcharged.

If for any reason you believe that your income for 2000/2001 will be less than that for 1999/2000 please let me know. It may be possible to reduce the payments on account.

Your self-employed income and expenditure

The accounts figures are as per your records. I have, however, made the following adjustments to them.

- The income includes the March sales invoice that was unpaid at the year end.
- The expenses have been adjusted for your private use of the items.
- I have included a provision for my accountancy fee.
- I have claimed capital allowances on your equipment.

If you have any questions please call me. I look forward to receiving the signed return back from you soon.

Yours sincerely

A Partner

Appendix 7:3

Example of a File Completion Checklist

Corporation tax completion checklist

Client name		Completed by	
Risk assessment	High/Low	Date	
Partner		Reviewed by	
File number		Date	

Consideration	Yes/No/N/A	Signed/Comments
Is there an engagement letter covering all the services provided? Is it up to date for corporate self-assessment (CTSA)?		
Have all the relevant files, including the permanent file, been read?		
Has the Revenue issued a notice requiring the company to deliver a return?		
Has the return been completed for the correct accounting period?		
Does the file contain supporting information for all entries on the CT600 and corporation tax computation?		
Are the signed accounts on file?		
Have all reliefs to which the company is eligible been claimed?		
Do the computations appear reasonable? Has an overall tax reconciliation been undertaken?		
Has the company been advised of the corporation tax liability, the due date(s) for payment and the interest consequences of late payment?		

Consideration	Yes/No/N/A	Signed/Comments
Has the tax been paid?		
Has the client been advised about quarterly tax payments?		
Has the client been advised about tax refunds?		
Has the client been asked to approve and sign the return in a letter?		
Has the return been filed on time?		
Is the file complete?		
Does it contain a copy of the signed return?		
Have the tax diary controls been updated?		
Is the corporation tax profit consistent with the previous period? Note the reasons for variances.		
Are the disallowances consistent with the previous period?		
Has appropriate disclosure been made on or with the return?		
Are the accounting records reliable? Can improvements be made to them?		
Have all the original accounting records been returned to the client? Is the client retaining the records for the correct length of time in a secure place?		
Are all claims and elections and time limits noted?		
Are details of losses noted?		
Are details of shadow ACT carried forward noted?		
Does the file contain details of all group transactions, transfer pricing and CFC issues?		
Are details of overdrawn directors' loan accounts noted?		
Has the client been billed?		
Has the permanent file been updated?		

Consideration	Yes/No/N/A	Signed/Comments
Has a partner reviewed the return?		
Are there any technical or other problems which necessitate a second partner review or 'expert' opinion?		
What tax planning recommendations can be made?		

Action required

CTSA Quarterly Instalment Payments (QIP) Log

Name		Accounting date	
Client reference		% payable in quarterly instalments (until 30.6.02)	
Partner/manager/ staff		Balance due on normal date	

Quarter 1

Date	Estimated profit (£)	Estimated tax (£)	% payable in quarterly instalments	First instalment (25%) (£)

Quarter 2

Date	Estimated profit (£)	Estimated tax (£)	% payable in quarterly instalments	Second instalment (25%) (£)

Quarter 3

Date	Estimated profit (£)	Estimated tax (£)	% payable in quarterly instalments	Third instalment (25%) (£)

Quarter 4

Date	Estimated profit (£)	Estimated tax (£)	% payable in quarterly instalments	Fourth instalment (25%) (£)

Balance

Date	Estimated profit (£)	Estimated tax (£)	% payable in quarterly instalments	Balance (£)

Quarterly running total

Date	QIP paid (£)	Cumulative paid (£)	Revised QIP due (£)	Over/under paid (£)	Further payment due/refund claimed (£)
First quarter					
Second quarter					
Third quarter					
Fourth quarter					
Balance					

End of year reconciliation

Date	QIP paid (£)	Cumulative paid (£)	Actual QIP due (£)	Over/under paid (£)	Interest position
First quarter					
Second quarter					
Third quarter					
Fourth quarter					
Balance					

Chapter 8

Tax Planning

8.1 Tax planning is usually seen as the sexy part of tax practice. It is a chance for advisors to make a real difference to a client's tax liability and to be constructive and pro-active. The work may be originated by the firm or produced in response to a client question. Tax planning encompasses a wide range of work ranging from a decision about whether to incorporate a partnership through to complex tax schemes.

This chapter sets out a wide range of issues for firms to consider when offering tax planning services to their clients including:

- the general issues;
- using checklists;
- the contents of tax planning files;
- providing the advice;
- the scope for firms to offer planning services;
- potential pitfalls.

A broad approach

8.2 Tax planning involves more than simply suggesting ways to save tax in a given situation. To be successful at tax planning advisors need to think carefully about the wider implications for the taxpayer. Advisors should take into account the following considerations when offering tax planning advice.

Economics

8.3

- The cost of the advice, including the cost of implementing the scheme, must be commensurate with the benefit.
- The advice should be viewed from an economic point of view, not just from a tax perspective. The aim should be to maximise the taxpayer's total income, cash flow or resources and not just to minimise tax.

- The professional indemnity risk should be in proportion to the fee.
- There should be a commercial reason for undertaking the planning.

Aims, personality and family

8.4

- Consider the taxpayer's aims, wishes and personality.
- Review the impact on the rest of the taxpayer's family.
- For personal tax planning, ideally the whole family should be involved.
- Take into account all of the taxpayer's businesses, pension funds and trusts.

The work

8.5

- Consider all the taxes, both direct and indirect. Minimising one tax could cause problems with another.
- Take into account future political and legal changes, for example, a change of government or the possibility of a general anti-avoidance rule (GAAR) being introduced.
- Remember the basics, such as using all annual allowances and reliefs.
- If there are problems they should be drawn to the taxpayer's attention at the first opportunity.

Anti-avoidance

8.6

- Great care must be exercised to avoid tax planning schemes falling foul of the *Ramsay* principle and the anti-avoidance provisions.
- It is acceptable planning for taxpayers to arrange their affairs to minimise their tax liabilities but the Inland Revenue may review the means by which tax is avoided.
- Tax planning advice should be capable of withstanding Inland Revenue scrutiny.
- Customs and Excise generally close VAT loopholes quickly. They particularly dislike complex and artificial schemes.
- There are many anti-avoidance provisions relating to overseas transactions.

Overseas issues

8.7

- Ensure that the client is advised about the tax issues in the overseas country as well as those relating to the UK. Few advisors have the necessary expertise; it may be better to refer the client to an international practice (see 21.2).
- If the client is reluctant to consider the overseas issues, the firm should consider whether it can act.
- Consider money laundering issues (see 20.46).
- The exchange of information between countries is increasing all the time.
- Documentation must reflect the full facts of the situation. The jailing of fraudulent advisors is not unknown.

Disclosure and enquiries

8.8

- Full disclosure of all the facts should be made to the Inland Revenue.
- Tax planning may increase the risk of an enquiry.
- Consider the risk and cost of the Inland Revenue challenging the scheme and of failure.
- Clients may not want to pay twice, once for the scheme and again for an enquiry.

Risk management

8.9

- Ensure that the firm's professional indemnity insurance covers the work.
- Check that there is an engagement letter in place covering the work and limiting liability if necessary. It should cover the work to be undertaken, the fee and time scale (see 2.24).
- Make sure that the scheme will enhance the firm's reputation.

Accounting

8.10

Consider whether the scheme distorts the entity's accounts and the impact on shareholders and financiers.

Compliance, claims and elections

8.11

- Complex planning is all very well but make sure that the client is complying with filing, tax payment and record keeping requirements and not incurring interest, penalties and surcharges.
- Missed claims and elections have traditionally been one of the biggest risk areas for tax practitioners. Self-assessment should improve this but firms should continue to pay attention to the possibility of making claims and elections and to their timing.

Specialisation and research

8.12

- Encourage staff and partner specialisation to create experts within the firm.
- Expect staff and partners to share their knowledge with each other.
- Have a good tax library (see 14.39).
- Undertake careful research.
- Keep up to date with the latest thinking and proposals.

Quality control

8.13

- Adopt good quality control and review systems (see Chapter 11).
- The firm should work within its limitations and know when to call in an expert, particularly for the drafting of legal documents and valuing property (see 21.32).
- Investment advice must be within the scope of the firm's authorisation (see 20.11).

A checklist approach

8.14 A tax practice will usually undertake three main types of tax planning.

- Annual reviews as part of completing the tax return or before the end of the tax year. Such reviews should now be undertaken before the tax return is submitted to the Inland Revenue. A review shortly before the end of the tax year may still have a limited benefit for some clients.
- Planning exercises specifically tailored to the client's needs, such as share valuations or partnership retirement planning exercises.
- Specifically marketed planning products including remuneration packages and healthchecks. For examples of some tax planning products see 10.9.

8.15 The use of checklists can assist all types of tax planning. Even specific planning exercises have elements to them that lend themselves to a standardised approach. A checklist approach is an easy way to identify planning opportunities and minimise the risk of an important issue being overlooked. They enable some of the work to be delegated subject to control by the partner or manager.

8.16 Suitable checklists are available in tax publications and these can be adapted for the firm's clients. Others could be specifically designed by the practice. A series of these together with accompanying information sheets or leaflets will give a tax practice a means of offering clients a cost effective tax planning service.

For an example of a personal tax planning checklist see Appendix 8:1.

The tax planning file

8.17 Whilst most firms are unlikely to use separate tax planning files except for the most complex cases, it is good tax practice management to have a separate 'advice' section on a client's current tax or correspondence file.

8.18 The file should contain the following papers:

- details of the planning work to be undertaken;
- background and briefing notes;
- a note of the assumptions used;
- copies of reference sources and supporting cases and legislation;
- sufficient working papers to support the advice given and any checklists used;

- the opinion of Counsel or an independent expert;
- notes of telephone conversations and meetings;
- the advice given;
- details of the client's instructions and any further work required;
- details of any key dates, elections or future action;
- evidence of review by a partner or manager and a second partner review if the work is considered high risk.

Providing the advice

8.19 It will usually be appropriate to meet with a client requiring tax planning or advice to ascertain their needs. Alternatively, the instructions may be given over the telephone. However the ideas are initially discussed, the advice should be followed up in writing. This minimises the risk to the practice and ensures that the client has a permanent record of it for future reference. An advice letter should contain the following points.

- The purpose of the letter, the client's aims, the main conclusions and the tax savings should be summarised in the opening paragraphs.
- The main body of the letter should contain the facts, a discussion of the planning opportunities, together with the solution, legislation, cases and calculations.
- The conclusion or recommendations can be a series of action points.
- If there is no clear-cut answer say so and present the options.
- Use numbered paragraphs and pages.
- Make the letter as short and concise as possible.
- The letter should state the assumptions on which the advice is based, give risk warnings, caveats and any necessary disclaimers.
- If the firm has relied on the advice of an expert or Counsel, it should say so.

8.20 If the advice is provided report style it should be in the following format.

- Title page. The report should be marked 'confidential'.
- Contents.
- A summary of the main points including any assumptions on which the advice is based.
- The expected results, such as tax savings or the risk of an investigation.
- The scope of the work and the taxpayer's objectives.
- Supporting calculations, schedules and appendices.

8.21 The report should be sent out with a covering letter. The letter should aim to minimise the firm's risk; in particular it should contain disclaimers, re-state key assumptions, give risk warnings and restrict, if necessary, its circulation.

Relationships with the Inland Revenue

8.22 Wherever possible complex tax planning schemes should be discussed with the Inland Revenue. Clearance applications can be made for certain transactions, particularly those concerning corporate reconstructions, purchases of own shares, demergers and employee share schemes. Capital gains tax valuations can also be checked prior to submission of the return. Doing this gives the client certainty.

8.23 Where formal approval and clearance procedures do not exist, tax advisors must be careful to ensure that the client's tax return makes sufficient disclosure to enable the Inland Revenue to understand fully the transaction and its implications. Failing to do this could result in a later tax 'discovery' (see 7.6).

8.24 Firms should be prepared to discuss planning schemes with the tax authorities on the basis of the provision of full information. The Inland Revenue and Customs and Excise almost always investigate such schemes and are likely to challenge them at the Commissioners, tribunals or in the courts.

8.25 Situations where tax planning is likely to have taken place, for example, business changes, may give rise to a higher risk of an enquiry. Advisors should, therefore, always be prepared for their work to withstand such scrutiny. This is even more important where complex tax planning schemes are involved.

8.26 Tax advisors should be aware of the fine line between evasion and avoidance and ensure that the advice that they offer clients does not fall into the wrong category. This can happen inadvertently as a result of political and legal changes.

8.27 Although there is as yet no general anti-avoidance rule, various legal judgments have given the Inland Revenue wide-ranging powers to counter unacceptable tax avoidance. It is important to keep in mind that any tax planning must be for a bona fide commercial reason. A series of transactions which includes steps inserted purely for tax avoidance will almost certainly be challenged.

Detailed tax planning

8.28 The following section lists some of the most common areas where tax planning services are frequently offered. It also highlights some of the specific risks to watch out for when providing planning advice. It should be noted that many of the most popular tax planning subjects are also the high-risk areas.

Income tax

8.29 Planning topics include the following:

- high marginal tax rates;
- making use of allowances and lower rate bands for other family members including ensuring the appropriate beneficial ownership of assets;
- pension planning;
- the use of tax-exempt savings, for example, Gilts, ISAs and National Savings products;
- non-residents and other residence and domicile issues;
- rental and investment property;
- reliefs such as the Enterprise Investment Scheme and enterprise zones;
- family trusts;
- school fees planning.

8.30 Risk areas include:

- trusts;
- divorce and separation;
- enquiries;
- overseas issues.

International tax

8.31 Planning topics include:

- offshore structures;
- non-domiciled individuals;
- double taxation;
- transfer pricing.

8.32 Risk areas include:

- anti-avoidance provisions;
- fraud and money laundering;
- conflict between UK tax efficiency and the tax treatment overseas;
- transfer pricing;
- investigations.

Employees and directors

8.33 Planning topics include:

- the choice of company car;
- choice of a car or salary, including the Fixed Profit Car Scheme (FPCS);
- minimising Class 1 and Class 1A National Insurance;
- tax efficient benefits in kind;
- share schemes;
- termination payments;
- pensions.

8.34 Risk areas include:

- the definition of employed versus self-employed;
- termination payments;
- PAYE audits.

Unincorporated businesses

8.35 Planning topics include:

- whether and when to incorporate;
- choice of year-end;
- change of year-end including the utilisation of overlap profits;
- admission and retirement of partners;
- claiming capital allowances, particularly first year allowances;
- limited partnerships;
- the acquisition of further businesses;
- pensions.

8.36 Risk areas include:

- incorporation including lost capital allowances and taper relief;
- accounting policies and compliance with generally accepted accounting policies (GAAP) including the withdrawal of the cash basis and the valuation of work in progress;
- grey areas for expenses including estimates and expenses with duality of purpose;
- correct classification of assets subject to capital allowances;
- farmer's averaging claims;
- the optimum use of losses;
- the operation of PAYE including the Working Families Tax Credit and student loans;
- enquiries.

Corporation tax

8.37 Planning topics include:

- buying and selling companies and corporate reconstructions;
- financing issues;
- the choice of remuneration, bonuses or a dividend from a family company;
- remuneration packages and share schemes;
- the correct timing of dividends and bonuses;
- IR35;
- taking advantage of falling corporation tax rates, for example by changing the accounting date;
- pension schemes;
- avoiding tax at high marginal rates, for example by deferring the sale of assets or bringing forward capital expenditure;
- transfer pricing issues;
- group relief;
- losses;
- capital allowances, particularly first year allowances.

8.38 Risk areas include:

- the definition of an associated company – this is now highly relevant for eligibility to the starting rate of corporation tax;

- group issues;
- overseas transactions;
- losses;
- provisions;
- PAYE audits;
- insolvencies;
- enquiries.

Capital gains tax

8.39 Planning topics include:

- equalising assets between husband and wife to make use of both annual allowances and reliefs;
- retirement;
- sale of a business;
- share valuations;
- losses;
- correctly timing the disposal of assets depending on gains/losses and roll-over relief.

8.40 Risk areas include:

- qualifying for business asset taper relief;
- definitions, for example, those associated with retirement relief.

Inheritance tax

8.41 Planning topics include:

- practical planning, for example, lifetime gifts out of income, lifetime transfers and estate equalisation;
- trusts;
- insurance schemes;
- passing large estates on to the next generation;
- will reviews and variations;
- valuable chattels.

8.42 Risk areas include:

- gifts with a reservation of benefit and lease carve-out schemes;

- trusts;
- valuations;
- qualifying for business property relief and agricultural property relief.

VAT

8.43 Planning topics include:

- business transfers and changes;
- the use of various schemes, for example, the cash accounting scheme, tour operators' margin scheme;
- the VAT rating of specific supplies;
- partial exemption;
- sales promotions.

8.44 Risk areas include:

- partial exemption;
- artificial separation of businesses;
- EEC and international trade;
- property transactions;
- groups;
- exempt supplies.

National Insurance

8.45 Planning topics include:

- employed/self-employed status;
- National Insurance effective remuneration.

8.46 Risk areas include:

- the interaction of the different classes of National Insurance;
- Class 1A National Insurance and benefits in kind;
- the interaction with state benefits.

Quick review

8.47

- Artificial tax planning schemes may not be in the client's interest because of the risk that they will be challenged by the tax authorities.

- Involving the whole family in tax planning can increase the likelihood of the advice being accepted and acted upon. This particularly applies to retirement, inheritance tax and capital gains tax issues.
- Keep detailed notes of telephone calls and meetings giving instructions.
- Getting clients to accept and act upon tax planning suggestions depends upon the way that the advice is communicated (see Chapter 4).
- Tax planning does not have to be the sole preserve of the wealthy. A checklist approach emphasising simple ideas can be cost effective for all taxpayers.
- When giving advice always tell clients how much tax the ideas have saved them.
- For some clients there may be very limited scope for tax planning. In this case look at the entirety of their financial affairs and seek ways to improve them. See 10.15 for some suggestions.

Appendix 8:1

Personal Tax Planning Checklist

Tax practitioners have to consider so many issues when dealing with their clients' tax affairs that it is easy to overlook planning issues. Using a checklist, such as that attached, will highlight problems or areas where advice can be given.

Using the checklist

- Under self-assessment it is vital to ensure that all the points are considered before the tax return is submitted to the Inland Revenue. An annual planning review at any other time of year is now largely irrelevant.
- The initial risk assessment should be completed prior to completing the checklist. It can then be confirmed after the checklist is completed. If the final assessment is 'high' it is recommended that a more detailed review of the risk areas be conducted or specialist advice sought.
- The checklist includes space to show that it has been reviewed and considered by a partner or manager.
- The use of 'don't know' rather than a spurious 'not applicable' or 'no' is encouraged. In this case an entry should be made in the comments box so that the point can be discussed with the client. This avoids time being wasted finding answers immediately.
- It includes room to draft an action list.
- It has space to show that the points have been discussed with the client and to record their comments.

Personal tax planning checklist

Client name		Completed by	
Initial risk assessment	High/Low	Date	
Final risk assessment	High/Low	Reviewed by	
		Date	

Consideration	Yes/No N/A Don't know	Comments
1. General		
1.1 Is there an engagement letter covering all the services provided and is it up to date for self-assessment?		
1.2 Is the file complete? Are the computer records up to date? Has a partner or manager reviewed the file? Have relevant points been carried forward to next year?		
1.3 Are the planning suggestions cost effective and do they suit the taxpayer's personality and wishes?		
2. Allowances and rate bands		
2.1 Have all personal allowances been claimed?		
2.2 Are the spouse's/children's personal allowances being used?		
2.3 Have the lower rate bands of tax been utilised effectively?		
2.4 Is there scope to make an election between husband and wife as to the beneficial ownership of assets to optimise the use of personal allowances and the lower rate tax bands?		
3. Tax returns and tax payments		
3.1 Has the taxpayer's personal tax return been completed? Is it consistent with the previous year?		

Consideration	Yes/No N/A Don't know	Comments
3.2 Was the return completed by 30 September to take advantage of tax underpayments being coded out?		
3.3 Is there scope for reducing the tax payments on account?		
3.4 Was the previous year's return completed and submitted to the Inland Revenue on time?		
4. Residence and domicile		
4.1 Are the taxpayer and his or her family UK resident/ordinarily resident? If not note the country of residence.		
4.2 Are the taxpayer and his or her family UK domiciled? If not note the country of domicile. Has this been agreed by the Inspector of Taxes? Have there been any changes in circumstances?		
4.3 Is there scope for tax planning based on the taxpayer's residence or domicile?		
5. Income		
5.1 Is the taxpayer's income consistent with the previous year?		
5.2 Are there any unexplained receipts into any bank accounts?		
5.3 Does the taxpayer's income fluctuate widely each year, for example, because of bonuses? Can these be timed to delay tax payments or to even out the pattern of income?		
5.4 Can dividends from family companies or fixed term deposits be arranged so that the income falls into a later tax year, thus deferring the tax (and potentially the tax payments on account) by one tax year?		

Consideration	Yes/No N/A Don't know	Comments
6. High marginal tax rates		
6.1 Have you considered income levels for those claiming the age-related allowances or the children's tax credit? Capital gains or tax-free investments may be more appropriate.		
6.2 High marginal tax rates can arise where dividend or investment income straddles the higher rate tax threshold. Have you considered whether tax-free investments may be more suitable?		
7. Industry factors		
7.1 Are there any planning or compliance issues arising out of the industry or sector in which the client operates, for example, Lloyd's underwriters, farmers etc.?		
8. Records		
8.1 Are the taxpayer's records adequate and would they be so if there was an Inland Revenue enquiry?		
8.2 Are there any record keeping recommendations that could be made?		
8.3 Have all the original accounting records been returned to the client? Is the client retaining the records for the correct length of time in a secure place?		
9. Enquiries, penalties and interest		
9.1 Have there been any full or aspect enquiries? Note the outcome.		
9.2 Is there a risk of an aspect enquiry?		
9.3 Will there be problems if there is a full investigation?		

Consideration	Yes/No N/A Don't know	Comments
9.4 Does the client have investigations insurance?		
9.5 Are there any outstanding tax liabilities?		
9.6 Has any interest been paid or penalties and surcharges incurred?		
10. Claims and elections		
10.1 Review the file for claims and elections and note the time limits.		
11. Employment and benefits in kind		
11.1 Are appropriate records being kept to justify the business mileage driven? Is there scope to increase the business mileage to reduce the benefit in kind charge?		
11.2 Are there any unusual benefits in kind?		
11.3 Review the tax cost of company cars and consider private ownership and the use of the Fixed Profit Car Scheme (FPCS) instead.		
11.4 Have *section 198* claims been made for expense claims and expenses incurred 'wholly, exclusively and necessarily' in the employer's business?		
11.5 Consider whether the employer can provide tax effective benefits in kind.		
11.6 Is the taxpayer eligible for any employer share schemes?		
11.7 Are there any capital allowances claims that can be made?		
12. Income tax losses		
12.1 Are there losses?		
12.2 Have they been utilised in the most tax effective way?		

Consideration	Yes/No N/A Don't know	Comments
12.3 Are there any losses arising on shares held in unquoted trading companies that can be used against other income?		
13. Pensions		
13.1 Does the taxpayer have an independent financial advisor?		
13.2 Are adequate pension contributions being paid?		
13.3 Have maximum contributions been made in the year?		
13.4 Has unused relief from the previous six years been used up to 6 April 2001?		
13.5 Have the pension contributions been related back against the income of the previous year?		
13.6 Does the spouse or partner have adequate pension provision?		
13.7 Are the earnings above the earnings cap?		
14. Savings		
14.1 Have the maximum amounts been invested in an ISA?		
14.2 Have Tessas been funded to the maximum extent?		
14.3 Have matured Tessas been transferred to an ISA?		
14.4 Where balances are held in bank and building society accounts are they earning the best rates of interest?		
14.5 Have non-taxpayers made elections to receive bank and building society interest gross?		
14.6 Have the maximum amounts of Premium Bonds and National Savings Certificates been bought?		
14.7 Do children have appropriate investments?		

Consideration	Yes/No N/A Don't know	Comments
14.8 Does the taxpayer have a stockbroker?		
14.9 Ensure that non-taxpayers do not receive dividend income outside ISAs. Dividend credits cannot be reclaimed, resulting in potentially high marginal tax rates.		
14.10 Is the taxpayer interested in the Enterprise Investment Scheme?		
14.11 Is the taxpayer interested in investing in an Enterprise Zone?		
14.12 Is the taxpayer interested in creating a tax-free 'income-stream' by investing in government stocks or Gilts?		
14.13 Is there scope to transfer assets between spouses to minimise higher rate tax on investment income?		
15. Giving		
15.1 Is the proprietor interested in tax effective charitable giving or the creation of a charitable trust?		
16. Property		
16.1 If the taxpayer has spare funds have you considered paying off mortgages since MIRAS is abolished from 6 April 2000?		
16.2 Have you considered taking a lodger? Rent a room relief exempts income from lodgers up to £4,250 a year.		
16.3 Is the taxpayer interested in buying a property to let?		
16.4 Does the taxpayer have more than one property?		
16.5 Are there any reasons why the taxpayer's home might not meet all the conditions for exemption as his or her principal private residence?		

Consideration	Yes/No N/A Don't know	Comments
17. Capital gains tax		
17.1 Has the annual exemption been used?		
17.2 Has the spouse's annual exemption been used?		
17.3 Is there scope to make an election as to the beneficial ownership of assets?		
17.4 Have any losses been utilised?		
17.5 Are there any losses which could be crystallised to cover chargeable gains?		
17.6 Have you considered the timing of disposals, particularly around the year-end to defer capital gains tax and enhance taper relief claims?		
17.7 Is the taxpayer coming up to retirement? Consider eligibility for retirement relief/business asset taper relief.		
17.8 Are any 1982 re-basing elections needed?		
17.9 Can any claims for negligible value be made?		
17.10 Have you periodically reviewed chattels and personal property for valuable items? Ensure that there is adequate insurance. Consider a sale.		
18. Inheritance tax		
18.1 Note the approximate value of the estate (both the taxpayer and his or her spouse).		
18.2 Is there an up-to-date will? Who drew it up and where is it kept?		
18.3 Is the will tax effective?		
18.4 Is the £3,000 annual exemption being used?		
18.5 Are gifts being made out of income?		

Consideration	Yes/No N/A Don't know	Comments
18.6 Are lifetime transfers being made? Consider the taxpayer's age and state of health.		
18.7 Have inventories been made of any unusual or valuable assets?		
18.8 Is there life assurance?		
18.9 Have the estates of husband and wife been equalised?		
19. Trusts		
19.1 Consider setting up family trusts.		
20. Potential problems		
20.1 Have there been any property transactions? Note the details.		
20.2 Is the proprietor involved with any trusts? Note the details.		
20.3 Are there any overseas issues? Note the details.		
20.4 Are there any matrimonial or family issues? Note the details.		
21. Financial management		
21.1 Are there any problems with the client's banks or financiers?		
21.2 Are there any other financing or debt management issues?		
21.3 Is there appropriate insurance for all the taxpayer's needs?		
22. Lifestyle		
22.1 Is the income sufficient to justify the taxpayer's lifestyle?		
22.2 Are there any personality or other issues to be noted?		
22.3 Does the proprietor have any health concerns?		

Action list

Discussed (meeting/telephone/letter)

Date

Comments

Chapter 9

Enquiries

9.1 The enquiry regime affects all taxpayers under self-assessment because some enquiries are purely random. However, the majority of enquiries still occur because the Revenue believe that something may be wrong with the return. Increasingly, they are using sophisticated risk analysis to determine which returns to review and tax practices need to adopt procedures to meet this challenge.

9.2 It is in the client's best interests to minimise the risk of an enquiry because of the:

- risk of additional tax being found to be due;
- possibility of interest and penalties;
- cost of unexpected professional fees;
- stress inherent in any enquiry.

It is also in the firm's interests to avoid enquiries wherever possible. Although they can be a useful source of additional revenue, investigations can give rise to claims against the firm, unhappy and lost clients, fee losses and in extreme cases penalties and the risk of a professional complaint.

9.3 The principal aim of a firm's enquiry procedures should therefore be to minimise the risk of a return being selected for enquiry. Secondly, its systems should ensure that, if there is an enquiry, it is handled in the right way from the outset.

This chapter covers:

- critical review of tax returns;
- handling and monitoring enquiries;
- more serious enquiries;
- PAYE and VAT investigations.

Minimising the risk of enquiries

9.4 The risk of an enquiry for a small or medium-sized business is low but when one occurs it is likely to be a full enquiry into all aspects of the taxpayer's affairs and business. The risk of an enquiry for a business with a turnover in excess of £250,000 is high but it is more likely to be an aspect enquiry. Most enquiries into non-business returns will be aspect enquiries but if anything is found to be wrong the enquiry could be extended. It is important to avoid the Revenue asking any questions about the return because one question usually leads to many more.

Tax practices should assess the risk of each client being the subject of an enquiry. A risk assessment is included in Appendix 9:1.

9.5 Firms should also be aware of the triggers that can give rise to an enquiry. This will enable them to avoid pitfalls and to warn clients of the risks. Investigation triggers for sole traders and individuals include the following:

- informants (for example, other government departments, third parties such as banks and disgruntled ex-spouses and employees);
- information exchanged between the Revenue and Customs and Excise in enquiry cases;
- late notification of chargeability;
- information about the client in the media or in their own publicity or advertising;
- registers of boats and light aircraft;
- applications for licenses and planning permission;
- returns from auctioneers;
- information gathered from other taxpayers' records (although this should not occur);
- unusual or unexplained variances;
- benchmarking against similar businesses in the area and by reference to economic notes.

Triggers for companies may also include:

- topical issues such as provisions;
- loans to participators;
- share valuations;
- overseas issues;
- transactions within groups;
- legal and professional costs;
- the classification of capital and revenue expenditure;
- capital allowances claims.

9.6 The Inspector's main focus in a business enquiry is likely to be to prove that the accounting records are in some way deficient. This makes it essential to review the accounts. The checklist at Appendix 9:2 offers a means for firms to undertake a critical review of a sole trader's tax return to minimise the risk of enquiry before the return is submitted to the Revenue. Similar checklists can be devised for other clients.

9.7 Once the enquiry window has passed, the Revenue can only make further enquiries where there is a 'discovery'. Firms should minimise the risk of there being a later 'discovery' by making sure that there is adequate disclosure of all relevant information on the return and that the taxpayer is not negligent in the conduct of their affairs (see 7.6).

Handling enquiries

9.8 However good the firm's critical review procedures, it is still likely to face some enquiry cases each year. The following paragraphs outline the steps that firms should take to minimise their risk, get the best outcome for the client and reduce stress for all concerned.

9.9 Although some clients respond positively to enquiries because they understand their random nature and have nothing to hide, many taxpayers find the process stressful and may see it as a personal affront. They may even blame the advisor. Having tax investigations insurance can help. If so the procedural requirements set out by the insurance company for handling and notifying enquiries must be followed from the outset. (See also 16.24.)

9.10 For routine enquiries, the firm is likely to have the necessary resources to handle the enquiry within the firm. Where the investigation is serious, particularly where a client approaches the firm to act for the first time (for instance, where they have not been previously known to the Revenue), the firm should consider whether it has the skills and expertise to act (see 9.36).

9.11 Under self-assessment enquiries follow a standard pattern. Advisors should ensure that they are familiar with this approach.

Initial action

9.12 The advisor should undertake the following procedures upon being notified of an enquiry.

- Check that the audit notice (*section 9A* income tax and capital gains tax, *section 11AB* corporation tax and *section 12AC* partnership tax) is valid and has been issued within the correct time frame. Challenge it if it has not. Self-assessment enquiries apply to income tax from 1996/1997 and for corporation tax periods ending on or after 1 July 1999.

- Ensure that the letter of engagement covers enquiries. If not issue a new one. (See 2.24.)
- Agree the fees with the client. Enquries may produce valuable fees but if handled incorrectly they can give rise to losses. Make sure that the client can afford to pay and if in doubt obtain payment in advance.
- Brief the client about what an enquiry may mean for them and the need for their full cooperation and involvement. Advise them that the enquiry may last a considerable time, rarely less than six months and on average about a year.
- Appoint an experienced and trained member of staff to deal with the case, if dealing with enquiries is beyond the expertise of the person who usually deals with the client. This is essential where any district other than the taxpayer's usual tax office is involved. Sole practitioners should consider bringing in an expert from outside with suitable experience (see 21.2).
- Consider a request for 'faster working', which may get the case concluded within six months. Many Inspectors are, however, reluctant to use it.
- Review the information requested and challenge its provision if it is inappropriate, for example, personal bank statements or accountant's link papers. An appeal can be made to the Commissioners within 30 days.
- Do not disclose any information which is not necessary to enable the Inspector to check the accuracy of the return. It could give rise to a negligence claim.
- Meet with the client and obtain additional information from them if necessary.
- Critically review the accounts and accounting records prior to submission to the Revenue.
- Ensure that neither the firm nor the client discloses that there is an enquiry to interested third parties such as banks, suppliers or customers. It may result in a loss of confidence. In high profile cases, knowledge of an enquiry may attract media attention.
- Answer the Inspector's questions within the required time scale. If a delay is necessary at any stage due to holidays or illness (either the firm or client) keep the Inspector informed.

9.13 The response to the advisor's letter will vary. The enquiry may be closed if it is an aspect enquiry. In many full investigation cases the usual response will be to request a meeting. It may be appropriate in some situations for the advisor to discuss the issues with the Inspector alone but in most cases it will be more cost effective to have a meeting with the client present.

9.14 Advisors need to be well prepared for meetings with the Revenue. Inspectors deal with many interviews each week but advisors may only attend a few each year.

Preparation for a meeting

9.15 Once the Revenue has requested a meeting, the advisor should consider the following points.

- Ask for an agenda and a list of interview questions to be sent in advance.
- Discuss private expenditure and bank accounts in detail with the client if such issues are otherwise unknown to the advisor. A means and asset test undertaken in advance of the meeting will enable the client to produce more accurate answers about day-to-day living expenses rather than simply guessing during a meeting.
- Make disclosures in advance of the meeting. The Inspector may need to discuss serious irregularities with a colleague.
- Discuss the meeting and its conduct with the client so he or she is forewarned of the format.
- Advise the client about the questions which will be asked (including personal questions), the importance of confining his or her answers to the questions asked, room layout and body language.
- Warn the client that the Inspector or his or her staff may have visited the business premises and the client's home prior to the meeting.
- Advise the client about the fact that the Inspector may have used statistical techniques to analyse the accounts. (See *Taxation,* vol. 144, no. 3741, 27 January 2000, page 354.)
- Inform the client about the Revenue's tactics for obtaining information, such as visiting sporting events such as Wimbledon to check for taxpayers renting out houses or parking space. (See also 9.5.)
- Just before the meeting, review all the files and the return under enquiry so as to be fully up to date about the client's affairs.

Declining meetings

9.16 The cost of a client and his or her advisor attending a meeting with the Inspector should not be underestimated. Nor should the stress likely to be experienced by a majority of clients. In many situations a meeting will be necessary to progress an enquiry but practitioners should not agree to them without good reason or thought. If a meeting goes badly and it could have been refused, the client could complain.

9.17 It is of course possible to decline a meeting with the Inland Revenue although they do not like this. Reasons for refusing a meeting include the following.

- It is not cost effective.
- It would cause the client undue stress or difficulty due to their personal circumstances, for example, disability or mental illness.
- Belief that the Inspector is on a fishing exercise.
- Indications that there will be more than one Inspector present.
- A list of interview questions has been sought and they can be answered equally well by letter or telephone. This is particularly relevant where, for example, the Inspector is asking questions about lodgements into a jointly-held bank account which the client may not be able to answer 'off the cuff'.

9.18 Increasingly, Inspectors like to meet business clients at their premises. There are unlikely to be any circumstances where this would be to the taxpayer's benefit. Such meetings should usually be declined particularly if the premises are unsuitable, for example, small retail outlets, hairdressers or takeaway restaurants where there is no separate office.

9.19 An alternative to a meeting at either the Inland Revenue or the client's premises is to hold it at the firm's offices. This is neutral territory and the client is likely to feel more comfortable because they are familiar with the office. The meeting room can be laid out to give an advantage to the advisor and client (see 4.35).

Meeting the Inspector

9.20 No one likes attending such meetings and it is important for both the advisor and client to remain calm, courteous and constructive throughout the process.

9.21 Inspectors are advised to obtain as much information as possible in a meeting. This means that they will ask open questions such as 'tell me about your business'. Most people like to talk about themselves and voluble taxpayers should be warned about this. Open questions should be countered by a request for the Inspector to be more specific about the areas he or she is interested in. Clients should be advised to talk as little as possible, to answer only the Inspector's specific questions and to ask for clarification if they do not understand the question or if they think it is phrased too widely.

9.22 The Inspector may keep quiet at the end of the taxpayer's answer. Awkward silences may encourage the taxpayer to offer additional information. Enquiry meetings should generally be full of pauses.

9.23 *Enquiries*

9.23 Attention should be paid to how the Inspector is controlling the meeting. There may be an intimidating office environment or a failure to offer common courtesies such as tea or coffee. Throughout the meeting the Inspector will be watching the taxpayer and advisor's body language (see 4.30). If there are two officers present this makes picking up non-verbal signs easier.

9.24 The Inspector will direct all questions to the client and deliberately cut out the advisor. Advisors should be careful not to answer for their clients nor to lead or influence their answers.

9.25 The advisor's role in a meeting with the Inspector is to:

- make detailed notes and to request a copy of the Inspector's notes;
- reassure the client;
- intervene to clarify questions which are unclear;
- ensure the Inspector sticks to the agenda and confines his questions to the tax period under enquiry;
- make sure that the Inspector does not expand his questions beyond the case under enquiry, for example, by asking about the directors' personal tax in a corporate enquiry;
- expand on issues which the client is unsure about;
- advise the Inspector that a written reply will be given to questions which cannot be answered in a meeting because they require research;
- challenge the Inspector's preconceptions or prejudices about the client or business if they are untrue;
- intervene if the Inspector is unnecessarily aggressive – in this case the advisor should consider terminating the meeting;
- request rest breaks if the meeting goes on for more than an hour – few clients can concentrate for much longer than this without an adjournment;
- request a break if issues come to light about which the advisor was unaware;
- terminate the meeting if serious irregularities come to light;
- ask the Inspector what further information is required (if any);
- agree any adjustments to the return;
- invite the Inspector to agree the client's return and issue a closure notice;
- take matters further if required, for example, to the General Commissioners.

9.26 After the meeting the advisor may be required to liaise with his or her client to produce additional information such as to identify amounts banked or to analyse expenses. Where omissions from the return are identified, the firm may be involved in quantifying these or challenging the Inspector's figures. Advisors will also be needed to negotiate penalties in contract settlement cases.

Throughout the enquiry

9.27 Good communication skills with both the client and the Revenue are vital to the smooth running of an enquiry. The advisor's aim should be to minimise the client's stress and not to add to it. The following considerations will help to keep the enquiry running smoothly.

- Keep the client informed at each stage about what is going on. Aim to eliminate surprises. Discuss the appropriate course of action with the client and keep them involved in the process. Remember that the enquiry is into their affairs.
- Be professional and courteous to the Revenue. They are only doing their job.
- Remain detached and impartial.

9.28 If at any time it becomes apparent that there are significant omissions from the return, irrespective of whether they have been identified by the Revenue, the client should make a voluntary disclosure. If they are not willing to do so, the firm must consider whether it can continue to act (see 6.31 and 20.4).

Closing enquiries

9.29 Firms should always obtain completion notices under *TMA 1970, s 28A(5)* so that the Inspector cannot ask further questions at a later date. Contract settlements should be worded so as to include a deemed completion notice because these can only be issued under *TMA 1970, s 28A(6)* where the Commissioners have given a direction. As a result they are not usually obtained. In their leaflet IR160 the Revenue advise that they will not seek to take advantage of this.

9.30 Before agreeing to additional liabilities it is essential to ensure that the client can settle them, particularly where contract settlements are concerned.

9.31 Where enquiries are unnecessarily protracted a request should be made to close the case. If this fails a letter to the District Inspector or Compliance Manager may speed up matters. Failing that, the firm should apply to the Commissioners. This power should be used wisely, but where there are no reasonable grounds for continuing the enquiry, practitioners should consider its use.

Monitoring enquiries

9.32 The progress of all enquiries should be monitored to ensure that deadlines are met. It is also useful to collect other information about the handling and outcome of enquiry cases to help the firm build up a data bank of information that may help with future cases.

9.33 Enquiry records containing the following details should be kept.

- Client name.
- Trade.
- Partner/staff involved with the case.
- Tax office.
- Investigating officer.
- Suspected reason for enquiry.
- Information supplied.
- Key topics under investigation.
- How the enquiry was handled, for example, in a meeting or by correspondence.
- The outcome, including the extra tax found to be due, interest and penalties, whether it was a contract settlement and the necessity to sign a certificate of full disclosure.

9.34 The following key dates should also be monitored.

Event	Date received	Date due to be submitted	Date actually submitted	Date meeting held
Audit notice received				
Appeal				
Initial information request				
Further information request				
Appeal				
Meeting 1				
Meeting 2				
Further letter 1				
Further letter 2				
Further letter 3				
Amended self-assessment				
Appeal				
Contract settlement				
Certificate of full disclosure and statement of assets (if relevant)				
Closure notice				

Note 1. Enter N/A where the date does not apply.

9.35 The records should be kept centrally and reviewed weekly by the head of the tax department. Other records may also be required where the firm has a tax investigations insurance policy.

More serious cases

9.36 Where fraud or serious irregularities are suspected the case will be dealt with by the Special Compliance Office or a district other than the taxpayer's own. The Revenue's primary aim is to collect tax although they will prosecute in certain cases. This is to act as a deterrent to others and the details are usually publicised. Prosecution is more likely where professionals are involved, there is fraud, forged documents, abuse of the PAYE or the sub-contractor system or persistent irregularities.

9.37 If there is any indication that a tax office other than the taxpayer's own tax office will be involved in the investigation, the case must be referred immediately to someone experienced in this type of case. If the firm does not have an in-house specialist, an independent expert should be appointed (see 21.2).

9.38 The next stage is to ascertain whether prosecution is likely by establishing whether the interview will be conducted under 'Hansard' or under caution. Where full cooperation and disclosure is given under 'Hansard' it is usual not to prosecute. However, this was brought into doubt in the case of *R v W and another [1998] STC 550.*

9.39 Firms should be aware of search and seize powers under *TMA 1970, s 20*. Such powers may be exercised at both the client and firm's premises. Search warrants are often executed early in the morning when partners may not be present. The firm should lay down strict guidelines for staff and partners to follow in this event depending on whether the warrant applies only to the client in question or the entire firm's tax work. Legal advice may be necessary in drawing up such guidelines. For details about documents subject to legal professional privilege see 15.45. For procedures for serious PAYE and VAT cases see 9.44.

PAYE and VAT

9.40 PAYE and VAT issues make popular investigation targets not only because the amounts of revenue involved are significant but because of their increasing complexity. This is particularly the case for PAYE, which now covers Class 1A National Insurance, the Working Families Tax Credit and student loan collection.

9.41 VAT and PAYE assurance visits are usually carried out based on a risk assessment of the client. As investigations may follow on from such routine visits, it is once again important to minimise the risk of an assurance visit occurring by undertaking regular critical reviews.

9.42 *Enquiries*

The checklist at Appendix 9:3 provides firms with a means to undertake a PAYE review to identify 'hot' issues. The checklist can also be adapted for use as a pro-active 'healthcheck' for interested clients (see 10.12). Similar checklists can be designed for VAT reviews. Critical reviews may identify errors early, thus potentially avoiding penalties and minimising interest.

9.42 Where a client is subject to a routine PAYE or VAT assurance visit, the firm should offer to attend the meeting or be on hand to help. This is particularly so where the practice completes the VAT returns or maintains the payroll records for the client. A relatively small amount of effort at the control visit stage may prevent an issue being subject to further investigation. A pre-visit review of the client's records can also be helpful in identifying errors for voluntary disclosure prior to the visit.

9.43 Most firms are unlikely to have so many VAT or PAYE investigations on-going at any one time that keeping track of them will be difficult. The only areas of concern are likely to be VAT assessments or PAYE determinations raised after a visit. If they are disputed they will require an appeal within 30 days of issue. The firm could have a separate control to monitor these. Alternatively, the use of the firm's diary and post systems should ensure that nothing is overlooked (see 15.22 and 15.27).

9.44 The firm must ensure that PAYE and VAT enquiries are dealt with by appropriately trained staff, particularly where fraud is alleged. Customs and Excise in particular have wide ranging powers and firms should have policies for dealing with:

- unannounced visits to clients and the firm;
- cautions;
- search warrants;
- distress (in the event of non-payment).

The procedures should cover advising the client to remain silent, getting specialist help quickly, and obtaining legal representation.

Quick review

9.45

- For further information see the *Investigations Handbook*, *Enquiry Handbook*, Tax Bulletin Special Edition 2, Codes of Practice 8, 9, 11 and 14 and SAT 2.
- If the firm is unhappy at the way the enquiry has been handled consider a complaint to the Revenue Adjudicator (see 21.29).
- Bear in mind the provisions of *TMA 1970, s 99*. An advisor who

knowingly assists or induces the making of an incorrect return is liable to a maximum penalty of £3,000.

- Do not let the current tax affairs of a client under investigation become out of date. It may, however, be prudent to delay the submission of the return. If provisional figures are entered on the return as a result of the enquiry ensure that the return is amended within the twelve-month time frame.
- Professional fees charged in connection with investigations are dealt with at 3.38.
- For details of tax investigations insurance see 16.24.
- Once an enquiry is concluded, ensure that the firm's fees are paid before undertaking further work.

Appendix 9:1

Risk Assessment to Determine if a Tax Return is Likely to be Selected for Enquiry

Client name	
Client reference	
Partner/manager/staff responsible	
Tax year	

The presence of the following factors will make a case more likely to be selected for enquiry.

	Yes/High	No/Low
Is the turnover above £250,000?		
Are the taxpayer's affairs complex?		
Are there overseas connections?		
Are there instances of late returns?		
Is the industry in which the client operates one which is targeted by the Revenue, for example, the construction industry?		
Are there large payments to sub-contractors?		
Are there management charges?		
Are there any unusual debits which could give rise to a benefit in kind?		
Have directors' loan accounts been overdrawn?		
Are there any unusual capital allowances claims?		
Are there complex capital gains tax calculations?		
Have any businesses been sold or acquired?		
Have there been any clearances or pre- or post-transaction rulings?		
Have there been any other events likely to trigger an enquiry (see 9.5)?		

Risk assessed as High/low

If the risk is high, undertake a critical review of the return, consider the issues in more detail and make disclosure on the return as necessary.

Appendix 9:2

Critical Review of a Sole Trader's Tax Return

Consideration	Comments/Action
1 Is there a history of late returns?	
2 Have tax payments been made on time?	
3 Are all the sources of income (including investment income) consistent with the previous year? Disclose the reason for variations.	
4 Are there any unexplained receipts into the bank/building society accounts, including private and joint accounts?	
5 Are the expenses consistent with the previous year? Are they allocated consistently between headings on the return? Disclose the reasons for variations.	
6 Are there estimated expenses and accounting differences that should be disclosed?	
7 Are gross profit margins low or inconsistent with previous years?	
8 Have private use percentages/ goods for own consumption estimates changed from the previous year? Are they justified?	
9 Are there any expenses that could be challenged by the Inland Revenue?	
10 Are there any unusual, large or complex capital allowance claims?	
11 Does the business use sub-contractors?	

Consideration	Comments/Action
12 Is the status of the proprietor likely to be questioned?	
13 Are there any tax issues arising because of the industry in which the business operates?	
14 Has the accounting year-end been changed?	
15 Are the drawings/income sufficient to justify the taxpayer's lifestyle?	
16 Has the source of any new capital/income been explained?	
17 Have there been any other changes or relevant circumstances in the year which should be disclosed, for example, work patterns, parental leave or family crises?	

Appendix 9:3

Critical Review of a Client's PAYE Systems

Consideration	Comments/Action
1 Assess the competence of the payroll staff and the reliability of the system used.	
2 Are all employees on the payroll? Consider casuals and sub-contractors.	
3 Are starters and leavers taxed correctly? Is there a high staff turnover?	
4 Are there employees working abroad?	
5 Is the National Minimum Wage being operated?	
6 Review sub-contractors' contracts. Are payments to sub-contractors significant?	
7 Do all employees have employment contracts?	
8 Are there bonuses, overtime payments or staff gifts?	
9 Have there been redundancy or termination payments?	
10 Is the Construction Industry scheme an issue?	
11 Are PAYE/National Insurance payments up to date?	
12 Are P35s, P11Ds and end of year returns up to date?	
13 Are there any large or unusual benefits in kind including golden hellos?	
14 How are benefits in kind calculated, manually or by using a computer program? Are mileage logs kept for car benefits?	

Consideration	Comments/Action
15 Are Class 1A contributions being correctly operated and paid?	
16 Is the operation of statutory sick pay, statutory maternity pay, the Working Families Tax Credit and student loans correct?	
17 How are reimbursed expenses recorded? Are 'round sum' expenses paid? Is petty cash being abused by management?	
18 Are expenses correctly categorised?	
19 Are there any dispensations in force?	
20 Consider the correct operation of pensions, payroll giving, share schemes and profit-related pay.	
21 Have the issues arising from previous PAYE inspections been taken on board?	

Chapter 10

Additional Services

10.1 Just as tax law is constantly changing so must tax practices continually evolve. Firms are fundamentally different today compared with practices 30 years ago, and they will continue to change over the next 30 years. This chapter suggests a range of additional services for tax practices to offer to their clients including:

- tax planning products;
- financial planning and services;
- facilitation;
- niche markets;
- business coaching and services;
- outsourcing;
- services to other professionals.

Chapter 22 considers the future for tax services.

Building on a compliance base

10.2 There are two schools of thought about whether tax practices should offer additional services to clients. The first view is that there is no need to expand beyond the traditional role of a tax practice - compliance and planning services. There is a sound argument for this and if a firm knows what it does well it should keep on doing it. Many tax practitioners offer their clients an excellent service and are reluctant to move away from their core activities. However, pursuing only one market or type of work could leave a practice very exposed to changes in customer demand, technology or tax law. Such practices should consider a range of additional services which build on their existing activities.

10.3 The second view recognises that compliance services alone are not a sufficient basis for a tax practice. The professional bodies have advocated this for some years and have tried to encourage their members to consider some alternatives. The main reasons why compliance services are under threat are as follows.

- Technology. Increased computerisation of the tax function has increased the speed at which data can be processed and forms and computations completed. Rightly or wrongly this has led to a perception that pure compliance services are low-grade work.
- Tax system changes. Self-assessment has led to increased standardisation.
- The Internet. The increasing use of the Internet has fundamentally changed the way in which tax practices can supply services.
- Competition. It is comparatively cheap and easy to set up a tax practice from home. Many mid-tier tax practices are being acquired by consolidators and whilst the full impact of this may not yet have been felt, practices should remain alert to the possibility of serious competition from a large provider.
- Simplicity. Under self-assessment many taxpayers mistakenly believe that they can complete their tax returns themselves.

10.4 Tax advisors are very well placed to offer a wide range of services to their clients because they possess a detailed knowledge about them. This knowledge should be the key to the additional services they provide. Surveys have shown that accountants and tax advisors are trusted by their clients and that clients would like to buy more services from them. It may sound obvious but to meet this demand firms need to develop a range of additional services to sell to clients. This may be as simple as packaging or marketing existing services in a way that makes them more attractive to clients.

10.5 The type of additional services that a tax practice could provide depends on where it is starting from, its size, expertise and resources. This chapter assumes that all firms offer basic compliance services and are looking to expand the range of alternative services from this base. The chapter highlights a variety of additional services which practices can provide. Some are aimed at clients and some at other professionals and third parties. The main areas to consider are:

- tax planning products;
- financial planning and services;
- training and helplines;
- outsourcing;
- other business services.

10.6 Some firms may already provide some of the services mentioned to clients as part of the routine tax compliance work without either communicating the fact to their clients or charging appropriately for them. In this case the firm should review its marketing (see Chapter 5), client communication (see Chapter 4) and its charges (see Chapter 3).

10.7 Not all the services suggested will suit all firms but many practices will be able to identify one or two areas that interest them. Increased specialisation, particularly for smaller practices, will help to ensure survival in an increasingly competitive market.

Tax planning products

10.8 The easiest additional services for a firm to offer are those which build on its existing tax skills. Some examples of possible services are detailed below. The list is not exhaustive; firms will be able to think of others specifically tailored to their clients' needs.

Formalised planning services

10.9 Most firms already offer year-end planning reviews or a planning review undertaken when the tax return is completed but many firms do not charge clients specifically for them (particularly large clients). Where firms offer planning services to clients the suggestion often leaves them cold or the word 'planning' is seen as synonymous with 'expensive'. Tax practices can generate increased income from tax planning exercises if they are packaged as specific products. A fixed fee usually works best.

10.10 One way of selling additional planning services is to coincide with specific life events, such as:

- getting married;
- having a baby;
- career progression;
- setting up a business;
- separation or divorce;
- business changes;
- retirement;
- getting older.

10.11 The lives of most clients will provide regular opportunities for constructive reviews. The firm will need to develop a series of checklists and related information sheets for clients detailing the planning possibilities. All of the taxes as well as commercial issues should be covered. Many checklists and guides are available in tax publications. For further information on planning services generally see Chapter 8.

Healthchecks

10.12 Many firms will already be familiar with healthchecks for clients worried about PAYE or VAT control visits. Other areas which lend themselves to this approach include tax enquiry healthchecks (both personal and corporate), National Insurance, benefits in kind, inheritance tax, risk management and business succession. The firm should use a checklist approach to review clients' affairs and systems and identify likely areas for concern which can then be discussed in a follow-up meeting. The critical review checklists for sole traders' accounts and PAYE systems in Appendices 9:2 and 9:3 can also be used as a healthcheck for new clients.

Asset purchases

10.13 Tax advisors are well placed to advise on major asset purchases including cars, equipment and property. It is important to make sure that clients know that when making expensive acquisitions, tax advice can be cost effective. Almost all asset purchases involve extensive tax knowledge, in particular capital allowances, leasing, VAT and stamp duty. A knowledge of the financing of such assets is also important. Computer software exists to help such decision-making.

Company cars

10.14 Clients often need advice about the choice between different types of company car or whether to take a car at all. A formalised planning service can save clients significant amounts of tax. Computer software to aid such decisions is available.

Financial planning

10.15 In many situations the scope for tax planning is limited, particularly for taxpayers with average incomes or with debt or financing problems. An alternative is to offer financial planning services which look at the totality of a taxpayer's financial affairs rather than tax savings in isolation. Financial planning may open up possibilities for selling clients other services or products. It may be necessary to develop links with other professionals, banks, factoring houses and financiers.

10.16 Financial planning opportunities could include:

- personal debt management – where clients have substantial or burdensome debt;
- training and advice in day-to-day budgeting to contain debt problems;
- business financial management and funding including partnership capital, factoring and invoice discounting;
- bank charges and interest reviews – computer programs exist to ascertain whether clients paying substantial charges and interest are being overcharged by the bank;

- checking credit references and obtaining corrections or disassociations (see 20.72);
- training clients to live within their means.

Lifestyle review

10.17 One way of approaching a financial planning exercise is to undertake a lifestyle review. This can work well for personal tax clients. The approach to the review is as follows.

- Ascertain from the client what they want from their life now, in 5 years, 10 years and 20 years.
- Develop a computer model (for example, a spreadsheet) which contains details of all the client's personal and domestic expenditure. It should cover everything from the mortgage to childcare, pets, holidays and Christmas. Couples should ideally do the exercise together.
- The outgoings should be compared with the taxpayer's current income. This will identify whether they have spare funds or live at a deficit. Tax and National Insurance payments should be taken into account.
- Suggestions can be made as to how to improve the current position by reducing expenses, renegotiating loan repayments and interest rates and looking for a new job or a payrise. If the financial position is healthy, then advice can be given as to how the long and short-term goals can be achieved and what should happen to the surplus.
- Future aspirations can then be incorporated into the model. This will identify what action is needed to achieve the goals set at the outset. For example, if retirement at 50 is desired, it may indicate a range of options as well as giving an opportunity to sell additional pension premiums.
- If the client is self-employed the model can be expanded to consider areas where the business can be improved to produce more income. It can also help in the setting of charge-out rates for those selling services.

Clients often appreciate such reviews because they are not just about tax and they help to clarify clients' thoughts in a structured way.

Financial services

10.18 Financial services work has always been intrinsically linked with tax practice but many firms do not exploit the full value of this work. It is an area where clients are particularly keen to buy additional services and where tax practices hold a lot of information about clients to enable them to market appropriately specific products, for example, pensions or school fees planning. The tax system is now so complicated, with many different marginal rates of tax, that tax professionals are well placed to offer constructive advice about the most suitable investments for taxpayers in different situations.

10.19 The best way for firms to approach this area of work is to set up or buy in a team of independent financial advisors and dedicated clerical assistance. Smaller tax practices may be able to band together to set up their own financial services company. If the work develops beyond being merely incidental to the running of a tax practice the firm may need to be separately registered with the PIA. For further information about financial services regulation see 20.7.

10.20 Financial services does not just include the regulated work, it should encompass the entire range of investment advice and financial planning. Because tax advisors charge on a fee basis it means that they are not influenced by their own reward from the advice they offer. The range of advice should include:

- property investment – for example, buy to let;
- cash-based investments – a knowledge of the most up-to-date savings rates on bank and building society accounts can earn many clients extra income each year;
- information about National Savings products;
- a consideration of alternative investments – antiques or fine art.

10.21 Firms with links to general insurance brokers will be able to sell clients insurance services including business policies, professional indemnity insurance, health cover, private medical insurance and term life assurance.

The selling of tax investigations insurance offers an opportunity to generate additional fees although the administrative costs may not necessarily make this financially lucrative (see 16.24).

Helping clients to help themselves

10.22 There is a range of services which firms can provide to enable clients to be more familiar with their own tax affairs. Increasingly, firms will be required to act in partnership with their clients.

Training

10.23 Tax practices are well placed to offer a wide range of client training on topical tax issues including benefits in kind, National Insurance, student loans, Working Families Tax Credit, corporate self-assessment, enquiry issues, tax for non-specialists, employment law and VAT.

10.24 Some personal clients, particularly those who cannot afford to pay high fees, may be better off being trained how to deal with their own tax returns and accounts. These skills will last a lifetime and the taxpayer will have more resources available in the future to pay for creative tax or financial advice. The training could be in small groups or one to one.

Checking services

10.25 The Inland Revenue is encouraging taxpayers to file their tax returns electronically over the next few years and is offering discounts for doing so. However, they are unlikely to want to receive a large number of poorly completed returns with obvious errors needing correction. It seems likely that the Inland Revenue may in the future encourage unrepresented taxpayers to send their returns to a tax professional for a quality control check prior to submission. The forwarding of the returns from client to advisor and back and ultimately to the Inland Revenue can be done electronically.

Helplines

10.26 Where a client cannot afford a tax compliance service they may be able to pay for occasional advice. Although the Inland Revenue runs a telephone helpline many taxpayers prefer to pay for impartial advice. This service can be offered over the Internet as well as by telephone.

10.27 This service should be charged per unit (for example, ten minutes) and be subject to a minimum charge. It is recommended that payment should be made in advance by credit card. Premium charge-out rates should be used for this service to allow for the additional administration costs, file notes, telephone transcripts etc. As the service is only used occasionally it may represent better value for the taxpayer that needs some advice and support but can deal with a lot of the work themselves.

Computer consultancy

10.28 Tax practices with suitable resources and personnel should consider expanding the range of their services into computer consultancy or software development. Information and data management is going to be central to all clients in the future and some firms are already earning fees from providing tax services over the Internet and advice to clients on e-commerce.

10.29 The consultancy arm should ideally be a separate company. The computer services it offers could include website design, Internet services, tax return completion kits for unrepresented taxpayers, compliance and practice management software, client databases and benchmarking products.

Business coaching

10.30 Tax advisors possess a detailed knowledge about their clients' financial affairs. This makes it relatively easy to provide business coaching or mentoring services. The proprietors, particularly of small businesses, can be very isolated. It is sometimes difficult for them to be objective about key business and financial issues and having a trusted advisor to call upon can be an important service.

10.31 Business coaching services can be provided by:

- offering telephone support to provide feedback and motivation;
- attending regular meetings;
- specific planning services.

10.32 Specific planning services could include:

- benchmarking against both external information and information generated within the firm so that the client knows how they compare with others in their industry;
- trend analysis to help to focus a business on where it is going;
- stock control, debtor and cash management to increase profits;
- customer or client reviews to remove 'dead wood' or unprofitable contracts;
- production process and product consultation to investigate new products or systems;
- developing business strategies and plans;
- a review of personnel to maintain motivation, highlight training issues and to ensure efficiency;
- a fixed asset review to ensure that equipment is being used to its maximum potential.

General business advice

10.33 There is frequently an overlap between tax and business advice. Tax professionals are central to a wide range of work including:

- acquisitions and mergers;
- incorporation;
- corporate reconstructions;
- staff issues;
- pricing;
- EEC and international trade.

10.34 Firms must also be responsive to changes in the market and business practice so that they can continually offer clients new services, for example, suitable contracts to companies caught by IR35.

Developing a niche market

10.35 Developing an industry-based niche market is one way of enabling the firm to offer additional services both to clients and other professionals by becoming an expert in a particular field. Care must be taken not to be too dependent on one market as this may leave the firm exposed to changes in the law, for example, IR35. Other niche areas include: the medical profession, entertainment industry, farmers, Lloyd's Underwriters, the elderly and sports people.

Outsourcing

10.36 Tax practices have long undertaken outsourcing, particularly the operation of payrolls, the completion of VAT returns and bookkeeping. Firms need to think more widely about the opportunity for outsourced services in the future. Internet-based services will be particularly important.

Payrolls

10.37 The Internet needs to be more widely used for outsourced work. This will avoid some of the problems traditionally associated with bureau work, namely waiting for the client to send all the details by post. The client can send the details electronically to the firm. The firm's bureau will then process the data and return it electronically to the client. Effectively, the firm runs the client's computer for them. The client can also have links to their bank to pay the salaries and to the Inland Revenue to pay the tax and transmit forms. With increasing burdens on employers for the Working Time Directive, student loan repayments and the Working Families' Tax Credit, this should be a growth area.

VAT

10.38 VAT returns can also be serviced over the Internet.

In-house tax department

10.39 The possibility exists for tax practices to operate as the in-house tax department of larger companies. Instead of the company employing its own tax staff, the entire function, including compliance, investigations and international aspects, is taken over by a tax practice. This could also benefit partnerships.

10.40 The advantage to the company or partnership is that the tax department has a fixed cost and a range of tax experts can be used rather than simply one or two permanent tax staff who may not be expert in all fields. The advantage for the tax practice is increased involvement with the client and the possibility for a wider range of planning and compliance work.

Personal tax work

10.41 Larger tax practices could expand into volume processors of routine personal tax cases for other firms of tax advisors. They have the skills to recruit and retain personnel and implement quality control systems.

Specialised services to other professionals

Advice

10.42 Many firms offer specialised advice to other professionals as well as to clients. If the firm has a skill in a particular area this possibility should be considered. Examples of suitable specialisms include the following.

- Investigations services. This is a growth market following the introduction of personal and corporate self-assessment.
- International tax planning and transfer pricing.
- VAT.
- Share valuations.
- Capital gains tax.

Self-assessment means that tax returns must be correct and computations accurate. Small tax practices and sole practitioners may not have access to the necessary technical expertise in-house and are willing to buy advice from an expert.

10.43 A clear pricing structure is recommended and, because it is one-off advice, premium rates can be commanded. A minimum charge should be set. The service is highly suitable for being offered over the Internet.

Information

10.44 Many large firms already produce internal newsletters or information sheets for clients. These could also be sold to other professionals. The Internet can be used to produce subscription service newswires.

Expert witness

10.45 Opportunities exist for forensic work in negligence cases against other tax professionals, tax cases or loss of income disputes.

Lecturing and writing

10.46 Tax practices with suitably qualified personnel could offer lecturing services on the public lecture circuit, write articles or tax books. This work also has the added bonus of being good for PR.

Training

10.47 Larger tax practices often undertake their own in-house tax training courses. These could be opened up to other tax practitioners in the area.

10.48 Practices with suitable training departments could consider training ATT or ATII students.

Quick review

10.49

- When offering additional services the benefit of the work compared to the cost to the client must always be considered before starting work.
- In undertaking most additional services it is vital that the firm:
  - issues an engagement letter detailing the work to be done and the cost;
  - sends a report where appropriate detailing the exact scope of the work, any assumptions and the findings. Disclaimers should be included wherever possible.
- The Internet and e-commerce are now central to the core and additional services offered by tax professionals.
- Tax advisors possess a detailed knowledge of their clients. This can be used to create additional services specifically tailored to the clients' needs.
- Alternative services must offer clients added value – either a financial benefit or a means of making life easier.
- Practice development will be stunted if a firm is not open to the idea of offering non-compliance, value-added services.

10.49 *Additional Services*

- The range of additional services offered by practices should be kept under constant review. The firm needs to keep one step ahead of clients and the competition from other tax practices.
- In the future the most successful tax practices are likely to be those who embrace new skills including those outside their traditional sphere of work.
- The International Coaching Federation promotes ethical standards in coaching. Contact them at www.coachfederation.org

Chapter 11

Quality Control

11.1 Chapter 7 reviewed the issues that firms must consider when offering a tax compliance service as well as the reasons why they should implement standard procedures and controls over their work. This chapter looks at the issue of quality control to ensure that those standards are maintained across the firm.

11.2 The extent of quality control required by a tax practice will principally depend on its size and the complexity of the work the firm undertakes. Quality control should start with continuous self-review by the staff managing the case day to day. The firm's procedures may then include some or all of the following:

- review of correspondence and advice by tax partners and managers;
- file completion reviews, usually in conjunction with the finalisation of the tax return;
- hot reviews of complex tax advice;
- cold file reviews;
- reviews of the tax systems.

Unnecessary bureaucracy?

11.3 Extensive tax reviews are often thought to be unnecessarily bureaucratic since tax is not regulated work; but tax work can be risky. Many professional indemnity claims (not necessarily the most publicised ones) result from negligent tax work or advice and it can be a source of complaints and fee disputes. Good review procedures can minimise the risk of a claim and therefore be commercially beneficial.

11.4 Non-tax partners often feel that they are not competent to review the work of the tax department. This can lead to an unaccountable department working in isolation. A checklist approach can help. A file checklist is included in Appendix 11:2 and a systems checklist is included in Appendix 11:3.

Partner review

11.5 The practice should have procedures for reviewing and signing letters. They should cover who can:

- review letters before they are signed out (in a large firm this may be more than one person);
- sign routine letters and in what name (routine letters include requests for information, letters to clients sending copies of signed returns, and to the Revenue submitting the return where no information is disclosed other than that included on the return);
- sign letters sending tax returns to clients for signature and in what name;
- sign advice letters and in what name (all letters expressing an opinion on any subject are advisory);
- initial copy letters.

11.6 Only partners should sign in the firm's name. Copies should be retained of all letters, supporting schedules and documents (see 15.14).

11.7 The firm's procedures should set out what supporting information or files are to be provided to the reviewer to enable them to review the case. Some partners adopt a policy of only signing non-routine letters after a face-to-face discussion with the person working on the case.

File completion reviews

11.8 Tax firms should implement a file completion procedure. This is achieved most efficiently by using a checklist. Simple completion checklists provide good quality control but the use of a more detailed checklist can turn a compliance exercise into a planning exercise. The benefits of a checklist approach include the following.

- Minimising the risk of an important point being overlooked, wrong advice being given or a computational error occurring. They can preempt problems in the event of an Inland Revenue enquiry. See also the critical review checklists in Appendices 9:2 and 9:3.
- Identifying planning and commercial opportunities and areas which may be important in the future. A planning checklist is included in Appendix 8:1.
- Assisting effective delegation and control by allowing the partner or manager reviewing the file to obtain an overview of the client and more fully to comprehend its affairs. At the final review stage it is vital that someone stands back from the detailed work and ensures that the client's tax affairs are consistent with the commercial transactions.

- Linking a company's tax affairs with the directors' personal tax so that no compliance or planning points are overlooked. Clients generally dislike fragmentation of their affairs and in small owner-managed companies the directors often fail to distinguish between company and personal transactions.
- Maximising fee-earning opportunities. If a careful review of the company's affairs is undertaken it may identify areas where advice can be given (and charged for) and a more detailed compliance review or planning exercise undertaken.

11.9 A sample corporation tax file completion checklist is included in Appendix 7:3. There are many different file completion checklists available in tax procedure manuals. Alternatively, the firm can develop its own completion sheets.

Hot reviews

11.10 The practice should have a policy for the hot review of files where risk or technical issues merit it. The hot review may be carried out within the firm or by an outside expert. The situations when such a review is likely to be appropriate include cases of difficulty in interpreting the law, share valuations, disclosure issues, tax investigations and ethical concerns. Hot reviews also help to ensure that advisors only give advice that they are competent to give.

Firms may decide to annually hot review two or three of the largest cases for each partner and manager as a matter of course to minimise the risk of inaccurate or inappropriate work being sent to clients.

11.11 The main focus of the work in a hot review should be to:

- check the facts provided;
- ensure that the advice given accords with the facts;
- re-research the point to see if the reviewer comes to the same opinion;
- technically review the computations;
- minimise the risk to the firm by ensuring that there are appropriate engagement letters, risk warnings, statements of assumptions and disclaimers.

Once the review is complete, the work undertaken and the conclusions reached should be noted, signed and dated.

Cold file reviews

11.12 Tax practices should consider undertaking annual cold reviews of some of their tax files. This process can highlight problems and areas where improvements can be made as well as reducing the risk of errors. The results of the reviews should be discussed with the person working on the case and the relevant manager or partner. Their comments or explanations for problems or errors should be sought. The files reviewed, the type of work and the findings should be summarised in a report circulated to members of staff and partners. Areas for improvement, action or training should be identified. The findings relating to a particular member of staff may need to be discussed during a staff appraisal (see 12.37). A sample personal tax file review checklist is included in Appendix 11:2.

11.13 Smaller practices may find it hard to allocate the time or resources to undertake cold reviews. Such firms and sole practitioners should consider an external review (see 11.24). Larger firms or those with a tax committee will have appropriate staff or partners to undertake the reviews. However, there is a danger that the members of the tax committee may be reviewing systems that they introduced and that they may not be as objective as an independent reviewer. Periodic external reviews may still be of benefit to these firms.

11.14 For personal tax cases February and March may be the best time to undertake quality control reviews as it is a relatively quiet time of year. The best timing for corporate work will depend on the year-end profile of the firm's clients. An on-going quarterly programme is a good option as it spreads the workload and ensures that the serious errors or problems with a particular member of staff are identified quickly.

11.15 Where the firm has more than one office, an inter-office review with a partner or manager reviewing the work of another office can be beneficial in ensuring a consistent approach throughout the firm.

11.16 The reviews should cover the work of all partners and staff engaged in tax work. Most files should be chosen because they are high risk but a small number of randomly selected files should also be reviewed. The reviews should cover all types of work undertaken by the firm including personal tax, corporate tax, PAYE, VAT, trusts, investigations, Lloyd's Underwriters and planning advice.

Risk

11.17 Practices should use a risk assessment to determine which files should be reviewed. High-risk cases should be subject to regular review. A risk assessment is included in Appendix 1. The assessment can also be used to determine high-risk cases when assessing fee levels or staff allocation.

Specialist or highly technical work

11.18 The idea of reviewing highly technical or specialist work may be daunting to a non-specialist. This will be exacerbated if the case involves a large number of files. A non-specialist can undertake such reviews by using a suitable checklist if they bear in mind that the objectives of the exercise are to minimise risk. It may be easiest to undertake the review with the person working on the case day to day so that key documents can be easily located.

11.19 In addition to the points covered on the file review checklist in Appendix 11:2, a cold review of specialised tax work should also cover the following points to ensure that:

- the engagement letter covers the work undertaken in sufficient detail;
- a corporate finance engagement letter is issued if appropriate (see 20.34);
- the work does not breach the firm's investment business registration (see 20.11);
- there are no money laundering issues (see 20.46);
- the *Ramsay* principle is not in issue;
- quotations have been provided to the client and the time costs are being recovered;
- the advice is given in writing;
- detailed, legible and dated file notes are kept of all meetings and telephone conversations;
- letters and reports clearly state the assumptions on which the work is based, who made them and the implications for the validity of the work if they do not hold true;
- appropriate risk warnings have been given;
- letters and reports contain appropriate disclaimers;
- any adverse comments from the client have been resolved in full;
- the file, letters and reports have been reviewed by a partner or manager;
- the person working on the case has undertaken their own checks and cross-checks to minimise the risk of errors occurring;
- details of the reference sources used are kept on file;
- timetables have been met;
- diary notes are kept of all key dates and deadlines;
- the staff/partners undertaking the work have the appropriate specialised training and qualifications and their CPE is up to date;

- if the case is large the files are well organised and easy to follow;
- the person in charge of the case appears to be in control of it with a full understanding of all the issues.

Investigation cases

11.20 These cases can also present difficulties for reviewers. Many high-risk issues can arise from an enquiry including fee recovery, complaints and claims. The information to be obtained from the review and monitoring of such cases can provide invaluable information as to the best approach to be taken in the future. In addition to completing the file review checklist in Appendix 11:2, the following points should also be considered.

- Is there an appropriate engagement letter?
- Are the time costs being recovered?
- Is all the information required by the investigations insurers being retained (if applicable)?
- Has all the information been supplied to the Inland Revenue on time?
- Has only the appropriate information been supplied to the Inland Revenue?
- Are diary notes kept of key dates and deadlines?
- Have detailed, legible and dated notes been kept of all meetings and telephone discussions?
- Has the client been kept informed of the progress of the case and asked to approve the course of action/letters?
- Has a partner reviewed all the letters?
- Has a closing notice been obtained?
- Have recommendations been made to the client following the investigation?
- Has the client been offered investigations insurance if they do not already have it (see 16.24)?

Regular systems reviews by the head of the tax department

11.21 The head of the tax department is responsible for the efficient operation of the tax department. This involves continual monitoring and updating of the firm's tax systems and from this process should flow the management of the department including:

- client allocation;
- work priorities for each fee earner;
- risk management.

11.22 A sample tax systems checklist is included in Appendix 11:3. The approach to this review is to document and appraise the system combined with a brief review of its operation. The permanent systems information can be cross-referred to the firm's tax and office procedures manual or documented separately. Once it has been carried out for the first year, it will simply require updating and review in subsequent years.

11.23 The main focus of the review should be the monitoring of the tax diary controls. This will enable the head of the tax department to produce regular summaries for the practice of:

- the number of outstanding tax returns;
- cases where deadlines were not met;
- details of the tax returns in progress;
- filing dates for VAT returns, P11Ds and CT600s;
- expiry dates for claims and elections;
- items of outstanding post by members of staff;
- workload by members of staff;
- ongoing tax investigations.

These summaries will enable the fee earners to chase clients and deal with cases in the right order of priority, thus minimising the risk of an error or oversight occurring.

External reviews

11.24 Firms without the appropriate internal resources or expertise should consider having an independent review of their systems and a sample of tax files. They may also require the services of an expert to undertake hot reviews (see 21.2). Tax practices which are part of a training or marketing group may be required to have external reviews under the terms of their registration or membership.

11.25 Apart from the potential lack of resources, internal reviews in small firms can cause conflict and tension as criticism may be taken personally. Other benefits of external reviews include the identification of structural weaknesses in the firm's systems and common errors. An external reviewer is objective and has the experience of many different systems to offer.

11.26 External reviewers usually work more quickly than staff or partners undertaking internal reviews because they are experienced in file and systems reviews and know what they are looking for. Firms should compare the cost of an external review with the chargeable time which would be lost by the internal reviewer.

11.27 Where the firm is part of a training or marketing group the reviewer will usually be supplied by the organisation. If not, the best way to find a suitable external reviewer is by word of mouth, through contacts made at local practitioner groups or by contacting the firm's professional body.

11.28 Confidentiality should not be a concern if the reviewer is another professional person bound by rules of professional etiquette, but clients should be made aware that a person outside the firm may review the firm's files. This is best done by a suitable clause in the engagement letter.

11.29 Terms between the firm and the reviewer should be agreed at the outset of the engagement by exchange of letters or by the reviewer issuing an engagement letter to the practice. The firm should ensure that they understand what they are contracting for including:

- the number of days the review will take;
- the number of offices to be covered;
- the number and type of files reviewed, for example, corporate tax, partnerships and individuals;
- the number and type of specialist files reviewed, for example, trusts, investigations, tax planning;
- ensuring that the work of all key personnel is covered;
- the detail in which the files will be reviewed;
- whether the review includes a technical review of the work undertaken;
- details of the report, meetings and feedback that will be given;
- details of any grading or marking system used.

Quick review

11.30

- The key objective of quality control in a tax practice is to minimise risk.
- Regular reviews can result in a more efficient tax department by identifying and solving problems early, facilitating target setting, focusing training and motivating staff.
- Firms will benefit commercially from using a file completion checklist that also covers planning issues.
- Quality control is good marketing. It reinforces the fact that the practice is selling a premium brand service of a reliable and consistently high standard.

Appendix 11:1

Risk Assessment

This checklist can be used to determine which files should be subject to review.

Client name	
Client reference	
Partner/manager/staff responsible	
Tax year	
Reviewer	
Date of review	

	Yes/High	No/Low
Is the client commercially significant for the firm?		
Are there large tax liabilities?		
Is regular planning advice given?		
Is the client a member of a group?		
Are there related businesses?		
Are there overseas connections?		
Does the company have outside shareholders?		
Is the client tax adverse?		
Are there complicated taper relief claims?		
Is the case complex?		
Are there complex transactions, for example, remuneration packages or share schemes?		
Have there been any complaints from the client?		
Are there personality considerations which could give rise to problems?		
Are there any unusual features about the case?		
Are there instances of late or non-compliance?		
Is the industry in which the client operates high risk?		

Risk assessed as High/low

Appendix 11:2

Personal Tax – File Review Checklist

Client name	
Client reference	
Partner/manager/staff responsible	
Tax year	
Reviewer	
Date of review	

Permanent information

Do the manual files or computer records contain the following?

		Yes	No	N/A
1	An up-to-date engagement letter			
2	Personal and background information about the client			
3	A new client form			
4	A copy of the Form 64-8			
5	Planning or technical review checklists			
6	Relevant agreements, for example, partnership/rental			
7	Capital gains tax histories			
8	Inheritance tax transfers/planning			
9	Details of trusts			
10	Pension contribution histories/NRE calculations			
11	Authorisations, for example, banks/ solicitors			
12	Copies of claims and elections			
13	Summaries of planning advice, the outcome of enquiries and important correspondence			

Current information

Do the current tax or correspondence files contain the following?

		Yes	No	N/A
1	Evidence of review by a partner/manager			
2	A file completion sheet and critical review			
3	A signed copy of the tax return			
4	A tax calculation working sheet and tax computations			
5	Evidence of the work done			
6	Adequate working papers to justify the entries on the return			
7	A letter/file note asking the client to approve the return before signing the form			
8	A letter advising the client about their tax position			
9	A letter warning them about interest/ penalties			
10	Confirmation of receipt of the return/capture/amendment by the Revenue			
11	Form SA310 reducing tax payments on account together with supporting calculations			
12	Taxpayer statements of account			
13	Notes of meetings/telephone calls			
14	Details of tax planning/advice/elections, together with adequate supporting/working papers			
15	A letter returning the original papers to the client with retention instructions			

Controls

		Yes	No	N/A
1	Have the firm's controls been completed/ updated as necessary throughout the engagement?			

Action to be taken following this review

Appendix 11:3

Tax Department Systems Review Checklist

Head of department	
Reviewer	
Date of review	

Permanent information

Please document the following (attach separate sheets if necessary). If the procedure is documented in the firm's tax or office manual a cross-reference to the relevant paragraph will suffice provided that the procedure is being followed without amendment.

Computers	
Software used	
Computer back-up arrangements	
Manuals	
Tax manuals used	
Office procedures used	
Files	
Client file structure including permanent files (both computerised and manual)	
Procedure for dealing with papers subject to legal professional privilege	
Clients	
Procedures for new clients including money laundering	
Procedures for ex-clients	
Engagement letter	
Date of last update	
Details of subjects covered	
Disclosure	
Policy for submission of accounts	
Disclosure policy	

Errors and irregularities	
Procedure for dealing with errors on returns (both client and firm)	
Procedure for dealing with other tax irregularities	
Letters	
Procedures for signing out letters	
Telephone/meeting notes	
Procedure for making telephone/meeting notes	
ELS	
Means of authorisation by the client	
Signed, hard copy retained?	
Procedure for dealing with rejected returns	
Claims and elections	
Precedents used for the wording of claims and elections made outside the return	
Method used to monitor time limits	
enquiries	
Means of monitoring due dates for information to be supplied to the Revenue	
The method of monitoring the receipt of closure notices	
Incoming post	
Procedures for opening/distributing post	
outstanding work	
Procedures for monitoring outstanding work/post	
Procedures for monitoring letters where a reply is expected	
Details of diary systems and forward notes	
Planning	
Details of planning services offered by the firm	
Details of checklists used	
Details of tax schemes or complex planning recommended to clients	

Means of ensuring compliance with the ethical requirements of the firm's professional body	
File completion	
Details of checklists used	
Review and quality control	
File review policy	
Planning review policy	
Hot file review policy	
Cold file review policy	
Systems review policy	
Client records	
Procedures for returning/storing clients' records and advising them of retention dates	
Policy for retaining clients' files	
Staff/partners	
Staffing and reporting structure	
Staff appraisal system and frequency	
Staff training on manuals/office procedures	
Staff training in-house and on external courses including specialist work	
Library	
Name/location of books and CDs	
Journals taken and means of circularisation	
Newsletters	
Details of newsletters sent to clients and their frequency	
Details of current brochures/leaflets produced for distribution to clients	
Consultation and referral	
Means of internal consultation	
Policy on external consultation	
Contacts for referrals (other firms and professionals)	

Detailed considerations

Please attach a separate sheet if necessary.

		Yes	No	N/A
1	Have there been any problems with the computer system since the last review?			
2	Have all clients been entered on the firm's systems including new clients, company directors and partners?			
3	Have all clients been sent the most up-to-date engagement/disengagement letters?			
4	Has the firm's policy for file reviews been followed at all stages?			
5	Do the systems recorded above give any cause for concern given the size and complexity of the practice?			
6	Is the firm's tax work up to date? Have there been instances of missed deadlines?			
7	Have the procedures for returning/storing client records and files been followed?			
8	Have all partners/staff undertaken adequate training and/or met their CPE/CPD requirements?			
9	Has the policy on staff appraisals been followed?			
10	Have the controls been kept up to date and are they regularly monitored?			
11	Are clients regularly notified of relevant changes in legislation?			
12	Have there been any PII claims?			
13	Have there been any complaints?			
14	Are clients offered investigations insurance?			

Tax diary controls

Does the practice operate the following controls over its tax work? Are they recorded, dated and regularly reviewed?

	Personal/partnership/trusts	Yes	Date	N/A
1	Information request letter sent to client			
2	Information received			
3	Further information requested			
4	Tax liability checked/reconciled			
5	Return sent to client			
6	Provisional or estimated figures logged and monitored			

	Personal/partnership/trusts (continued)	Yes	Date	N/A
7	Tax return returned to the firm			
8	Tax payment on account reduced and client warned of interest implications			
9	Client advised of their tax liabilities, payments on account, due dates for payment and the interest implications			
10	Return sent to the Inland Revenue			
11	Client warned about the penalties for late filed returns			
12	Fee issued			
13	SA310 received/tax return processed			
14	Refund received			
15	Taxpayer statement of account checked			
16	Client advised of the tax payments due and the interest and surcharge implications of late paid tax			
17	Inland Revenue informed of any errors on the taxpayer statement of account			
18	Amended/repaired tax return sent to client			
19	Amended tax return sent to Inland Revenue			
20	Amendment processed			

	Corporate	Yes	Date	N/A
1	Notice to file a return received			
2	Accounting date			
3	Filing date			
4	Tax payment date			
5	CT600 sent to client			
6	Client advised of tax payment, due dates and interest implications			
7	The need for quarterly payments identified and dates diarised			
8	CT600 returned by client			
9	CT600 submitted to the Inland Revenue			
10	Fee issued			
11	CT600 processed			
12	Refund received			
13	Statement checked and the client advised of outstanding tax and interest implications			
14	Amended/repaired tax return sent to client			
15	Amended tax return sent to Inland Revenue			
16	Amendment processed			

P35, P11D, payrolls, VAT returns		Yes	Date	N/A
1	Form/documentation completed and sent to client			
2	Client advised of the tax payments, due date, interest and penalty implications			
3	Form submitted to the Inland Revenue/Customs and Excise			
4	Fee issued			

Action to be taken following this review

Part III – Office

Chapter 12

Employees

12.1 Employing staff can be a daunting proposition. Not only are there the responsibilities and duties of employment law to consider but the effect on the other team members if there is a personality clash, as well as the impact on practice profitability. However, in spite of the problems and pitfalls, employing staff can bring real financial rewards. This chapter considers:

- recruitment;
- staff numbers;
- motivation, productivity and incentives;
- training;
- delegation and organisation;
- appraisal;
- employment law.

Recruiting

12.2 A sole practitioner starting out as a tax consultant may initially employ a spouse or family member to help out and create a positive impression of the practice. More staff will be recruited as the work expands.

Before employing any member of staff it is essential to assess whether there is a job that needs doing, whether it requires someone full time or part time and how long the need will last for. Seasonal factors, particularly for personal tax, should also be considered as well as anticipated future staffing requirements.

12.3 The firm should draw up a job description detailing exactly what work the member of staff will be doing and where they fit into the existing team (see 12.41). This will not only help the practice but will be essential information for a recruitment agency or to help in drafting an advertisement.

12.4 *Employees*

Job description

12.4 A job description should contain the following:

- job title;
- title of who the employee reports to (avoid names as they may change);
- title of those reporting to the employee (if any);
- the purpose of the job;
- the main duties and responsibilities;
- work standards expected;
- place of work.

12.5 When drawing up a job description the practice should also produce a job specification to help the recruitment process. This should cover:

- qualifications;
- training;
- experience;
- general intelligence;
- appearance;
- temperament;
- aptitudes (for example, an ability to speak languages or an aptitude for computers);
- interests;
- circumstances (for example, whether they have a clean driving licence).

The considerations should be specific. For example, the job description should say 'educated to degree level' and not 'well educated'. There must be no direct or indirect discrimination. Avoid references to gender by using the phrase 'the applicant'.

12.6 Recruiting staff is an expensive process. Firms should consider not just the cost of the agency or advert but the time spent by partners and staff processing applications and interviewing. Too large a response is almost as bad as too small. Select the recruitment media carefully. It should reach the right people, in the right numbers at the right price.

12.7 When recruiting do not always go straight to an agency or take out a newspaper advert. Ask employees if they know anyone looking for a similar job and consider internal promotion. Keep a list of applicants who sent in CVs when there were no vacancies. Are they still interested in a position? Consider a direct approach to schools and colleges. Encourage as large a pool of potential recruits as possible by offering flexible working arrangements such as job sharing, flexi-time, time off in lieu or when work is quiet.

12.8 Where a firm has difficulty recruiting high calibre staff consider permanent adverts or job placements with agencies. Recruit only the best staff but do so regardless of whether there is an immediate need. This approach may result in temporary over-staffing but it gives the firm an opportunity for some pro-active marketing and will keep other staff on their toes.

12.9 Keep a record of responses to adverts to monitor which ones produce the most appropriate response and the best staff. This will enable the firm to advertise in the most effective way. Use not only local newspapers but trade journals. National newspapers are only likely to be effective for larger firms. Consider advertising on the Internet and via the firm's website. Research has shown that the two most important factors in a successful recruitment advert are stating the job title and the salary. Keep notes of the reasons for not inviting candidates for an interview to avoid allegations of racial or sexual bias.

12.10 Recruitment agencies are expensive (expect to pay about 15 per cent to 20 per cent of the first year's salary), but they usually have a large pool of highly qualified staff and are particularly useful for temporary staff. To avoid wasting time interviewing unsuitable candidates ask the agency about their screening procedures and for a copy of the applicant's CV as well as the agency one. Negotiate the fee (see 14.53) and ensure that the contract contains provisions to refund or discount the fee in the event of the member of staff leaving or proving unsuitable within the first few months.

12.11 Use a variety of means to screen applicants before and during the interview, including application forms, handwritten covering letters, graphology, chatting to potential employees on the telephone and using tests. The firm may design specific tests to check a candidate's tax knowledge and computer skills or use psychometric or intelligence tests where the job merits it.

12.12 Always ask for references to check that the applicant is who they say they are and check qualifications with their professional body.

12.13 Although it sounds like a truism, interviews should be conducted by those experienced at interviewing. The firm should decide whether to 'panel' interview with two or more interviewers present at the same time or to conduct one-to-one interviews. All interviewees should be seen by more than one person even if this involves two one-to-one interviews.

12.14 The most important thing when interviewing is to think carefully about the way in which questions are phrased in order to get the best out of the applicant. Use open questions such as 'what made you apply for this job?', or 'what do you like about your present job?'. Most questions beginning with 'how', 'why' or 'what' are suitable for interviews. Interviewers should avoid leading questions, closed questions which only lead to a 'yes' or 'no' answer, limited questions and multiple questions. Hypothetical questions may have a place but should be used with care. Potentially discriminatory questions, such as those about family or children, should be avoided.

12.15 All interviews should be conducted upon similar lines to make it easy to compare candidates. Notes of the interview should be kept together with the reasons for selection.

12.16 It is essential that the entire recruitment process (and subsequent employment) is free from bias and discrimination (including sex, marital status, disability, race and ethnic origin). Bias on age grounds is not unlawful but is subject to a non-statutory Code of Practice issued in 1999. If an employer is found guilty of discrimination there is no upper limit on the compensation that can be awarded to an applicant. Discrimination may also constitute a breach of the ethical guidelines of the practitioner's professional body.

Numbers

12.17 The recruitment process should be intrinsically linked to an optimum number of staff for the tax practice. This does not just depend on the quantity of work. If the practice wants to be profitable it will also depend on the number of partners and the type of work it undertakes. Highly specialised firms where the partners effectively work as experts or consultants may require only one or two staff per partner. Firms undertaking routine compliance work will be able to delegate much more work and the staff to partner ratio will need to be much higher for the firm to be profitable. Most tax practices have three to seven staff per partner. Practices with a combination of routine and specialised work need to be careful that a partner undertaking specialised work is not responsible for too many staff undertaking routine tasks. If they are they will require a good manager to help them, otherwise both work and profitability may suffer.

For example, the following table shows the effect on fee income of three typical practice scenarios. For the sake of illustration the table assumes that each partner and member of staff works 1,300 chargeable hours each year at charge-out rates of between £100 and £40 per hour.

Staff:partner ratio	2:1	4:1	6:1
	£	£	£
Partner 1 × £100 × 1,300 hours	130,000	130,000	130,000
Manager 1 × £60 × 1,300 hours	78,000	78,000	78,000
Assistant 1 × £50 × 1,300 hours	–	65,000	–
Assistants 2 × £50 × 1,300 hours	–	–	130,000
Assistant 1 × £40 × 1,300 hours	52,000	–	–
Assistants 2 × £40 × 1,300 hours	–	104,000	–
Assistants 3 × £40 × 1,300 hours	–	–	156,000
Total	260,000	377,000	494,000

The 4:1 firm produces 45 per cent more fee income than the 2:1 practice. The 6:1 structure produces 90 per cent more than the 2:1 and 31 per cent more than the 4:1.

Small, specialised teams need to charge clients premium rates to offset the size of the group and the inability to profit from delegation. To achieve the same fees as the 4:1 firm, the fees of the 2:1 team would need to increase from £100 to £145, £60 to £87 and £40 to £58. To achieve the same fees as the 6:1 practice, the fees would need to increase to £190, £114 and £76.

Motivation

12.18 Keeping staff motivated is vital for practice profitability but it can be difficult to achieve where they undertake routine tasks, such as processing tax returns, year in, year out. What motivates an individual member of staff will depend on his or her personal circumstances. This may be ascertained in a staff appraisal interview. The firm should be flexible in the range of incentives it offers so that these can be tailored to the individual members of staff. Broadly the key motivators will be:

- pay and perks;
- holidays/time off;
- the work environment (see 14.10);
- job satisfaction/career development;
- social aspects.

12.19 Pay is the single key motivator. The firm should be careful to ensure that the pay rates it offers are in line with the local market or higher to attract the best candidates. If a firm offers rates higher than the market average it should expect its staff to produce work of above average quality.

12.20 Pay for a fixed number of hours regardless of the results offers very little in the way of motivation. If staff seem poorly motivated this may be one reason why. The firm must also ensure that pay is fair within the firm, particularly if new staff are recruited at a higher rate than existing staff. The only way to avoid this is to discuss pay openly and to have a transparent pay structure. Employees will accept unequal pay for unequal work or responsibility. A better approach is for pay to be linked to productivity. This will give staff regular incentives by way of bonuses or overtime.

Productivity

12.21 One way of measuring productivity in a tax practice is in comparison to budgeted chargeable hours. Consider setting chargeable hour targets for all partners and staff. Agree this in consultation with them (a good time to do this is at an annual appraisal). The budget must take into account holidays, sick leave, training and CPE and administration. Few people will manage more than 45 chargeable weeks a year. For a 35-hour week, this gives 1,575 hours. Targets should be achievable but tight and linked to incentives.

12.22 Some personnel will have no administration time; others, particularly partners and senior staff, may be responsible for specific administration tasks. Non-chargeable time should be monitored. This can be done by using the work in progress system. All staff and partners should provide a description of their non-chargeable time. Simply calling it 'administration' is not acceptable. Students and those studying for exams will achieve lower chargeable hours unless they also work overtime.

Overtime

12.23 Personal tax compliance work is now highly seasonal, with the majority of the work falling in the period June to January. September, December and January may be particularly busy. Expecting staff to work overtime at busy times of the year and paying them for it can be an effective way of coping with peaks in the workload and maximising the firm's profitability.

For example, a tax assistant whose main work involves processing tax returns is paid £18,000 a year, the equivalent of £10 per hour she works. Her chargeable hours are 1,550. After including employer's National Insurance, the basic cost to the firm per chargeable hour is £13. She is charged out to clients at £35 per hour. Overtime is paid at time plus one-quarter i.e. £12.50.

For each extra hour she works, the practice pays her £12.50, which is less than her basic budgeted hourly cost, namely £13. This means that the practice makes more for each extra hour she works above budget than her basic hours. This is why they can afford to pay her a higher rate for overtime. Furthermore, assuming that her share of the overheads is recovered in the budgeted hours, the profit earned for each extra hour worked is even higher.

12.24 Practices should be aware of the potential pitfalls of paying overtime.

- Once the firm starts to pay overtime it is difficult to withdraw it or change the rate.
- Limiting overtime to busy periods can be effective but making it available all the time may be counter-productive. The work may simply expand to fill the time and a culture of long hours will develop.
- If staff are happy to work late as a matter of course, overtime payments will be unnecessary and simply cost the practice money for something they currently receive free.
- The quality of the work must be maintained.
- Staff may want to work too much overtime and become tired and stressed as a result.

Bonuses

12.25 Using the above logic, it can be seen that rewarding staff who exceed their budgeted hours with bonuses can be highly cost effective and motivational. Bonuses should not be given for simply achieving the budget (unless there are exceptional circumstances) but for achieving 5 per cent or more than the budget.

12.26 In computing bonuses, work in progress write-offs above a certain amount should be taken into account to minimise excessive hours and sub-standard work. Where staff or partners are able to achieve higher than usual charge-out rates or additional profits, these should be rewarded by higher bonuses.

12.27 Other means of incentivising staff include the following.

- *Time in lieu.* Instead of paying overtime or offering bonuses, some staff may prefer to take extra time off work. Given the seasonal nature of many tax practices this may work well, particularly if time is taken off at a quieter time of year.

- *Holidays*. More and more people are trading money for time off. Offer increased holidays for each year of service or in place of pay increases.
- *Flexible hours*. This can be an important incentive for those with family commitments. The agreed hours are worked but the firm is more flexible about the exact hours of work or location provided that the work gets done. Some firms are experimenting with a nine-day fortnight.
- *Perks*. A range of perks may be motivational for some staff. Small firms may find them costly to provide but the collective buying power of even a small practice may make benefits such as private health and permanent health insurance attractive. For further details about perks see 19.17.
- *Recognition*. This tends to be underestimated. However, the acknowledgement of hard work or good results by a simple 'thanks' will be appreciated. Consider also a handwritten thank you letter for special effort, or a party at the end of the tax return season.
- *Training*. Many tax practitioners are motivated by training and career development possibilities, particularly early in their professional lives. Firms should use training to motivate and reward such staff. There is often a misguided notion that if staff are too well trained they will leave and look for a better job elsewhere. This is, of course, possible but most staff inevitably move on. Firms should have no regrets about this provided they have maximised the profit from their staff whilst they were employed. If the member of staff does not leave, the firm will have a more highly trained employee well placed to take on more responsibility or fill a vacancy.

Training

12.28 Training in a tax practice does not just include staff but all partners and principals. It can consist of the following.

- On the job training and induction, including knowledge of the firm's procedures, manuals and computer systems.
- Training for exams, for example, ATII or AAT, either at courses, by correspondence or a combination of both.
- Continuing professional education/development (CPE or CPD) for qualified staff to meet the requirements of the practitioner's professional body. This may be in-house or on external courses. Many firms belong to training groups which helps to minimise the cost. Training can also consist of tuition via the Internet, CD-ROM or video.
- Practice management, communication and IT skills.

12.29 The most successful firms are those that take training and personal development seriously. Most training is highly valuable and essential to a well-informed tax department. The firm should allocate a budget for each individual member of staff and ensure that it is spent. Staff should be supplied with relevant course brochures so that they are aware of the range of training available. Training should be discussed and evaluated in staff appraisal meetings so that it is appropriately targeted to the needs of the employee and team. The firm should bear in mind that it does not just incur the cost of the course but it loses time whilst the member of staff attends.

12.30 Tax is constantly changing and all members of the tax staff need to be kept up to date and to develop their areas of expertise. Those not directly involved in tax, including audit staff or administration personnel, will also benefit from tax training. Tax staff will require management or personal development training to enhance communication and computer skills.

12.31 Particular focus should be given to induction training. If this falls short a new member of staff will take much longer to get 'up to speed' and valuable income will be lost. Staff may also become frustrated or disillusioned and they may leave. Given the high cost of recruitment this may be a 'double whammy' for the firm.

CPE/CPD

12.32 Firms must ensure that their principals and staff achieve sufficient training units to meet the CPE/CPD requirements of their professional body and any registrations that they hold (for example, investment business). This training will consist of a combination of courses (structured activities) and reading (unstructured activities). Each member of staff or partner must keep a record of their CPE/CPD. If such records are kept individually, a copy should be provided to the firm. If the firm keeps the records, it should ensure that the member of staff reports all their training activities and reading, not just courses.

12.33 Individuals and firms should ensure that they are familiar with the activities that constitute CPE/CPD. Where personnel fail to meet the minimum requirements remedial action should be taken.

Delegation

12.34 Successful delegation comes from:

- choosing the correct work to be delegated;
- selecting the right member of staff to undertake the task;
- briefing them properly;

- expecting them to do a good job, to a high standard and on time;
- supervising the work;
- feeding back immediately if they fail to meet the required standard;
- praising good work; and
- appraising the end result.

If any of these stages are missed out the work may be substandard, time will be wasted and profits lost. As can be seen at 12.17, there can be very real financial rewards to be obtained from effective delegation. It is therefore essential that all senior staff obtain training in delegation, and staff and team management.

12.35 Many personal tax returns are routine, low risk work. If the firm assesses risk at the beginning of the appointment (see 2.7), these low risk clients can be allocated to the junior staff in the team subject to manager or partner review.

12.36 Periodically the firm should consider the following.

- Which member of staff is undertaking what type of work. Ensure that cases are delegated to an appropriate member of staff.
- Who is undertaking non-chargeable administration. Can this be delegated to clerical staff?
- Which clients are the firm's top fee earners. Are these clients getting enough care and attention from the firm or has the work been delegated too far?
- Decide which clients have most potential for fee growth. Ensure that the member of staff dealing with the case is sufficiently pro-active.

Staff appraisal

12.37 Small practices have less need for a formal approach to staff appraisal because the partners and managers work with the staff on a day-to-day basis and can quickly recognise strengths and weaknesses and deal with staff problems as they arise. Nevertheless, there are good reasons why a more formal approach is worthwhile:

- to meet training requirements for students;
- to evaluate new staff before they have been in the job for too long;
- to ensure a fair and impartial appraisal on which promotion or salary may be based;
- to provide personnel records in the event of the member of staff being dismissed;
- to get feedback about the firm, management structure, training

methods and future direction. Exit interviews for staff who leave should also be considered.

12.38 The firm should ensure that it has a suitable staff appraisal form (see Appendix 12:1). This should initially be a self-appraisal by the member of staff followed by comments from supervisors, managers and partners as appropriate. The form should then be discussed with the member of staff in an interview. Staff and managers should be allowed sufficient time to complete the form.

12.39 The timing of staff appraisals will vary. It is good practice for these not to be linked to pay reviews. Since they take time and effort, a quiet time of year is generally best, for example, February and March. Six-monthly appraisals may be suitable for larger practices but annually is likely to be sufficient for a smaller firm. It is important to appraise all staff on an equal basis.

Demotivated employees

12.40 Staff appraisals may highlight staff who are demotivated or it may become apparent from the quality of their work or demeanour. It is essential to stem demotivation quickly, otherwise it can spread throughout the firm. Consider the following action.

- Analyse the reasons (personal problems, lack of prospects, personality clash).
- Talk to the employee on a one-to-one basis. Find out what is necessary to improve matters, for example, extra help or more training.
- Where there is a personality clash, first establish whether there is another issue involved such as bullying. If not, then the following action may be possible depending on the staff concerned and the firm's structure: move both parties into different jobs so that they have less one-to-one contact, ask them to swap roles or give them both a new challenge or responsibility.
- Offer the employee counselling or a sabbatical (depending on how long they have been with the firm).

Tax teams

12.41 Clients will receive the best service when a firm has a tax department which functions as a team rather than a series of isolated individuals. Tax is increasingly specialised and in order to provide a cost efficient service many team members may be involved in one client's affairs. Good teams share ideas, provide support and cover during staff holidays and absences and respond collectively to urgent deadlines or work peaks. It would be quite possible to write a whole book simply about the management of a team. Partners and managers interested in taking the subject further will find the subject covered in more detail in a wide range of management books.

12.42 Teams may be either led by the partners or subject led (for example, small business department). In either case a good, motivated leader is essential to managing the team and getting the best out of it. The best leader will not necessarily be a partner although in most practices this is likely to be the case. Those heading up teams need good listening skills. Often the team members will be capable of solving problems and making good suggestions about clients' affairs, new services and the operation of the department; they simply need a conducive environment where they can put forward ideas and take risks knowing that they will not be ridiculed or ignored. Individuality and creativity within the team should be encouraged; if the individual does well, so does the team.

12.43 It is essential when recruiting staff to ensure that the composition of the team does not become unbalanced. Open communication, regular meetings and the involvement of all team members in the work and decisions are the keys to creating a successful team.

Employment law

12.44 Tax practices have to consider a wide range of employment law issues. A busy practice needs to take these matters seriously because the potential cost of failing to comply is not just bad publicity but very real financial penalties. A partner or senior member of staff should be given responsibility for this area and suitable training to keep up to date. A partner or member of staff skilled in employment law will also be able to provide valuable advice to clients. Employment law is, however, extremely complex and it is advisable to develop a relationship with a firm of employment lawyers both from the point of view of the firm and its clients. The following areas need particular consideration but are not intended to be exhaustive.

Employment contracts

12.45 The *Employment Rights Act (ERA) 1996* gives employees the right to have certain conditions of employment set out in writing in a 'principal statement' within two months of the start of their employment. The terms include the date the employment began, job title, rate of pay and pay periods, hours to be worked, holiday entitlement, sick pay and notification of sickness, pension arrangements, the notice period and disciplinary and grievance procedures. Employment terms must not discriminate between employees for reasons of sex, race or disability. Practices with more than 15 employees can be required to make reasonable adjustments to the office to overcome the practical effects of an individual's disability.

Hours of work

12.46 From 1 October 1998 the *Working Time Regulations* stipulate that employees are not allowed to work more than an average 48-hour week unless they have agreed in writing to opt out of the Regulations. Lunch breaks where the employee is required to cover telephone calls or open the door are unlikely to be considered rest breaks. Firms must keep records monitoring the hours worked. Particular care should be taken at busy periods of the year as the 'average week' is calculated over a 17-week period. It is automatically considered unfair dismissal if an employee is dismissed for refusing to opt out of the Regulations and even if an opt-out is agreed, the member of staff can terminate it subject to an agreed notice period not exceeding three months.

Equal pay

12.47 The *Equal Pay Act 1970* gives a woman the right to be paid the same as a man doing an equivalent job. Firms should be able to justify pay differences. The best way of doing this is by reference to good personnel records and staff appraisals.

Holidays

12.48 From November 1999 there is a statutory entitlement to four weeks' paid holidays after 13 weeks' continuous service. This can include bank holidays.

Parenthood

12.49 Pregnant employees are entitled to paid time off for antenatal care regardless of their length of service or hours of work and to 18 weeks' maternity leave from 30 April 2000, subject to 21 days' notice. There is no requirement to give notice of an intention to return to work. Those with one year's service are entitled to extended leave. Women with six months' service will be entitled to statutory maternity pay. If a woman is dismissed for reasons connected with her pregnancy or maternity leave it will constitute unfair dismissal.

12.50 The *Parent Leave Direction* permits both parents to take unpaid leave of up to three months per child within five years of its birth or adoption. Time off is also permitted for urgent reasons in connection with dependants.

Public duties

12.51 Employees are entitled to take unpaid time off for public duties (for example, as a JP, school governor or prison visitor).

Notice

12.52 Employees are entitled to be given notice depending on their length of service. For example, an employee employed for two years six months is entitled to a minimum of three weeks' notice. The contract of employment may specify a longer period. Unless the contract of employment states otherwise employees are only obliged to give one week's notice of their intention to leave the firm.

Practice sales/mergers

12.53 Where a firm is sold or merges and some or all of the employees are transferred to a third party, the firm must consult with the employees affected before the transfer takes place. From 1 November 1999 failure to do so can lead to an award of up to 13 weeks' pay. Statutory employment rights will be based on the length of service with both employers although the terms and conditions can be altered by the new firm to the extent that they could have been altered by the old practice.

Dismissal

12.54 Employees who have been employed for one year have a right from 1 June 1999 not to be unfairly dismissed and to be given a written statement specifying the reasons for dismissal within 14 days. If the dismissal is unfair the employee may be able to claim considerable compensation at an employment tribunal. To avoid claims, the termination must comply with the terms of the employment contract and statutory notice periods. The law is complex in this area and legal advice to prevent a costly tribunal hearing may be necessary.

Staff manual

12.55 The best way to minimise employment problems is to have a staff manual. This sets out what is expected of the firm's employees and the firm's reward structure. Such a document will promote equality of opportunity and treatment. Staff manuals are particularly important for tax practices because of the many ethical issues involved such as conflict of interest and client confidentiality. Subjects that should be covered in a staff manual are as follows.

- Description of the firm:
  - history;
  - philosophy/aims;
  - mission statement;
  - partners and key personnel;

- location;
- national and international links;
- equal opportunity statement.

- Employment:
  - contracts and personnel records;
  - hours of work;
  - absence and lateness;
  - training/CPE;
  - appraisal;
  - appearance;
  - conduct with clients;
  - health and safety (including fire emergency procedures, smoking, cleanliness and VDUs);
  - discrimination;
  - office procedures (for example, telephones, filing, tidiness);
  - use of office equipment;
  - notice period.

- Employee reward:
  - pay/bonuses;
  - pay days;
  - overtime;
  - benefits;
  - expenses;
  - promotion;
  - holidays;
  - sickness;
  - maternity/paternity leave;
  - other leaves of absence (jury duty/compassionate leave);
  - sabbaticals.

- Ethics:
  - confidentiality;
  - conflict of interest;

- interest in clients' affairs;
- private clients;
- honorary and charitable appointments;
- money laundering;
- *Investment Business Regulations.*

- Grievance/disciplinary/termination:
  - procedure;
  - misconduct;
  - termination;
  - non-competition and solicitation of clients and staff.

Quick review

12.56

- Firms should check employment contracts issued before 1996 to ensure that they comply with the *Employment Rights Act 1996*.
- The form at Appendix 12:1 can be used by partners to appraise their own strengths and weaknesses and for peer reviews by fellow partners.
- Consider offering joining bonuses to attract new staff. Make them conditional on the member of staff remaining with the firm for a set period.
- For details of health and safety issues see 14.48.
- Firms should consider the use of in-house or inter-office tax quizzes and competitions to keep staff up to date and reminded of key issues.
- Happy, motivated staff will result in a more profitable firm.
- For further information on employment issues consult the DTI website at www.dti.gov.uk ACAS produce a series of free booklets on employment issues. Contact them at 11–12 St James Square, London, SW1Y 4LA. *Accountancy* magazine also contains useful updating information on employment law.

Appendix 12:1

Staff Appraisal Form

Name	Job title
Reporting to	Supervising
Date of appraisal	Length of time employed
Chargeable hours budget	Chargeable hours achieved
Budgeted charge-out rate	Charge-out rate achieved
Next year's budgeted hours	Next year's budgeted charge-out rate

To be completed by the member of staff

Please grade yourself on the following skills. 1 is excellent and 5 is unsatisfactory. The partner/manager will then confirm or amend the grade.

	1	2	3	4	5	Grade confirmed/ amended
Technical ability						
Work relations						
Client relations						
Professionalism/ethics						
Judgement						
Initiative						
Management						
Personal appearance						
Timekeeping/attendance						

Appendix 12:1

Please answer the following questions.

What are your strengths?	
What are your weaknesses?	
What do you like best about the job?	
What do you like least about the job?	
What work have you done particularly well?	
Why?	
What work could you have done better?	
Why?	
What training do you need/want?	
What else would help you with your job?	
Aims/ambitions/motivations	
– short term	
– long term	

Manager comments/recommendations

Partner comments/recommendations

Staff signature	Date
Manager signature	Date
Partner signature	Date

Chapter 13

Computers

13.1 Computers are now an integral part of every tax practitioner's life and essential to a firm's fee generating capacity. Like them or loathe them they are here to stay. Information technology (IT) has revolutionised the way tax practices operate over the last few years' particularly with regard to:

- tax return production, and submission via ELS (see Chapter 7);
- automating tax computations;
- access to data and information via the Internet and CD-ROMS;
- e-mail for ease of data transmission and client communication.

13.2 Many firms have made a significant investment in hardware, software and staff training. Although the use of technology has resulted in increased efficiency and the simplification of some otherwise mundane tasks, it has not always resulted in either higher profits or shorter working hours. This is largely because of increased client expectation and competition. Firms must tackle this challenge in the future if they are to have the resources to maintain a high level of investment in IT.

Technology is continuing to evolve rapidly and this inevitably impacts on the range of services that clients demand. Tax practices should regularly appraise how they can use new developments to offer clients more or improved services. This chapter considers:

- developing and monitoring an IT strategy;
- choice of software, hardware, consultants and maintenance agreements;
- the Internet;
- control, security and health and safety;
- keeping up to date.

Setting an IT strategy

13.3 Computers are such a significant aspect of tax practice that it is vital for the firm to have an IT strategy. Not doing so may result in unfocused purchases of hardware and software, and non-integrated systems.

13.4 The firm should be clear about what it is aiming to achieve from its investment in technology. Is it, for example, to work more efficiently, win new clients or to offer alternative ways of working? Technology is changing so quickly that it is very difficult to predict how the market will develop over the next few years. Therefore, the strategy should be sufficiently flexible to adapt to changes as they happen.

13.5 Investing in IT does not only include hardware and software; training is at least as important. No tax practitioner can afford to be a 'luddite'. Personnel with limited computer skills should receive suitable training. No partner or member of staff should be dependent on others to operate the firm's tax systems. For those who are fully conversant with computers, there are always advanced skills to learn or to pass on to others.

13.6 Sharing computer knowledge within the firm is essential. This could include making programs or routines developed by one person or department available throughout the firm and producing a regular internal bulletin or newswire listing computer software 'tips'.

13.7 The firm should appoint a partner or manager to be responsible for IT matters and to liaise with consultants and software houses as necessary. They should receive appropriate support and training. If there is no one in the firm suitable to undertake this task, consideration should be given either to recruiting such a person or buying in the services of an external consultant on a regular basis.

13.8 The checklist in Appendix 13:1 provides a means for a tax practice to review its computer systems and thereby develop its IT strategy. The review should be carried out annually by the person responsible for the computer system and the results should be discussed in a partners' meeting.

Choice

13.9 Tax practices cannot stand still, they need to keep investing in computer equipment, software and training. A recent report indicated that in order to remain competitive, firms should spend approximately 7 per cent of their turnover each year on computer-related items and training.

Hardware

13.10 The main problem with computer hardware is that no sooner has it been purchased than a higher specification machine is available for a cheaper price. A detailed consideration of computer hardware is beyond the scope of this book; however, the following points should be borne in mind.

- The firm should buy the best equipment it can afford. This means that computers should have a large memory and processing capacity and printers fast printing speeds.
- When comparing costs take into account running costs such as printer cartridges.
- Increasing miniaturisation and portability means that desk machines are not the only option. When replacing equipment decide whether the practitioner needs a laptop, palmtop or desk machine.
- Have a replacement policy. For example, review all machines that are three years old to see whether they are still doing an effective job or whether they require replacement.
- Check that new equipment has everything needed to undertake the job in question such as CD, zip drive, modem or video camera.
- Ensure that the firm is using the most up-to-date operating software, word processing and spreadsheet packages.
- Find out about guarantees and support packages (see 13.17).
- Make sure that equipment is insured.
- Have a policy for disposing of old equipment, for example, to staff, schools or clubs.

Software

13.11 Most tax practices now prepare computerised tax returns for reasons of image and efficiency. In spite of its increased use, tax return software can still be expensive. Before purchasing a package, it makes sense to do plenty of homework. Changing to a different provider at a later date may be costly.

13.12 *Taxation* magazine publishes a useful supplement each October reviewing all the major tax packages and software providers. The review covers the following packages:

- income tax;
- corporation tax;
- employment packages including P11Ds and benefits in kind;
- electronic publishing;
- international tax.

Taxation Practitioner and *Accountancy* also publish software reviews.

13.13 Tax return production is not the only software that a tax practice will require. Packages are also available for:

- tax investigations and benchmarking;
- inheritance tax planning;
- tax administration;
- practice management;
- tax data;
- changes of accounting date or partners;
- probate and pension schemes.

13.14 Before purchasing any tax software, firms should consider the following points.

Initial

- Compare and review packages at exhibitions and conferences.
- Ask for a personal demonstration and a trial run.
- Seek references from satisfied customers.
- Find out about staff training and helpline support.
- Compare prices, not just the initial cost but the cost and frequency of updates and any 'hidden' extras.
- Does the software company offer 'pay for use' or subscription services? This may allow a new firm to set up without incurring the full cost of the software up-front.
- How long has the company been in business and how long will it continue to support the product for?
- Ascertain when the updates will be delivered each year.
- Find out how the software house responds to feedback.

The software

- Establish whether all the firm's needs are covered by the packages such as Lloyds underwriters, partnerships, trusts, ministers of religion, MPs, complex capital gains and groups of companies.
- Does the package include a pension planner and 'what if' planner?
- Does it include pre-programming of standard dividends?
- Can data be imported from accounts packages and, if so, which ones does it support?

- Does it support ELS?
- Will it support Filing by Internet (FBI) in the future?
- How is the data entered?
- What do the schedules look like?

Reports

- What reports can it produce for practice management purposes?
- How easy is the report generator to use? (Sometimes specialist training is required depending on how the software has been written.)
- Can the package be used for producing standard letters?

13.15 Tax practices should purchase integrated software where possible. Several different systems implemented piecemeal are unlikely to work as well as an integrated system. For example, it is possible for accounts production and P11D software to be linked into the production of a personal tax return, which in turn can be linked to benchmarking and tax investigation packages. The tax return should also link to practice management software to generate standard letters, reports and controls.

IT consultants

13.16 Unless the practice has an in-house computer specialist it may be cost effective for it to use an IT consultant for new systems implementation, maintenance or trouble-shooting. Nevertheless, IT consultants are expensive so it will pay to choose wisely. Issues to consider include the following.

- Be clear about what the firm wants to use the consultant for and what it wants to achieve.
- Use someone familiar with the tax and business world.
- Take up references.
- Ensure that they listen to what the firm wants and communicate in non-technical language.
- Make sure that they are not intimidating and can deal with technophobes as well as those who have good computer skills.
- Establish whether they offer training services.
- If they offer maintenance, find out if their contract covers hardware and software.
- Ask about their specific skills and qualifications.
- Compare charging structures.

- Find out about continuity of cover for holidays and illness. This is particularly relevant for small 'one-man band' operations.

If the firm develops a good relationship with a consultant, it may also be able to supply his or her services to clients (see 10.28).

Maintenance contracts

13.17 Even with the best computer equipment, things go wrong. A firm can be very vulnerable if it has inadequate internal expertise or maintenance cover. It will require both hardware and software support packages. Ideally these should be with the same supplier to prevent the software provider blaming the computer equipment and vice versa.

13.18 The supplier's initial guarantee may not be sufficient for most firms because if something goes wrong, the equipment is likely to have to be returned to the manufacturer, thereby leaving the firm without a machine. When negotiating a maintenance contract take into account the response time, particularly where computers are networked, and whether the contract covers the supply of a replacement machine if it has to be repaired off-site.

13.19 The cost of a hardware contract is likely to be around 10 per cent of the value of the equipment covered. Software contracts may be on a call-out basis.

The Internet

13.20 The Internet is rapidly becoming indispensable to every tax practice. It is important not only as:

- a means of marketing and advertising (see 5.46);
- communication (see 4.18);
- information (see 14.42);

but also to provide enhanced services to clients and for filing returns and forms (see 22.2).

13.21 Firms without Internet access are already at a disadvantage. For example, the frequently asked questions and answers on IR35 were only published on the Revenue's website and Tax Bulletin can be obtained free of charge over the Internet whereas the paper version is subject to a charge. Increasingly, published information will only be available by Internet subscription.

13.22 A useful resumé of the current Internet issues and a list of the main tax related websites are to be found in *Taxation*, vol. 144, no. 3750, 30 March 2000.

13.23 Tax practices should consider what part a website will play in their overall IT and tax strategy but before relying on it too much, it is important to ensure that it is sufficiently robust to withstand a large volume of traffic. A website which fails to deliver what it promises or where queries go unanswered could be a PR disaster. Firms also need to ensure that the site is secure since those accessing it will be divulging confidential financial information. The firm may need to provide assurance on this point.

13.24 Firms should bear in mind the following guidelines issued by the Data Protection Commissioner to ensure that their website complies with the *Data Protection Act 1998* (see 20.58):

- the data collected should be regularly reviewed and old, irrelevant or unnecessary details should be deleted;
- firms should publish a data protection and privacy policy on the website;
- website users should be told what data is being collected and how it is used – their consent should be obtained before the data provided is used for marketing purposes.

13.25 Cookies can be downloaded from a user's computer system and used by a firm to build up a databank of their most frequently visited webpages, thus enabling a firm to target its marketing more effectively. The *Data Protection Act 1998* prohibits the use of cookies unless the user knows why the information is being collected.

Control

13.26 Tax practices should establish procedures to prevent the misuse and theft of their computer hardware and systems. These details should be incorporated into the office manual. The following aspects should be considered.

- The environment in which the computer equipment is located should be secure and controlled to prevent unauthorised access. All equipment should be detailed in a fixed asset register and ideally tagged or bar-coded. Particular care must be taken with the security of laptop computers used outside the office.
- All data files should be password controlled and the passwords changed regularly, particularly where key staff leave the firm.
- It is an offence to use a machine for 'hacking' either to obtain unauthorised information or to change or modify it. Nevertheless, cybercrime is on the increase and may be particularly relevant for tax firms with high profile clients. Scanning software is available to detect when a system is being hacked into.
- All personnel should be aware of the computer close-down routine at the end of the day.

- Computer files should be named consistently throughout the firm so that they are easy to locate (see 15.47) and there should be controls over the deletion of data. Guidelines should be laid down for the circumstances in which data can be removed from machines. This should also cover the deletion of e-mails.
- The firm should lay down guidelines for employee use of the Internet and the sending and receiving of personal e-mail. This is a serious issue as it can waste large amounts of time. Staff should be clear about what is and what is not permissible. For example, can the Internet be used for share trading, booking holidays and chatting to friends? Misuse should be a disciplinary offence. Monitoring software is available.
- Computer programs must be properly licensed. All the licences should be kept safely. The Federation Against Software Theft (FAST) regularly takes proceedings against businesses for the illegal copying and use of programs.

Computer back-up arrangements

13.27 Detailed back-up procedures should be in place. The form these take will depend on the size and complexity of the computer system. It does not matter whether the system is backed up onto disc, CD, zip drive or tape. It is, however, important to have systems to ensure that:

- all machines are backed up at least daily (usually overnight);
- the back-ups for at least the previous four days are always retained;
- back-ups are taken at the year-end and retained indefinitely;
- back-ups are stored in a fireproof safe;
- duplicate back-up copies are taken off-site regularly;
- a copy of all the software programs is kept off-site;
- the back-ups are clearly labelled;
- occasional re-loads are made to ensure that the system could be reinstated if necessary (professional advice may be necessary).

Internet security

13.28 Following the 'lovebug' and other pernicious viruses, even small practices are not immune from the damage that these highly destructive viruses can cause. It is also very poor PR for firms to pass on viruses to clients and the more data that is transferred between the firm and its clients, the higher this risk. Firms should consider the following steps to keep their systems virus free.

- Use a 'firewall' and do not run any system outside the security perimeter.

- Use virus-checking software.
- Keep all protective software up to date.
- Configure machines to avoid e-mail overloads and unsolicited commercial e-mail (spamming).
- Ensure that where the Internet is used extensively for the transmission of client data, the firm's security is not compromised by poor security and procedures at the client's end.
- Review the security arrangements of off-site web-servers.
- Ensure that dial-in services for staff and clients are protected by adequate passwords and identification procedures.
- Review the security arrangements periodically and take into account any new risks.

Health and safety

13.29 Firms must ensure that the use of computers, VDUs and workstations offer as little risk to the health and safety of employees as possible. This can be done by ensuring that desks and chairs are at an appropriate height and that there is adequate lighting. For further details see 14.48. Staff using computers must have regular breaks or changes in activity. The firm should pay for eye tests for all computer users.

Keeping up to date

13.30 As the rate of change accelerates inexorably, it can be daunting for firms to keep up with the latest developments, but keep pace they must if they are to remain competitive. This takes two forms. First, firms should be open to the latest technology and buy the best they can afford. Areas to consider include the following.

- Speech recognition software. Speeds of up to 150 words per minute are possible.
- Web-cameras for Internet 'meetings'.
- Scanning equipment and document management systems to eliminate manual files.
- ISDN lines for open access to the Internet and e-mail.
- Systems, such as payrolls, run over the Internet and accessible by both client and firm.
- The use of integrated software for maximum efficiency (see 13.15).
- Digital signatures. The *Electronic Communications Bill* will enable digital signatures to be legally binding.

Secondly, practices should invest heavily in IT training. All staff should be able to:

- use spreadsheets;
- use tax return software and generate reports;
- use the Internet and e-mail;
- understand the output from a range of software packages including accounts preparation software;
- use practice management software;
- be able to converse knowledgeably with clients on a range of computer issues;
- understand the security aspects of the firm's computer systems.

Quick review

13.31

- The firm should have an upgrade policy covering both computers and software to ensure that it keeps up to date with the latest developments. Before upgrading, the practice should always review whether it is necessary and appraise the benefits to be obtained.
- For e-mail etiquette see 4.22.
- For details about negotiating contracts see 14.53.
- Firms providing Internet tax services need to ensure that they avoid the legal pitfalls. See the January 2000 edition of *Accountancy* at page 102.
- Computer equipment should be adequately insured. Consequential losses arising from the destruction of the computer system should also be appraised (see 16.10).
- New technology can be stressful for partners and staff alike. If major changes to the systems are planned, everyone should be involved in the decision from the outset and provided with suitable training.

Appendix 13:1

Computer Systems Review Checklist

Completed by		Date	

Issue	Comments
Does the firm have an IT strategy?	
When were the computers and software last upgraded?	
Who is responsible for computer issues? Have they received suitable training?	
Is there a substitute to cover during their absence from the office?	
Have there been hardware problems? Have they been resolved?	
What are the firm's hardware needs for the next twelve months?	
Are maintenance and support agreements in place? Have there been any problems with them?	
Have there been software problems? Have they been resolved?	
What are the firm's software needs for the next twelve months?	
Are *all* staff able to use computers and the Internet competently?	
What computer training have the partners and staff received in the last year?	
What are the firm's training needs for the next twelve months?	
What work/services does the firm use computers for?	
What work/services could they be used for?	
Does the firm have licences for all software? How regularly are machines checked for unauthorised software?	

Issue	Comments
Does the firm have anti-hacking and anti-virus software?	
Does the firm comply with the *Data Protection Act 1998*?	
Does the firm comply with the health and safety requirements for computer users?	
Does the firm have a website? Is it used as effectively as it could be to generate new work and client leads?	
Does the firm monitor website 'hits'?	
Does the firm encourage communication with clients by e-mail?	
Are e-mails subject to the same controls as other communications?	
Does the firm show all its letterhead details on its e-mails?	
Does it include a confidentiality clause on e-mails?	
Has the firm assessed the risks associated with its network or e-mail system failing?	
Are computer files maintained consistently throughout the firm?	
Does the firm have a policy on file deletion?	
Is the system backed up daily? Are back-ups stored safely and periodically removed off-site?	
Are passwords regularly reviewed?	
If a member of staff leaves the firm what controls are in place to prevent the unauthorised destruction of data or protection of data with an unknown password?	
Does the firm have a policy on the personal use of the Internet and e-mail by staff?	
Is there adequate insurance to cover computer breakdown, data loss or destruction?	

Improvements recommended

Twelve-month action plan

Chapter 14

The Office

14.1 Tax advisors are primarily office-based, so it pays for the office to be a pleasant place to work. This chapter looks at the office environment and covers:

- choosing an office and creating a conducive environment;
- working from home;
- libraries;
- negotiating with suppliers.

Property

14.2 Taking on office premises is an expensive financial commitment for any tax practice. The first consideration is the choice of location. This is important for most firms but it can be critical to the success of a new tax practice.

Location

14.3 Points to consider when choosing the location of a firm include:

- the expectations of the firm's clients;
- high street versus secondary location;
- proximity to public transport;
- parking facilities;
- shops and lunch facilities;
- undesirable environmental factors, for example, near heavy industry or a busy main road;
- whether there are other professionals in the area, for example, solicitors;
- whether there are banks in the area;
- whether there are competing tax practices nearby.

14.4 *The Office*

14.4 Careful advance planning is also essential to ensure that the premises are right for the practice. Before choosing a property the firm should consider the following factors.

Size and rooms

- How many partners' offices are needed and what size? Will they share an office and, if so, with whom?
- How many other staff are there? Is there sufficient unoccupied space to comply with health and safety requirements?
- How will the staff be grouped, for example, small business department, corporate tax, personal tax? If it is a small firm all the professional staff may be seated together.
- How much space is needed for a reception area and meeting rooms?
- Is there a suitable kitchen and toilet facilities?
- Filing and storage is a problem in most practices. Is there sufficient space on-site or will off-site archiving also be necessary?

Facilities

- Are there parking facilities? If so, how many spaces are there and who will they be allocated to?
- What are the heating/air-conditioning systems like?
- What security arrangements are there?
- What are the provisions for fire safety?
- Who is responsible for communal areas, for example, lifts and gardens?

Repairs and renovation

- Are the offices serviced? What are the maintenance conditions?
- How easy is it to install computer systems, cabling and telecommunications?
- What are the pros and cons of an old building versus a purpose-built office? Using any building for a purpose for which it was not intended is nearly always a more expensive option.
- How good is the soundproofing?
- How much partitioning will be needed?
- What is the cost of internal and external maintenance and the current state of repair of the building?

Financial considerations

- Is the cost of the property comparable with similar premises?
- Is it affordable?
- If the freehold or leasehold is being purchased, can financing be obtained? How much deposit is required?
- Have the costs of acquisition, for example, stamp duty and legal costs been considered?
- Has the survey shown up major problems?
- What is the cost of insurance, business rates and service charges?

Future

- Is there room for expansion?
- What is the length of the lease, its terms and flexibility?

Open plan offices

14.5 There is a growing trend towards shared workspace, 'hot desks' and open plan offices. These work best where the tax department works as a team or where there is job sharing. It does not work well where tax advisors are undertaking detailed technical work which requires quiet time for thought and research. There is also an increasing move towards partners working with staff rather than in isolation. When planning the layout of the office, the firm should take into account the type of work each person undertakes and their personality. Whether the office is open plan or not each workspace should be designed to allow some degree of privacy.

Working from home

14.6 Information technology has made it much easier to set up a small tax practice from home and a computer and telephone take up relatively little space. This way of working is particularly common for those setting up practices after taking early retirement, redundancy or when combined with looking after children. Working from home in the early stages of setting up a tax practice can be a good idea as it involves little risk and minimal extra cost but this has to be balanced against the image the firm wants to project. Working from home is rarely suitable where staff or large numbers of client meetings are involved.

14.7 The following issues should be considered before setting up an office at home.

- Try to work in a room specifically set aside for the purpose and away from living and sleeping areas. Converted sheds and garages can make good offices. Planning permission may be required.

- Allow space for storage of files both short term and long term.
- A meeting room may be needed to see clients and they may require access to bathroom facilities.
- A supportive family is essential. Deal firmly with interruptions.
- Working in isolation for long periods can be stressful. Build up links with people in a similar position to share experiences.
- Do not become out of touch. It is important to attend training courses and conferences and to interact with other tax professionals.
- Motivation and self-discipline are vital.
- Try to have defined work periods so that work does not take over family and social life.
- Work to your own rhythm; for example, try to get most of the work done in the mornings if you operate best at this time of day.
- Be mindful of lease covenants and local bye-laws prohibiting home-working. Be careful not to breach mortgage contracts.
- Ensure that neighbours do not object.
- If you have clients visiting the premises ensure that there is adequate public liability insurance and check that domestic insurance policies are not invalidated.
- Consider whether the property should be rated for business rates. Seek advice from the local council.
- Have separate telephone lines installed.

14.8 If the tax practice outgrows the available space at home, a decision to take on office premises can be difficult and risky. Often it will involve a dramatic growth in the size of the firm. Initially, the firm may not be as profitable as it was when it was based at home because of the higher property costs. To cover this cost and become more profitable, the firm will have to take on more clients, charge higher fees or get more work from each client. This in turn will lead to the firm needing more staff and office space. This trend should be fully thought through before renting an office for the first time. An alternative course of action is to make the transition gradually by sharing an office.

Share a workspace with another professional

14.9 If working from home is not a practical option or if the practice outgrows the available space, consider keeping costs down by sharing an office with another professional person. Sharing with someone engaged in a related activity, for example, an insolvency practitioner or solicitor, avoids the problem of direct competition. Sharing an office will also overcome some of the disadvantages of working from home.

Creating a conducive office environment

14.10 Wherever the office is situated a pleasant environment is essential to running a good tax practice but is frequently overlooked or underestimated. It is important for both partners and staff as they spend at least 35 to 40 hours there each week (over 25 per cent of their lives). A poorly designed office can cause lack of motivation, tiredness and inefficiency. How do staff and partners feel when they enter the office – depressed or ready to start the day? Increasing amounts of time are spent on home DIY but often little attention is given to the office environment.

14.11 Good design is also essential for creating the right impression for clients. They need an environment that is welcoming and puts them at ease as quickly as possible. Some larger corporate clients will expect a tax practice to have a suitably equipped boardroom with conferencing facilities but many clients are unfamiliar with an office environment and will respond better to informal meeting rooms and reception areas.

Health and safety requirements must be taken into account when designing and planning an office (see 14.48).

Reception area

14.12 This is the first and last place that clients see and it is vital to the impression given of the firm. The seating should be comfortable but not so low that people find it difficult to stand up easily. Formal hard-backed chairs should also be avoided.

14.13 There should be a selection of newspapers and business magazines. Take care not to show political bias. Reception areas are often used for marketing materials. Ensure that these are up to date and neatly presented. A press cuttings book of articles relevant to the firm and its clients is a good idea. If the partners' certificates and office registrations are hung in the reception area they should be framed consistently. Well-maintained plants and flowers are a nice touch.

Meeting rooms

14.14 These should be kept clear and uncluttered and should cater for different types of meeting. Conversation icebreakers, for example, sweets and executive toys, can help to put clients at ease.

14.15 Meeting rooms should be cooperative and not confrontational. Conducting a one-to-one meeting with a client across a desk creates barriers and a potentially competitive environment. Low seating round a coffee table creates a friendly impression for one-to-one meetings. Alternatively, use a circular or round-ended table rather than a traditional oblong desk or table. This is ideal for promoting discussion, as client and advisor feel equal. Ensure that the chairs are the same height.

14.16 The firm should have suitable china for tea and coffee. Bottled water and drinking glasses should be available. A stock of alcohol may be necessary but should be stored and offered with care.

Communal areas

14.17 Corridors and communal spaces should be as large as possible although often this is difficult in old buildings. They should not be cluttered or obstructed. Fire exits should always be kept clear. There should be sufficient space to hang coats and umbrellas.

14.18 Notice boards should be accessible to all staff, for example, in the kitchen or photocopying room. Care should be taken about the type of notices which are displayed and who is responsible for displaying them.

Desks

14.19 Desks should be sited taking the following points into account.

- There should be sufficient space around the desk to move in and out comfortably.
- The space around the desk should be clearly defined. Two metres from walls or other people are recommended.
- They should ideally not be sited so that the occupant has his or her back to a door, window or corridor, sits facing a door or large window or so that they cannot see the entire room, for example, if the office is L shaped.
- They should not be located directly under large beams, overhead shelves or cupboards.

14.20 Many offices do not allow for all these factors to be satisfied. In this case large pictures or mirrors may help. Rounded corners to desks give a softer image and help to prevent accidents. There should be sufficient space for personal items in desk drawers and space for a rubbish bin and bookcase within easy reach of the desk.

Seating

14.21 In a tax practice most people spend the majority of the day sitting down. Back pain accounts for large amounts of staff absenteeism. It is therefore vital to ensure that each member of staff has a good chair of strong construction suitable for their individual needs.

14.22 Chairs should be fully adjustable on a five-arm star base with castors. They should be suitable for the physique of the member of staff. High backs and armrests give security and support. If staff require foot rests they must be provided. The seat should be well padded with a moisture-permeable cover. The person using the chair should be able to work with their keyboard straight in front of them and they should not have to twist to use the telephone or other equipment.

Colour

14.23 The office colour scheme can have a surprising impact on concentration and creativity. Large swathes of light, bright colours work best. Flowers and pictures can change the colour impact of a room. Consider the use of the following colours.

- Yellow, peach or orange for activity areas or where uninspiring work is carried out, for example, filing rooms, photocopying rooms and kitchens.
- Soft blue and purple for areas of quiet thought, for example, offices and libraries.
- Blue and green to reduce noise levels, for example, in offices or boardrooms.
- Rich creams and peach are inviting and are good colours for reception areas.
- Grey, beige and dark brown can dim creative spirit and sap energy.

Tidiness and cleanliness

14.24 The cleanliness and tidiness of an office is generally indicative of the firm's attitude to their work and costs very little to get right. New clients may be lost if the office is dirty and the energy of staff can be drained.

14.25 Administration staff should be given specific responsibility for certain areas of the office and rewarded and appraised accordingly. Alternatively, an office manager should be appointed. Cleanliness and tidiness should be covered in the staff manual (see 12.55).

14.26 The offices and windows should be kept clean. Floors should be cleaned at least weekly. Bins should be emptied regularly and coffee cups washed and cleared away. Papers should be filed away neatly and desks left tidy each night. Piles of files should not be allowed to accumulate around desks but should be stored in filing cabinets or on shelves or trolleys.

14.27 Paintwork and furniture should be kept in good order. Old or broken furniture and equipment should be repaired or removed and not left cluttering up the office.

14.28 Toilets and washrooms should be kept scrupulously clean and well stocked. There must be clean hot and cold water. Notices and instructions should not be allowed to proliferate but should be discreet, polite and neatly typed.

14.29 Kitchens in tax practices are often neglected. The kitchen should be cleaned and tidied daily. The office should provide staff with a range of tea and coffee-making facilities either from a vending machine or kettle. A wide choice should be offered. Ask staff what they prefer and ensure that all tastes are catered for. Fresh drinking water should always be available, preferably chilled. A fridge should be provided to store perishables. A microwave oven or other simple cooking facilities may also be provided. Space should be available for staff to eat meals but food should be prohibited from being kept in desks. Plates used for hot food should be removed and cleaned immediately and staff should be discouraged from eating greasy or strong-smelling food at their desks.

Lighting

14.30 There must be sufficient lighting to avoid eyestrain. Lighting can have a significant impact on work efficiency. If the office has very little natural light, depression or lethargy can build up throughout the week. To brighten a dull office use light paint on the walls and light objects around the desk. Too much direct light can cause glare and reflects off computer screens. In this case polarising filters and blinds may be necessary.

14.31 Most office lighting is harsh and uncomfortable. Artificial light should not cast strong shadows. It should provide a good balanced light complementing the natural daylight. Fitting dimmer switches can help. Desk lamps under the control of each member of staff which can be repositioned for each task as required are a good investment and give staff more control of their environment.

Noise

14.32 Background noise can cause distractions. Some members of staff may be more irritated by it than others. It is a major contributor to stress. Noise can come from:

- computers;
- constantly ringing telephones and faxes;
- conversation;

- road traffic;
- creaking or slamming doors;
- buzzing lights or drinks machines.

To minimise noise in the office:

- place vibration-absorbing material (cork or carpet tiles) under computers or other equipment;
- do not have computer boxes on the top of the desk but in carriers below;
- carpet the areas around desks;
- oil squeaky doors, chairs and equipment;
- install sound-absorbing partitions;
- have separate spaces for meetings;
- install double or triple glazing to reduce external noise.

Smells

14.33 Being exposed to constant smells can also be distracting and may create the wrong impression for clients. Unpleasant smells may originate from:

- traffic fumes;
- photocopiers and printers;
- synthetic floors and glue;
- kitchens, washrooms and cleaning materials;
- coffee;
- cigarettes.

These problems can be avoided by:

- siting kitchens and washrooms carefully;
- ensuring adequate ventilation throughout the office;
- cleanliness;
- putting photocopiers in a separate room;
- having a no smoking policy;
- avoiding strong detergents and cleaning agents;
- using ionisers.

Images

14.34 Tax practices should be particularly careful to be seen, both consciously and subconsciously, as neutral. Images to avoid include distracting abstract art where the mind feels obliged to work out what is going on, scenes of desolation (sinking ships), black and white pictures, large areas of harsh contrasting colours, waterfalls or things going down and excessive past images (retired partners). Positive images include flowers, nature and water. Have only good quality objects in the office to imply confidence, security and reliability, for example, heavy pots, ashtrays and paperweights.

Temperature

14.35 The office should be heated and ventilated to a reasonable work temperature. This is prescribed as at least 16 degrees Celsius. Thermometers should be available in some rooms. The set temperature will not suit everyone and staff should have as much control as possible of heating and ventilation. Tending to be cool rather than too hot avoids drowsiness. Water bowls and lush plants can help to dampen a dry atmosphere.

Office equipment

14.36 Computer equipment is dealt with at 13.10. A tax practice will also require a range of other office equipment including photocopiers, shredders, franking machines, telephones, security and presentation equipment. Choosing the right equipment or contract can be difficult but using inadequate equipment can result in wasted time and cause stress, for example, where a photocopier continually breaks down.

14.37 Factors to consider apart from the cost when choosing office equipment include the following.

- Is it sophisticated and robust enough to deal with the tasks required without breaking down?
- Does it have features which the firm does not need?
- How quickly does it operate (for example, a photocopier or printer)?
- How long is it guaranteed for?
- How quickly is the product technology changing?
- Have similar items from the manufacturer proved reliable or do they frequently break down?
- What are the terms of the maintenance and support agreements? All equipment must be regularly maintained and dangerous defects remedied. This is required under health and safety legislation.
- What is the opinion of the person who is going to be using or operating the equipment day to day?

14.38 Staff should be trained in the correct use of the equipment in order to get the most out of it and to avoid accidents. In small tax practices all staff and partners should know how to use all the equipment.

Libraries

14.39 A good library is crucial for any tax practice. Large practices will have a librarian. Small firms should appoint a manager or partner to manage the library. Setting up and maintaining a suitable library has a considerable cost. Accordingly the practice should assess its needs carefully and keep them under review but as a minimum the information likely to be required will include:

- original legislation and statutory material;
- case reports;
- tax/VAT/PAYE tables;
- press releases and information published by the Inland Revenue, Customs and Excise and regulatory bodies, for example, Tax Bulletin;
- the firm's tax, financial services and office procedures manual;
- Extel or similar works for dividends and capital gains tax;
- standard reference works, for example, Simons, De Voil;
- tax annuals, for example, *Tolleys*;
- looseleaf works;
- tax planning books;
- tax journals and magazines, for example, *Taxation*, *Taxline* and *Tax Practitioner*;
- specialist works of relevance to the firm;
- internally generated information.

14.40 If the firm is not sure whether it requires a work, particularly new titles, it should buy 'on approval' or look at the book on trade stands at exhibitions and conferences. Firms can also borrow works they only require occasionally from the library of their professional body. Most libraries will provide such services, not only in person, but also by fax and post.

14.41 The number of copies of each work the firm requires will depend on its size. Staff should have easy access to all the works they require day to day to do their job. Failing to purchase sufficient copies can be a false economy and can hamper the work of the tax department. Sharing libraries between offices on different sites is rarely efficient.

14.42 The form in which the works are purchased will depend on the state of technology in the firm. The Internet is now essential to the efficient running of the tax department to enable it to obtain up-to-date information from the Inland Revenue, government departments and the professional bodies. Subscription services, for example, *Butterworths Tax Direct*, are now available over the Internet and many organisations offer free or subscription newswires, for example, Accountingweb. CD-ROMS, for example, *Butterworths Book on Screen*, have revolutionised the storage and access of data. There are many advantages to using this type of access including:

- storage;
- not having to update looseleaf works (this is a much hated task but it is vital that it is done well if firms still have paper copies of works);
- search facilities;
- easy cross-referencing via hyper-links.

14.43 Using the Internet or CD-ROMS for reference takes time to get used to. It certainly does not mean a paperless office, as sections of works will need to be printed out for ease of review and to include on files to justify the opinion given.

14.44 The library may be housed in a separate room or department. In smaller firms it may be spread throughout the office. Some firms use the boardroom but this hardly encourages the use of the books if the room is always occupied. Other firms use the reception area, which is more accessible and may have the added bonus of impressing clients, provided the works are neatly stored and up to date.

14.45 Wherever the library is kept it is important to maintain an index to the materials. The list should be made available to all partners and staff. It also provides a means of monitoring out-of-date works. Deletion of such books is essential to avoid incorrect advice being given. The classification and referencing of works will depend on the size of the practice but is usually unnecessary for small firms. Computerised indexing and search products are available to track articles in most magazines, for example, *Compucraft*'s Articles program.

14.46 The practice should have a circulation list of journals and internally generated information. There should be sufficient copies in circulation so that they can be read within a short time of receipt. It should be a condition of employment for all staff to keep up to date and to read the circulated materials.

14.47 The person responsible for the library should also be responsible for the following.

- Regularly e-mailing or sending memos to colleagues with details of essential reading.
- Keeping cuttings of articles from newspapers.
- Keeping magazine and journal indexes safely.
- Keeping records of important internal issues, for example, the outcome of tax investigations, Counsel's opinion, decisions affecting clients and VAT tribunal cases. Staff and partners should be obliged to make copies of relevant material from their cases for the library to encourage the sharing of knowledge throughout the firm.
- Maintaining a list of staff and partner specialisms in the event that consultation is needed.
- Maintaining details of external specialists who can be contacted for expert opinions (see 21.2).
- Providing summaries of topical issues for in-house and client magazines.
- Liaising with the computer department to keep an index of computer software, its location and licences.

Health and safety

14.48 Tax practices have a legal responsibility for the health, safety and welfare of their employees. There is a common law duty to provide a safe place and system of work (including the avoidance of undue stress) and safe equipment. The firm must provide proper supervision and employ competent fellow workers. In addition, under the *Health and Safety at Work Act 1974*, firms employing five or more employees must publish a clear health and safety policy and provide adequate training and instructions to staff. The practice is also required to ensure that clients and visitors are not subject to unnecessary risks.

14.49 The contents of a health and safety policy are not prescribed but it must be brought to the notice of all employees and should include the following:

- the person ultimately responsible for the policy;
- a description of the general policy (for example, covering computer use, heavy boxes, high storage and trailing leads and wires);
- the arrangements for bringing it about;
- persons with specific health and safety responsibilities.

14.50 Employees have a duty to ensure that they take reasonable care of their own health and safety and that of others working in the office and to co-operate with the firm in effecting the policy.

14.51 The practice must also comply with the *Workplace (Health, Safety and Welfare) Regulations 1992*. (The relevant issues are incorporated into paragraphs 14.12 to 14.35.) The office must have sufficient fire extinguishers and evacuation procedures. The fire brigade will provide advice on all matters relating to fire prevention and fire drills. The firm should have a policy with regard to smoking. It must also comply with a myriad of other UK and EEC health and safety legislation, covering, amongst others, lifting, first aid, emergency and warning signs, hazardous substances, electricity and VDUs.

Dealing with suppliers

14.52 Running a tax practice involves dealing with suppliers (for example, when buying stationery, books and computers) and negotiating contracts (for example, with employment agencies, training companies and car leasing firms). Following the steps below will help to ensure that the practice gets a good deal from its suppliers.

- Check that the supplier or contractor is reputable. For large contracts deal with a named representative who can be contacted in the event of a complaint.
- Where the contract is negotiable use a partner or manager trained in negotiation skills (see 14.53).
- When contracting for services interview the contractor (for example, a designer or public relations consultant). Ask for references or to see examples of their work.
- A partner should sign all contracts and authorise all new supplier accounts.
- Give suppliers and contractors clear, precise instructions or briefs about what the practice requires. Ideally these should be in writing, otherwise matters can be forgotten and if personnel leave either the firm or supplier, it can be unclear what has been agreed. Clear instructions are essential if a complaint is to be justified.
- If deadlines are relevant specify these clearly.
- Give the supplier a contact name at the practice.
- Issue purchase orders and confirm orders and instructions in writing.
- Check goods delivered to delivery notes and ensure that staff do not sign for missing items.
- Make complaints about unacceptable service, damaged or faulty goods straight away by telephone. Train staff in how to handle complaints (see 14.54).
- Have a verification procedure for all invoices and reconcile these to supplier statements.

- Ensure that the firm is not dependent on just one supplier in the event of a dispute or the supplier going out of business.

Negotiation

14.53 The negotiation of contracts is an art. Some partners are better at this process than others. Use a skilled person or appoint an agent if a lot of money is at stake. Tips for negotiating a successful contract include the following.

- Know what the practice wants from the contract.
- Do plenty of research about the company, the market and the product or service.
- There should be no winners or losers. If there are the contract may not be successful. Negotiation involves a mutually acceptable solution.
- It may involve compromise. Know which areas can be subject to compromise and which are key to the success of the contract.
- Be prepared to be flexible and leave room to manoeuvre.
- Ask appropriate questions and listen carefully to the supplier's answers.
- Know the firm's priorities.
- Learn to read body language (see 4.30).
- Do not give up. If the negotiations seem at an impasse, explore the alternatives.
- Make notes of what was agreed and ensure that the final contract or agreement reflects all the terms and conditions agreed to in the meeting.
- Know how to close the negotiation and how to back out gracefully if the contract is unacceptable.

Complaints

14.54 From time to time it will be necessary to complain about the quality of goods or services. Handling complaints correctly will ensure that they are dealt with seriously and that the practice achieves the right outcome. It will also help the firm to understand the best way to handle complaints from its clients (see 6.5).

- Ensure that the complaint is justified.
- Ensure that clear instructions or orders were given at the outset.
- Telephone the supplier and tell them what has gone wrong. Be cool,

calm and reasonable. Listen to their point of view. See 4.19 for further information about using telephones.

- Ask the supplier what they are going to do to put matters right and give them time to do it. Ask for the name of the person dealing with the complaint.
- If payment is being withheld advise the supplier accordingly.
- Confirm the conversation in writing or by fax or e-mail.
- Ensure that you obtain the desired result. If not take the matter further.

Quick review

14.55

- Running an office is expensive. Purchasing decisions need to be made wisely.
- Appoint a senior member of staff as the office manager. Reward them accordingly. Alternatively, allocate specific tasks to members of staff and pay them extra for the responsibility.
- A firm's attitude to cleanliness and tidiness comes from the top. Partners should be careful to set a good example.
- Pretend to be a client. Come into the firm's reception area and see what you think of it. Alternatively, ask a friend or member of the family to comment. When you work somewhere every day it is hard to be objective.
- Have a staff suggestion box for office improvements.
- For further information on health and safety issues see Jacqueline Jeynes, *Practical Health and Safety Management for Small Businesses* (Butterworth Heinemann).
- See 4.35 for details of where to sit in meetings.
- Choose the best suppliers. Aim to reach an agreement that achieves a good result for both sides. Make non-price issues as important as the cost.

Chapter 15

Office Systems

15.1 This chapter is about managing paper. Tax practices are still a long way from being paperless offices, largely because the risk of being sued makes it essential that each file has a paper trail showing how the opinion was arrived at or the work performed. There is also a belief that clients want to have letters and paper copies of returns and forms because this demonstrates that the firm has undertaken some 'tangible' work. In the next few years, with improved computer filing systems, it is likely that the amount of paper in the average tax practice will decline. If it does the good housekeeping skills illustrated in this chapter will be equally applicable to computer files.

15.2 There are very many different ways for firms to organise their administrative functions. This chapter is not prescriptive; rather it sets out the issues which firms should consider when setting up or reviewing their office systems including:

- incoming and outgoing post;
- typing, printing, photocopying and shredding;
- notes and diaries;
- files of all types;
- client records.

Incoming post

15.3 In many businesses the administration staff usually open the post. In a tax practice the firm's post should be opened by a partner or senior manager and then distributed to the relevant partners and managers who will then pass it on to their staff. Cumbersome as it may seem, this type of post-opening procedure is necessary to enable partners to identify potential problems, complaints and claims. Instead of a partner, a suitably trained office manager may undertake this task. Alternative personnel should be appointed to provide cover if the partner or manager responsible for opening the post is absent from the office. The post should be opened and distributed as quickly as possible, preferably on the day it is received.

15.4 It is recommended that all in-coming post is date stamped. This is of particular importance where time limits apply, for example, in enquiry cases. Care should be taken to ensure that enclosures and attachments are not lost. They should be secured to the letter with tags or staples or placed in a folder or wallet. The person opening the post should log the receipt of all cheques and forward them immediately to the accounts department.

15.5 If the post contains details of a complaint or claim it must be referred to the appropriate partner without delay. Failure to do so could prejudice the claim. For further details about handling claims see 16.17.

15.6 The firm should lay down broad time limits and targets for dealing with post. The head of the tax department should keep the amount of unanswered post under regular review so that any problems can be identified early. The number and type of outstanding items should also be discussed regularly in tax department meetings. If one member of staff has an unusually large burden of work compared to another, cases or specific pieces of work should be re-allocated or additional help found.

15.7 If a particular piece of correspondence does not require a reply, the reason should be noted on the letter.

15.8 Tax control registers should be updated for in-coming post; for example, the firm may log the receipt of SA310s.

Typing and printing

15.9 In some firms the tax staff type their own letters. In others it is more efficient for partners and managers to dictate their letters. The most effective method for a particular firm will depend on the number of standard letters it uses and the skills of its staff.

15.10 If the firm uses audio typing staff it will require procedures to:

- prioritise work so that the most urgent typing is dealt with first;
- allocate and divide the work fairly between members of staff;
- control enclosures so that they are not sent out with the wrong letter or lost;
- ensure that the correct number of photocopies of each enclosure is taken;
- make sure that extra copies of the letter are printed or photocopied so that if a reply is not received, an answer can be chased up (see also 15.23);
- ensure that client registers are updated, for example, to reflect a tax return being sent to the Inland Revenue.

One way to achieve these requirements is to use a typing cover sheet to indicate the priority of the work, the number of enclosures and the number of copies required.

15.11 All staff should be trained in advanced word processing techniques to minimise typing and printing time and to ensure a consistent layout throughout the firm. The practice should develop standard templates, paragraphs and letters for maximum efficiency.

15.12 Firms should develop a house style for its letters and typed documents including the use of:

- typefaces;
- headings;
- bold and italic type;
- paragraph numbering and bullet points;
- references;
- punctuation;
- titles;
- tables and charts.

15.13 Tax practices should consider how they use paper. Good management will help to reduce the physical volume of paper in the practice as well as saving costs. This can be achieved by adopting the following procedures.

- Scale down draft documents to take up less space on the page.
- Print draft documents on both sides of the paper (as long as this does not cause problems with the printer).
- Find out who prints the most documents. Are they all necessary?
- Ascertain if photocopiers are being used instead of printers. They are usually a more expensive option.

Photocopies

15.14 All documents leaving the firm should be photocopied or scanned into the computer. It is particularly important to retain copies of all signed documents including tax returns, P11Ds and VAT returns. Keeping photocopies of these documents may also be important in case the original documents are lost in the post or by the tax authorities.

15.15 It is good practice to provide clients with their own copy of tax returns and other documents for their own records. Some firms supply these to all clients and others provide them on an as-requested basis. This may be a better option where clients are averse to paperwork.

Shredding

15.16 All draft and scrap documents must be shredded to maintain client confidentiality. Staff should attempt to do this daily to prevent it building up into an unmanageable pile. It may be possible for shredded paper to be collected by recycling firms. Alternatively, staff within the firm may have a use for it.

15.17 Old files must also be shredded. This can either be done in-house or by an outside contractor. See also 15.41.

Notes

15.18 Keeping good notes of telephone conversations and meetings on tax files is essential. They should be made as soon as possible after the call or meeting while the information is still fresh in the practitioner's mind and not confused by subsequent events. Notes made by staff should be subject to the firm's usual review procedure (see 11.5).

15.19 Some advisors maintain that it costs clients too much to make detailed notes. However, firms that do not note the advice they give may find just how expensive failing to make that file note actually is when faced with a claim. Good, properly headed-up, dated and recorded contemporaneous notes can help to avoid claims and all staff should be trained in how to take them.

15.20 To enable notes to be easily identified on a file, firms may use specific telephone message note pads, print notes on different coloured paper or file them on a separate section of the file. For ease of reading, long notes should be dictated or typewritten. Internal and external e-mails should be printed out or filed in an appropriate computer file.

15.21 When the tax return or form is being completed, any relevant points to carry forward to the next tax year should be noted. This is good practice in case the person working on the case leaves the firm. The carry-forward notes completed with the 1999/2000 return should be filed on the 2000/01 section of the file rather than being left on the 1999/2000 section so that they are not overlooked. Alternatively, they should be noted on the permanent or notes section of the client's computer tax file.

Diaries

15.22 Diaries are essential not only for remembering meetings but to record future events requiring action, for example, to chase a reply to a letter or to remind the practitioner about the need to supply information in connection with an enquiry.

15.23 Diaries may be manual or computerised. Manual diaries should be maintained centrally and held by administration staff. Individual diaries, personal organisers and filofaxes are not sufficient on their own if they are removed from the office. Computerised diaries operated on networked systems are a good practice management tool because they are available to the whole office and can be programmed to issue reminders tailored to the advisor's needs. They can be used to control claims and elections, deadlines, the due dates for tax forms, specific dates for individual clients and meetings with the tax authorities. Tax practitioners will also require a personal diary to record appointments made out of the office.

15.24 Keeping diaries up to date takes discipline. Appointments and key dates should be entered as soon as they occur and should be updated when the partner or member of staff returns to the office. Personal diaries should be regularly cross-checked to the central office diary. Electronic organisers can be downloaded into a central system but this will only be cost effective for the largest practices where many staff are working away from the office.

Outgoing post

15.25 All post leaving the practice should be subject to proper review by partners and managers. Copy letters should be initialled to indicate who has approved them. The firm's tax return control registers should be updated to show, for example, that a tax return has been sent to the client for approval.

15.26 Staff should be aware of the time that mail is collected from the firm in the afternoon, the nearest last delivery post box and the latest time for couriers to collect from the firm. A post-out book should be used to record items sent by special delivery or courier in case a problem occurs.

15.27 The firm should have a system to chase up replies to letters. A centralised system is recommended to minimise the risk of problems arising if staff are on holiday or absent from the office. The system should cover outstanding replies from clients, the tax authorities and third parties.

Replies to letters can be monitored in the following ways.

- Filing an additional copy of the letter on a 'bring forward file'. The letters can be filed by month or day and checked either daily or at the month-end. It is usual to allow approximately a month to elapse before chasing up a reply.
- Noting letters requiring a reply on a diary system.

The best option depends on the size of the practice, the number of clients and the person working on the case. Clients should be charged appropriately for chaser and follow-up letters. If a client repeatedly fails to respond to a letter, consider alternative means of communication (see 4.5).

Files

15.28 If a document cannot be located easily it might as well not have been created. However boring filing and computer housekeeping may be it is essential to the proper management of a tax practice in order to minimise risk and liability. Over the next few years computerised filing systems will become more prevalent and increasing numbers of tax practices will store clients' files only on computer, scanning in non-computer generated documents. See 15.29 to 15.46 for manual files; computer files are considered at 15.47.

Client filing

15.29 It pays to set up an efficient filing system from the outset. The system should be capable of expanding with the practice and be easy and logical for everyone in the practice to follow. Consult several people about their preferences before finalising the system.

15.30 Regularly used files should be easily accessible to the person working on the case. Others can be located further away and retrieved when necessary.

15.31 It is a false economy to overfill filing cabinets and racks; time is wasted extracting files, they are liable to become damaged and accidents may happen if filing cabinets are top heavy. Likewise it is inefficient to allow files to become overfull. The clips or springs may break and papers can fall out and be lost and it takes much longer to find documents. Regular archiving of old or full files is essential. The best time to do this is at the end of each tax year for personal tax clients and at the end of the accounting year for corporate cases.

Manual files

15.32 Many tax practices are still dependent on manual files. The firm should decide which documents are to be filed on which section of the file and should develop its own standard tax file (see Chapter 7). Where a letter covers more than one subject, additional copies should be printed and filed.

15.33 Firms will need to develop systems covering the following.

- File numbers or references.
- The type of files used for filing, for example, lever arch, cardboard files or wallets.
- The colour of the files. It is a good idea to use different colours to denote whether the files are permanent, tax or correspondence.
- The number of files used for each client and the divisions within them. All clients will need files or sections for tax working papers (ideally organised year by year) and for correspondence and permanent information. Some clients will need files for accounts, investment business, Lloyd's underwriting or if they have complex capital gains. Other sections may be included for rental income and planning advice.
- The type of file dividers, for example, cardboard or plastic.
- The labelling of the files. The label should include the client's full name, reference number, the partner responsible, the type of file, the date it was set up and the tax years filed on it.
- Links to connected files, for example, director's personal tax, individual partners, spouses and other family members.
- The type of filing systems used, for example, racks or cabinets.
- The organisation of the filing cabinets, for example, alphabetical, by member of staff or by type of work.
- The location of the filing cabinets, whether they are all in one filing room or by the desks of the tax personnel.
- The labelling of filing racks so that files can be quickly identified without having to remove the file to determine its contents.

15.34 It is essential that filing is done regularly, preferably daily. It may be done by the person generating the letter or by administration staff. Whoever is responsible, it should not be allowed to accumulate, otherwise vital issues may be overlooked. Alternative cover should be arranged for holidays and absences.

15.35 Staff should be trained to ensure that documents are filed in the correct place. Filing is often considered low-grade work but it is essential that documents reach the right file. Care must be taken where there are several clients with similar names.

15.36 A referencing system will need to be devised to ensure that documents arrive not only on the correct file but also on the correct sections of each file. Filing references may typically include the year that the document was generated, a reference to the type of work, for example, P for per-manent file or T99/00 indicating the tax year. The initials of the various personnel involved in creating the document should also be incorporated as well as the client's reference number within the firm. Linked files, for example, partnerships, should have suffixes such as A, B.

Removing files

15.37 Failing to keep track of files can cause valuable time to be wasted searching for them. Procedures should be laid down for the following.

- The removal of files from their slot. For example, a card could be left in place of the file. The card should contain details of who has taken the file, the date and its location.
- Taking files out of the office. It should be agreed which staff may remove files and in what circumstances. The firm should ensure that it has adequate insurance for files out of the office including files being transported between sites and kept at home.

File security

15.38 It goes without saying that all clients' files should be kept securely. The information on them is confidential and should not be disclosed deliberately or inadvertently to those outside the firm. This means that particular care must be taken when files are out of the office. For example, they should not be left in unattended cars or unlocked brief-cases at clients' premises.

15.39 Many tax practices have high profile or famous clients. Their files may be of considerable interest to unauthorised personnel. Care should be taken to ensure that such files, both manual and computerised, are subject to special security arrangements. This may involve regularly changed passwords restricted to the staff working on the case or secure filing cabinets with restricted access. For further details about the security of computer files see 13.26.

Lost files

15.40 However good a firm's systems, from time to time a practice will lose or mislay a client's file. The firm should have a system for locating and recreating lost files. This should involve:

- a thorough search of all filing areas by administration staff;
- identifying the last known person who may have used the file;
- notifying everyone in the office that the file is mislaid and asking them to look for it;
- if the file cannot be found, recreating the file by printing out all letters and returns from the computer system – this may have to be done from back-up discs;

- the partner and staff involved with the job should then recreate any permanent information from their knowledge of the case and read the file to assess what information is missing;
- the file should be noted to the effect that it is a recreated file and may be incomplete;
- if the file is eventually located, the two files should be merged and any duplicate documents destroyed.

Archiving and destruction

15.41 The firm's procedures should cover the archiving of old files, including those belonging to ex-clients. This should include the circumstances in which files are to be archived or microfiched and a means to log and monitor their location and contents. The storage facility should be secure, dry and easily accessible.

15.42 As a minimum files must be retained to comply with Inland Revenue record keeping requirements. Firms should also check whether their professional indemnity insurers stipulate a retention period. Most tax advisors keep files for considerable periods, at least on microfiche. Some documents, for example, agreements, contracts and deeds, should be retained indefinitely. Care should be taken with regard to retaining papers beyond the required time limits (see 15.46).

15.43 The destruction of old files should be subject to proper procedures and should be authorised by a partner or senior manager. If the files relate to a current client, ideally their approval to the destruction should be sought. Alternatively, this could be covered by a suitable paragraph in the engagement letter, advising the client of the length of time that files will be kept for. The firm should also have a policy for the deletion of computer files.

Enquiries

15.44 In enquiry cases the Inland Revenue may require access to the tax advisor's papers to confirm the accuracy of the taxpayer's return. In many cases the taxpayer will consent to the papers being produced but where such consent is withheld care must be taken not to disclose protected documents.

15.45 Tax practices should be aware of which documents are protected and ensure that their files and references clearly identify these. Particular care will need to be paid to high-risk cases. The main protection is given to the papers of an appointed tax advisor with regard to the giving of tax advice and also to audit papers. The subject is highly complex and subject to change due to a series of high profile cases including *An Applicant v An Inspector of Taxes [1999] STC (SCD) 128*. The protection afforded does not cover documents which contain tax returns, accounts or information which the advisor has assisted the client to prepare for delivery to the tax authorities.

15.46 Ensuring that papers are not disclosed incorrectly requires good file management. The following points should be noted.

- Papers should be clearly segregated and marked 'audit', 'advice' or 'link'. If mixed papers are produced they may be called for and read to ascertain whether they are protected documents.
- Legal advice may be necessary in complex cases.
- Old papers beyond expired time limits should not be held unless the client wishes it. If papers are destroyed after being requested this is an offence under *Taxes Management Act 1970, s 20* or *s 20A* but no offence is committed if they have been destroyed as part of the firm's file management policy.
- Wherever possible confidential third party papers should not be held by the practice if they are not subject to tax advisor protection or legal professional privilege.
- Documents in the possession of the taxpayer are not protected and care should be taken to ensure that clients do not hold unnecessary documents.
- Documents held by tax advisors relating to prospective but not actual clients are also not protected.

Computer files

15.47 Computer files should be used consistently throughout the firm. Folder names should follow the same pattern, for example, surname first followed by initials so that they appear alphabetically. Descriptive and intelligent file titles should be used for ease of identification of the contents. Files should be stored in standardised directories, for example, by client name or reference number. For example, a letter to Jane Smith about her tax return may be called 'taxreturn9900' and a letter about capital gains tax may be called 'cgtgenadvice140200'. Both would be filed in a directory or folder called 'Smithjane'. Computer clocks and dates should be accurate so that lost documents can be traced on a date basis. The date the letter was typed may also be added. Larger clients may need more than one directory.

15.48 The firm will require procedures with regard to the archiving of old computer files and those relating to ex-clients.

Administration filing

15.49 Administration filing differs from client filing and the firm should be much more ruthless about it. Only documents that need to be referred to again, for example, contracts and agreements, should be kept. The office manager should review all files regularly and documents that are no longer required should be discarded.

15.50 Files containing administrative papers should be sub-divided into lots of small categories so that they can be found easily. The files should have a contents list at the front. Be careful about filing papers in a 'sundry' or 'miscellaneous' section as they may never be found again.

Client books and records

15.51 Tax practices need to have systems with regard to the retention and storage of original client records.

15.52 When a client's tax return information, books and records are received by the practice, they should be logged and a detailed list made of the contents. The best way to do this is to use a standard sheet which can be ticked off quickly. A sample sheet is included at Appendix 15:1. The items should be cross-checked with any covering letter sent by the client and the discrepancies notified to them as soon as possible. Where records are received by post a letter of acknowledgement should be sent to the client.

15.53 It goes without saying that client documents must be kept securely until they can be worked on. The records should be stored in wallets or bags. Once the tax work is complete the original records should be stored safely until they can be collected. The greatest of care must be exercised to ensure that the records of one client do not become confused with those of another. All bags or boxes should be clearly labelled. Particular care should be taken with clients of similar name.

15.54 The firm should decide whether it will or will not retain original records for clients, bearing in mind that a failure to keep the appropriate records can result in a fine of up to £3,000. Alternative policies range from keeping all records in case clients lose them, to returning all records to clients for safe keeping. In practice a policy mid-way between the two extremes will probably work best. Different procedures may be necessary depending on the type of client. Some are clearly capable of keeping their own records; others may need a different approach.

15.55 Some practices keep small quantities of records such as P60s, pensions certificates etc., particularly where the firm believes that the client may lose them. These may be returned to the client after the record-retention period is satisfied. Since the onus is on the client to retain the records and the potential fine is high, a preferable route may be to keep photocopies of all original documents and return the originals to the client with instructions to retain them for the correct period of time. For an example of a sample letter see Appendix 15:2 at the end of the chapter.

15.56 It is both good practice management and client service to package client records in a plastic bag printed with the firm's details or in clear plastic packaging. This keeps the records secure and dry. They should be labelled with clear instructions. For example: 'The Inland Revenue requires these records to be kept safely until at least 31 January 2006. If they are destroyed or lost before that date it could result in a fine of up to £3,000'.

15.57 The firm should keep a list of all the client records it holds. This should record the date that they were received, their location and details of how they are collected or returned to the client. This should be cross-referenced where appropriate to a post-out book. Client records should ideally be returned by recorded delivery post or a certificate of postage requested. Periodic reconciliations of the physical records held with the list should be undertaken. For an example of a control sheet see Appendix 15:3.

15.58 Occasional purges of uncollected records should be undertaken during a quiet time of year and the records returned.

15.59 However good its tax work, if a firm loses or mislays clients' records, it will upset clients, result in loss of confidence in the firm's work and generally be a public relations disaster. The risk of losing records will be minimised by a speedy turn-round of work and by returning client records to them in person either during a meeting or by asking the client to come in and collect them. The practice should have insurance against the accidental loss or destruction of client records (see 16.10).

Quick review

15.60

- A survey by printer specialists Lexmark in May 1999 indicate that firms spend between 6 per cent and 15 per cent of their income on paper and print.
- Handling paper can be a big time waster. Aim to touch each piece of paper as few times as possible. This will involve working quickly and efficiently and having good filing systems.
- Whilst the Electronic Lodgment Service (ELS) requires hardcopy, signed tax returns to be retained, firms cannot be paperless offices. It remains to be seen whether Filing by Internet (FBI) will remove this condition once agents' filing is available.

Appendix 15:1

Client Records – Logging in Sheet

Client name		Logged by	
Date of receipt		Missing items notified	
Opened by		Acknowledgement letter	

Tick the boxes below to indicate the items received. Where there is more than one item for each category please note the number of items received. Bank statements should be checked to ensure that there is a complete sequence.

Check the items received:

- against the covering letter. Note all missing items and advise the client as soon as possible;
- against the tax return information request letter. Note all missing items and notify the client as soon as possible.

Missing items:

Items	Received (tick)	Items	Received (tick)
Covering letter containing information		*Self-employment*	–
Employment	–	Accounting records	
P60		Sales invoices	
Payslips		Purchase invoices/receipts	
P11D		Bank statements	
Pensions received		Petty cash details	
P60		Cheque books	
Benefits Agency statements		Paying in books	
Pensions paid	–	Other (detail)	
PPCC		*Rental income*	–

Appendix 15:1

Items	Received (tick)	Items	Received (tick)
Savings/investments	–	Agent's statements	
Bank interest certificates		Invoices	
Private bank statements		Expense receipts	
Building society interest certificates/books		Bank statements	
Stockbroker statements		*Lloyds Underwriters*	–
Contract notes		List below	
Dividend counterfoils			
Giving	–		
Details of covenants or gift aid payments			
Trusts	–		
R185s			
Other (list below)			

Appendix 15:2

Sample Letter About Retaining Records

Dear Client

Since I have now completed your tax return I am returning your original records to you for safe keeping. You must take care how you store the records to ensure that they are not lost or damaged in any way.

The Inland Revenue requires you to keep *all* the records relevant to your tax return for one year starting on 31 January following the year of assessment. For the 1999/2000 tax year this means until 31 January 2002.

If your tax return was submitted late the requirement to keep the records is extended. For example, if the return was submitted in February 2001, the records must be retained until 31 March 2002.

If the Inland Revenue enquires into your tax return the requirement to keep the records may be extended. The records must be kept until the date that the formal enquiry is treated as being complete if this date is later than the normal time limit.

Remember that it is your responsibility to keep all the original records safely for the relevant period. If you do not you can incur a penalty of up to £3,000.

If you have any questions please contact me.

Yours sincerely

A Partner

Alternative paragraphs

If you are self-employed or rent out a property, you are required to keep *all* the records relevant to your tax return for five years ten months from the end of the tax year. For the 1999/2000 tax year this means until 31 January 2006.

The original information may be retained as photocopies or held on a computer, provided that the copies or scanned images are full and complete copies of the originals.

Appendix 15:3

Client Record Control Sheet

Client name	Client number	Description of records	Location	Date in	Date out	Means of return
Examples						
A. Carter	C75	Accounting, in small box	Cupboard 1	25.8.00	7.12.00	Collected by AC
B. Dawson	D8	Tax, in blue wallet file	With client's file	30.6.00		
C. Ells	E50	Rental, in black lever arch file	Cupboard 2	2.10.00	30.11.00	Recorded delivery 30.11.00 X35477

Chapter 16

Insurance

16.1 This chapter considers the main types of insurance cover required by tax practices. It is designed to help firms to get the most out of their policies and to avoid some of the pitfalls.

16.2 Some insurance is obligatory, for example, public and employer liability. Where practitioners work at home domestic policies should be checked to ensure that working from home does not invalidate them. Professional indemnity insurance is also mandatory for all practitioners and firms regulated by a professional body.

16.3 Tax practices are also likely to have:

- office buildings and contents insurance against fire, theft and accident;
- insurance against computer attack and viruses;
- loss of profits cover;
- recreation of records insurance;
- cover against legal claims including staff matters and libel;
- fidelity and fraud cover;
- group car policies;
- investigations insurance.

16.4 A range of personal insurance cover will also be required by the firm and can be offered to staff as part of a benefits package including:

- life assurance covering partners and staff both for the benefit of the firm and relatives;
- permanent health insurance or critical illness cover for the benefit of the firm, staff and partners;
- private medical insurance;
- pensions for partners and staff.

16.5 A firm will probably need several brokers to satisfy all its insurance requirements. It is unlikely that a combined policy will satisfy the firm's needs at the cheapest price. If the practice is part of a marketing group, it may offer its members competitive cover. Larger firms may be able to negotiate favourable cover directly with Lloyd's Syndicates. Firms should cultivate good relations with brokers to ensure that they understand the practice and how it operates. This will help to ensure that the firm buys the right insurance cover in the right amount. See 14.53 for negotiation tips.

Risk management

16.6 Tax practices do not only require insurance; they need to consider other means of managing risk. Firms should identify and evaluate the risk of a damaging event occurring and draw up contingency plans to minimise losses. Any event requiring an insurance claim will be stressful for all concerned. Knowing exactly what action to take if it does will be of considerable help. Some brokers offer computer models to help to identify disaster recovery responsibilities although this service can be expensive.

16.7 Aspects to consider when drawing up contingency plans for disaster recovery include the following.

- Keep a diary of emergency numbers, for example, plumbers, electricians, locksmith and alarm companies away from the office.
- Find alternative office premises (see 16.8).
- Know who can supply replacement computers and office equipment.
- Keep fixed asset registers or photographs of equipment away from the office.
- Know how long it will take to install telephone lines to new premises.
- Keep data back-up tapes and discs off-site (see 13.27).
- Install anti-virus software (see 13.28).
- Have a means of informing staff of the problem and alternative working arrangements, for example, by a telephone 'chain'.
- Allocate specific responsibilities to staff.
- Have policies to deal with the loss of client records.
- Have procedures for file recreation (see 15.40).
- Keep clients informed of events.
- What happens if the disaster occurs at the busiest time of year?
- Which areas of the firm can be put on hold and which are key to its success?

- Early negotiation with loss adjusters.
- Short-term financing.
- Managing cash flow.

16.8 There are companies that let fully-equipped offices in the event of a disaster but these are expensive. A better plan for most practices would involve staff working from home, moving to another of the firm's offices or having a reciprocal agreement with another professional firm.

Loss of profits

16.9 A tax practice should insure for business interruption in the event of fire, flood or other disaster. The practice must take care to insure the correct sum. This depends on the policy definition of 'profits'. The sum insured must accord with the stated definition and not some other internal measure of profit. It is also important to take into account anticipated growth if profits are rising sharply or if a merger is planned. Some policies allow for this automatically. The firm should also consider how long the cover will last for (the maximum indemnity period). This is usually twelve months but this may not be adequate for all firms.

Books and records

16.10 If client records are destroyed this can have significant PR consequences for the firm. Having adequate insurance cover will go some way to helping with their recreation. The cover should include the firm's manual files and computer records, and the recreation of original client records in the possession of the firm.

16.11 Whilst the records have little intrinsic value, the consequential loss arising from their loss or destruction can be significant. Ensure that the policy covers:

- accidental loss and theft, not just destruction by fire or flood;
- laptop computers;
- loss both on and off-site and from cars;
- the destruction of computer records by viruses;
- consequential loss, for example, fines and penalties imposed by the Inland Revenue or Customs and Excise;
- loss of income whilst the file is being recreated;
- the fact that some files or records will cost more than others to recreate – the 'average' cost may not be adequate if only a small number of large or complex files are destroyed.

Professional indemnity insurance (PII)

16.12 All tax practitioners who are members of a professional body must have professional indemnity insurance with an authorised insurer if they hold a practising certificate. Members with practising certificates working in partnerships or as employees must ensure that the firm's policy covers them. If not they must have their own PII cover irrespective of whether they receive fee income. In the event of practice mergers or demergers adequate insurance must be in place. Policies must cover all staff and sub-contractors and past and current partners.

Level of cover

16.13 Firms who are members of the Institute of Chartered Accountants in England and Wales with gross fee income of less than £400,000 must have cover for any one claim and in total at least equal to two and a half times their gross fee income. The minimum cover for a sole practitioner is £50,000. It is £100,000 in all other cases. £1 million is the maximum level of cover required but firms should consider whether the minimum and maximum limits are adequate for their needs based on a risk assessment. Defence costs, legal representation and expenses are usually included in addition to the level of cover. Other practitioners should ensure that they comply with the rules of their professional body.

16.14 Gross fee income must be based on the firm's accounting year immediately preceding the start of the policy. It must include the value of sub-contracted work, commissions and personal appointments. Care should be taken in reducing the cover in the event of declining profits.

16.15 The firm should also consider the excess that it is prepared to bear. It will depend on past claims and financial resources. For sole practitioners the excess must not be more than £20,000. For partnerships it must not be more than £20,000 multiplied by the number of partners.

Claims

16.16 All tax practices must appoint a partner with responsibility for managing PII insurance and claims. There must be a system to notify immediately claims and situations that may give rise to claims, to the partner responsible and to the insurers. Insurers must be notified promptly so that appropriate action can be taken even if the possibility of a claim is vague. Failure to do so could prejudice the claim. Prior to completion of the renewal form all staff and partners should be asked to confirm that they are not aware of any circumstances likely to give rise to a claim.

16.17 If a letter of claim is received it must be faxed immediately to the brokers. No acknowledgement should be given to the claimant until the firm is instructed to do so by the insurers. Detailed responses to claims are generally required within three months. Accordingly, files and documents will have to be supplied to the insurers quickly.

16.18 Following the Woolf reforms, many cases are settled either before the issue of proceedings or by negotiation and mediation. In other cases there will not be a full trial, only a summary judgment. These procedures will not necessarily enable the firm to put its side of the case fully. In order to avoid this situation occurring, a robust defence to the claim needs to be presented from the beginning.

16.19 If the case proceeds to court it will be allocated to one of three tracks.

- Small claims in the County Court for cases under £5,000. These will be dealt with quickly and informally and will last no more than one day.
- Fast track in the County Court for cases worth between £5,000 and £15,000. These cases must come to Court within nine months. There is a tight timetable and the trial is limited to one day.
- Multi-track in either the County Court or High Court for cases over £15,000. The judge will set the timetable.

16.20 In all cases practitioners facing claims must be prepared to get on with the case quickly and to co-operate fully with insurers and solicitors. Disclosure and expert witness statements will need to be dealt with from the outset.

Risk assessment

16.21 Insurers usually require the practice to carry out a risk assessment in conjunction with arranging or renewing cover so that the firm can be sure that an appropriate level of cover has been arranged. The review should take into account:

- the types of clients the practice has and its potential exposure to shareholders and creditors;
- the type of work the firm undertakes and whether it is ongoing or one-off;
- the general economic climate, for example, recession;
- the risk assessment carried out for new clients (see 2.7);
- fees;
- the firm's claims history.

Reducing the risk of claims

16.22 Tax practitioners should take steps to limit the incidence of claims. In particular they should:

- issue engagement letters (see 2.24);
- have systems of review and quality control (see Chapter 11);
- have procedures for taking on and losing clients (see 2.10 and Chapter 6);
- have back-up systems for computers – this is particularly relevant for bureau work (see 13.27);
- not undertake work beyond their skills, competence or resources;
- pay particular attention to claims and elections, time limits and deadlines;
- avoid off-the-cuff advice and keep detailed notes of telephone conversations and meetings;
- have good staff and partner training;
- consider disclaiming, limiting or excluding liability, for example, when dealing with mortgage references or when producing reports;
- consider obtaining indemnities;
- include assumptions and risk warnings in advisory letters and reports;
- consult internally or with other professionals and regulatory bodies when in doubt (see 21.2) – many insurers also offer consultancy services.

Ceasing in practice

16.23 PII cover must last for at least two years after ceasing to hold a practising certificate. This is because PII policies work on a 'claims made' basis. The cover may be arranged by the firm, the new practice if the firm has been subject to a takeover or by the practitioner personally. In many cases two years' cover will not be sufficient, in which case it should be continued for six years. At the end of each year the practitioner should consider whether there is a need to continue the cover. This is particularly relevant if there has been a history of claims.

Tax investigations insurance

16.24 There is an increasing demand for tax investigations insurance to cover the professional costs (but not the tax) arising from self-assessment enquiries. Since any client may be investigated, tax practitioners probably have a duty to inform their clients about the existence of tax investigations insurance. It is estimated that between 10 per cent and 20 per cent of accountants now offer such insurance and this figure is likely to increase substantially as the number of enquiries increase and CTSA enquiries take place.

Types of scheme

16.25 The tax investigations insurance market has expanded significantly with the introduction of personal and corporate self-assessment. The insurance companies in the market have slightly different products on offer but broadly the types of policy they offer are detailed below. Most practitioners should be able to find a scheme to suit them.

The least expensive policy is a group scheme that covers all clients but it has disadvantages. The firm is responsible for collecting the premiums from clients and there is likely to be a shortfall which the practice will either have to cover itself or by charging clients taking out the insurance higher premiums. Clients who have not paid their premium may benefit at the expense of others if they are subsequently investigated.

The next cheapest scheme is voluntary group cover where the clients have the option of being in the scheme. Premiums are higher than the group scheme, usually two to three times more expensive. It is usually a condition of the policy that all clients (or a majority) have to be offered a chance to participate and not just those clients perceived by the firm to be the most at risk from an investigation.

The most expensive cover is on an individual basis where the client arranges the policy directly with the insurer.

VAT investigations and employer compliance investigations are not usually covered in a standard policy but can often be included on request, as can any other specialised risk relevant to the firm. Some insurers also cover Special Compliance Office enquiries.

Benefits to the firm in offering tax investigations insurance

16.26 Offering tax investigations insurance is part of good practice management. It is a value-added service that demonstrates client care. Writing to clients to tell them about the insurance can provide a good marketing opportunity for selling other services. Other benefits include the following.

- Clients are not penalised for the cost of professional fees when the Inspector has found nothing wrong.
- It reduces the likelihood of the client leaving the practice because fees have added insult to injury where extra tax has been found to be owing.

- A commercial decision does not have to be taken to concede to additional tax liabilities rather than incur fees that could exceed the disputed tax.
- The investigation can be properly defended to ensure that no more tax is paid than is absolutely necessary.
- It allows the case to be taken as far as necessary, including to the Commissioners or courts if the insurers consider it appropriate.
- Where the case is difficult or complex or where the practitioner is temperamentally unsuited to dealing with investigations, insurance will pay for a specialist to ensure that the client has the best advice.
- Investigations insurance guarantees a 100 per cent recovery on enquiries work, thereby protecting the firm's profits. It avoids the risk that the practitioner may cut corners to keep the fees low and increase their professional indemnity risk.
- If the firm does not offer the insurance and has several investigations ongoing at once it could face financial difficulties if it has problems with fee recovery. A practice with 400 clients should expect about 6 to 8 cases ongoing at any one time.

Persuading clients to take tax investigations insurance

16.27 Good marketing of the insurance scheme is critical. The marketing materials should be honest and accurate. They must sell the scheme and provide details of its terms and cost. The firm will need to mailshot clients and follow up the letter with telephone calls, reminders, client seminars and newsletters. The best marketing will be specifically targeted; for example, a leaflet aimed at pubs and restaurants.

It is essential that the limitations of the insurance are clearly specified, in particular, that it insures only professional fees and *not* tax, interest and penalties or the client's loss of time or earnings whilst dealing with the case.

Choice of insurer

16.28 The tax investigations insurance market is fairly competitive. Recommendations from other advisors and interviews with three or four companies are the best way to find the right broker. For a review of the main insurers and contact details see John Newth, 'A Maturing Product', *Taxation*, vol. 143, no. 3710, 10 June 1999, page 272.

Issues to consider when offering clients tax investigations insurance

16.29 Tax advisors must fully understand the terms of the insurance cover if they are recommending it to their clients. Questions to ask the insurers include those listed below.

- Does the policy cover all enquiries including aspect enquiries?
- From what stage in the enquiry process is there cover?
- Is the policy written on a claims arising or claims notified basis? Care must be taken on this point when moving the policy between insurers in case some claims are not covered.
- Does it cover meetings with the Inspector?
- What are the general exclusions, limits on cover and excess?
- How much are the premiums and commission (if any)?
- Are premiums affected by the client's record with the Inspector, defaults or poor accounting records?
- Who does the work, is it the firm or an advisor supplied by the insurer?
- Is there a helpline and, if so, will it be useful?
- Does the insurance company provide training to help staff and partners sell the cover to clients?
- Do the underwriters change frequently? If so, find out why.
- Can the scheme afford to pay out what is promised? See 16.31.
- Ask the insurers to provide specific examples of cases they would or would not have covered using the firm's own files as examples.

16.30 Operating the scheme requires good administration and a client database. The tax practice will need to find out how the insurer's administration works and set up systems to:

- invite clients to join the scheme;
- bill and collect premiums;
- renew policies;
- inform insurers which clients are high risk;
- notify insurers of claims.

Claims resistance

16.31 Tax practitioners are often concerned about claims resistance. This may happen if the premiums quoted are too low. Insurers, underwriters and the practice all have to have a fair deal if claims resistance is to be avoided. The likelihood of this can be checked by some simple arithmetic. For example, if a firm assesses that each client has a 2 per cent risk of being investigated and the cost of an average investigation is £2,000, the premium has to be a minimum of £40 per client (the percentage risk of investigation multiplied by the average investigation cost). A premium of below this may lead to claims resistance. A premium based on the percentage risk of investigation multiplied by the average investigation cost multiplied by two would give a lower risk of claims resistance.

16.32 Other reasons for claims resistance include:

- late notification of the claim;
- error by tax advisor in the accounts preparation;
- the advisor's fees are too high;
- too much time had been spent dealing with the claim;
- poor client records but this is rarely used as a reason for resisting claims.

Quick review

16.33

- Some professional indemnity insurance policies include a free helpline to advise on enquiries and investigations.
- Employer liability cover must be not less than £5 million (*Employer Liability (Compulsory Insurance) Regulations 1998*).
- Ensure that employer liability policies include accident cover for staff working at the client's premises.
- Some household or business general insurance policies also include tax investigations cover. The firm's usual advisor may not, however, be able to handle the enquiry.
- Take care with insurance valuations. If the firm under-insures by one-third, claims will also be reduced by this amount.
- Do not agree to a 'consent order' where a complaint is made to the practitioner's professional body without first discussing the matter with the firm's PII insurers. A consent order is, in effect, an admission of guilt. It could prejudice a claim and the PII insurers may refuse further insurance cover.
- Allowing clients to pay their bills by credit card may affect the firm's professional indemnity insurance policy. If a client makes a claim to the credit card company it may be settled without reference to the practice and this may compromise a claim under the professional indemnity insurance policy. When agreeing a contract with a credit card company raise this concern. Consider issuing a side letter stating that all claims must be referred to the firm before being settled and that the professional indemnity insurers have the right to take over the claim.

Part IV – Firm

Chapter 17

Managing Structural Change

17.1 Some practices are started by sole practitioners and remain that way. Other firms evolve over time. It is very difficult for a tax practice to stay the same for a long period. The acquisition of new clients makes change inevitable, although in many firms this will be a gradual process. All practices have a limit to growth, beyond which they cannot progress without considerable change. This chapter looks at the ways in which a tax practice may develop including:

- operating as a sole practitioner;
- partnerships and their management;
- buying a practice;
- mergers;
- expanding internationally;
- selling the practice;
- retiring.

17.2 Many tax practitioners have difficulty in developing their firms because they lack management skills. Most tax personnel receive very little management training and this makes it difficult to make the transition from being a manager to a partner. Equally, a sole practitioner with five staff may not have the ability to manage a three-partner firm with twenty staff.

17.3 Firms need to think carefully about their growth so that it can be kept to a level that the partners can cope with. If it is not kept under control it can cause excessive stress and the practice may not survive unless it brings in professional management.

Sole practitioner

17.4 The majority of tax practices are run by sole practitioners. Many advisors find working in this way very rewarding, in part because none of the management issues relating to partnerships affect them. It is a very flexible and comparatively unbureaucratic way of operating a practice because decisions can be made without the need to take into account the views of other partners. It is not a way of working that suits everyone because the practitioner is solely responsible for all aspects of running the practice and before setting up a tax practice potential sole practitioners should consider carefully the points made in Chapter 1.

17.5 Just because the firm is run by a sole practitioner does not mean that the issues raised in the rest of this book do not apply. Systems and good procedures are still important, albeit tailored to the specific needs of the firm. In the short term they are necessary to provide clients with a quality service and to set acceptable standards for staff, and in the long term to facilitate the admission of a partner or the sale of the practice.

17.6 The main professional difficulty facing sole practitioners is the need to provide alternative cover in the event of their absence, incapacity or death. The professional bodies recommend that all sole practitioners appoint an 'alternate'. It is mandatory to do so where the firm is authorised for investment business (see 20.44). An alternate is another sole practitioner or partner, who agrees to step into the practitioner's shoes in the event of their incapacity or death so that clients obtain a continuing service. It is necessary to draw up a legal agreement between the parties, including an enduring power of attorney and for the practitioner to include the details in their will. The practitioner's professional body can offer further advice.

Partnership

17.7 The time may come when the sole practitioner can only develop the practice further by taking on a partner. Joining up with another sole practitioner or small firm is an alternative option (see 17.25). Larger practices may also take on new partners because of expansion or retirement.

Taking on a partner

17.8 Taking on a partner is never a decision to be made lightly. Personal rapport should play a large part in the choice as many practitioners spend more time with their business partners than they do with their spouse.

17.9 The respective personalities of the partners must be considered. It is counter-productive to have two strong people vying to be managing partner. Equally, if all the partners are poor at administration, the team will be weak. It is impossible to be prescriptive about the ideal composition of a partnership but in a typical, four-partner firm, the aim should be to have:

- a fair leader who has the support of others and is a good internal communicator – they should have an overview of the practice and how different areas within it inter-relate;

- a good client contact who can bring in new work, understand clients' needs and is reassuring, calm and confident;
- a technical wizard with a detailed tax knowledge and the ability to apply it to new ideas;
- an organised administrator and compliance officer to manage the day-to-day running of the practice and to ensure that quality control is maintained.

17.10 Each partner's technical skills should also be complementary. There is little benefit in having two partners who are capital gains tax experts unless the firm wants to market itself as a niche capital gains tax practice. A general tax partnership should aim to have partners (or staff) with skills across the range of taxes.

17.11 Being a partner requires more than being good at tax. It also demands drive, ambition, management and leadership as well as good client and personnel skills. Before taking on a partner, firms should also see how prospective candidates match up to the following personal characteristics:

- conscientiousness;
- integrity;
- motivation;
- ability to perform under pressure;
- self-managing (work and emotions);
- awareness of others' needs (staff, colleagues and clients);
- persuasive ability.

The prospective partner should also have sufficient breadth of practical experience combined with commercial and management skills.

17.12 When recruiting a partner, the firm should draw up a job specification in much the same way as it would do for a new member of staff. It should incorporate a list of desirable personal characteristics, technical abilities and management skills, such as being good at IT or marketing. For further details about recruitment see 12.2.

17.13 Finding good partners can be difficult, particularly for small firms, because there is a limited supply of suitable tax practitioners available. Firms need to offer attractive rewards (see Chapter 19), a wide range of opportunity, autonomy and security to attract the right people. Many senior employees are reluctant to give up their employment rights to maternity pay and termination packages for the onerous obligations inherent in being a partner; particularly if they are only offered an appointment as a salaried or fixed-profit share partner.

17.14 The current trend for medium and large firm mergers may make it easier to recruit senior staff who find themselves surplus to the requirements of the merged firm. Alternatively, the practice may be lucky enough to be able to promote home-grown talent. Promoting staff from within can bring stability to a firm. This can be an attractive selling point to clients because it is so often lacking in a profession where mergers are common.

Considerations for new partners

17.15 Practitioners who are considering a partnership offer should first of all see how they match up to the criteria for success outlined in 17.11 and in the introduction. Secondly, they should do their homework carefully before joining a partnership. Partnerships often operate in a culture of silence but the obligations on partners are considerable, particularly with regard to unlimited liability and a duty of good faith to fellow partners. Before signing the partnership agreement, the following issues require consideration.

- Obtain a copy of the partnership agreement and independent legal advice if necessary.
- Ask for a copy of historic and management accounts.
- Find out about capital commitments, lease obligations and liabilities.
- Who owns the assets, the partnership or the individual partners?
- Is the firm run efficiently (see Chapter 18)?
- Is it a good investment and career opportunity? How does it compare with other opportunities on offer?
- Consider the effect on profits of the admission and any associated retirements.
- Ask about future strategies and obtain copies of budgets and plans.
- Find out the profit sharing arrangements (see Chapter 19).
- Discuss the terms being offered (profit share, capital contribution, drawings).
- Will the partnership offer be as a full equity partner?
- Check tax arrangements, particularly the withdrawal of the cash basis of accounting.
- Can finance be obtained to fund the purchase of the partnership share?
- Check the professional indemnity insurance and find out about claims and complaints (see 16.16).
- Obtain indemnities from the existing partners with regard to claims arising before the date of admission.

Incoming partners will probably have to sign a confidentiality agreement in order to obtain access to such information.

Management

17.16 A partnership requires good management to make it act as a cohesive unit, otherwise there is a danger that it will become a group of individual partners all pulling in different directions. The primary management document will be the partnership deed but supplementary agreements may be required to set out the way in which the firm will operate on a daily basis and the specific responsibilities of each partner.

17.17 The firm should appoint a senior or managing partner to lead the firm. Many tax partners have strong personalities so it will take skill and tact to direct the practice. Age or the length of time that the partner has been with the firm are not prerequisites, although this is how many senior partners are appointed. The senior partner should be the most competent person for the job who has leadership, vision and the support of the other partners and staff.

17.18 The partnership should decide how it is to be structured, for example, by partner-led teams or subject-led teams such as small business unit or entertainment group. It is the role of the senior or managing partner to ensure that each team or department interacts effectively and that the firm does not simply comprise several small empires. Failure to interact can lead to poor marketing and cross-selling.

17.19 To be effective the partnership must regularly set aside time for partners' meetings. It will depend on each individual practice whether this is a set day per month or as the need arises. Care must be taken not to hold too many unnecessary partners' meetings when there is nothing to discuss. The firm may be better appointing a small management team to solve day-to-day problems; alternatively, it can rely on the judgment of fellow partners without the need to continually report back. Quick 'stand-up' meetings without a formal agenda to discuss an issue are highly effective and work well where there is a small number of partners on one site.

17.20 The following tips may help the firm to decide whether a meeting is really worthwhile and ensure that it is run effectively. This checklist can also be applied to meetings with clients and third parties.

- What is the meeting aiming to achieve?
- Is there an agenda and has it been circulated?
- Could the issues be dealt with other than in a meeting?
- How much will the meeting cost in terms of lost fees?

- Is the cost worthwhile or can the issues be dealt with by a smaller group?
- Do all the partners need to be present for the whole meeting?
- Do they all contribute to the meeting?
- Is the location the best choice to minimise costs and travelling time?
- Is there any background information which is required before a decision can be made?
- Do all the partners know the time of the meeting and will they arrive on time?
- Are partners' meetings well chaired?
- Do they stick to the agenda and finish on time?
- Do the meetings achieve their objective?

Buying a practice

17.21 A new firm can grow organically over a period of time but faster growth can be achieved by acquiring a practice. Existing firms may also want to expand more quickly than internal growth alone would allow in order to generate higher returns for the partners and to offer clients a greater range of services. Merging with another firm is one option (see 17.25), buying a practice is another.

17.22 The market currently favours the vendors of tax practices because of the various consolidators seeking to acquire mid-tier firms (see 22.24) but market conditions frequently change. There are two options to consider when purchasing a tax practice.

- Buying a block of fees (see 17.34).
- Buying a practice. This may involve the acquisition of premises, staff and partners and is likely to suit a new start-up situation.

17.23 Firms should consider the following issues when purchasing a practice.

- The quality of its clients.
- The likelihood of them transferring successfully to the new practice.
- The type of service they received from the other firm and their expectations.
- The management skills required to integrate the new business into the existing firm.
- The requirements of specialised or niche clients.

- The scope to offer clients further services and the extent to which this was unexploited by the vendor (see Chapter 10).
- The price required.
- The bargaining position of the two parties.
- The payment period.
- The ability to arrange suitable finance.
- The guaranteed fees required by the vendor and the amount of retained fees to be paid on an earn-out or success basis.
- Restrictive covenants and warranties, for example, with regard to the work intentions of the former partners.
- The working capital requirements.
- The quality of the records kept by the vendor to justify the purchase price.
- Warranties offered with regard to fees and claims.
- Professional indemnity insurance issues.

17.24 Buying a practice is expensive and not the only option. Consider the alternatives, such as:

- attracting new clients by successful marketing (see 5.11);
- bringing in new clients by offering low or no fees for an initial period (see 3.44).

For a consideration of the issues from the vendor's point of view see 17.31.

Mergers

17.25 One of the most popular ways for firms to develop and expand is to merge with another tax practice. This can take many forms. It may be a merger of equals or a takeover of a smaller firm by a larger practice. The resulting firm will probably contain all or most of the partners in the original firms.

17.26 Before entering into merger talks with another firm, the practice must have very clear reasons for wanting to make such a radical change, such as increasing the range of services it can offer to clients, expanding into different geographical areas or benefiting from economies of scale.

17.27 Many merger talks fail partly because there are so many issues which have to be discussed and reconciled. The longer the firms have been established and the greater the degree of equality between them, the harder this will be. Every aspect of the firms' practice and management has to be compared and an agreement reached on it. Even after a firm has merged it often takes many years before the two practices are successfully integrated. Good management is vital to achieving this process. The easiest mergers are often those between quite disparate practices where the original firms can effectively become departments or teams within the combined entity.

17.28 The following points are some of the many issues which firms will need to resolve during the merger talks.

- The name of the combined firm.
- Profit sharing ratios.
- Capital requirements.
- Location and premises, unless the firms are in different towns.
- Internal structure and management including partners' responsibilities.
- Harmonising working practices, both technical and administrative. This will need to cover all aspects of the firms' work from file layout to new client procedures (see Chapters 2, 7 and 15).
- Staff employment rights (see Chapter 12).
- Marketing the new practice (see Chapter 5).
- Setting appropriate charge-out rates (see Chapter 3).

International links

17.29 A combination of practice mergers and acquisitions will allow a firm to expand nationally but doing the same internationally is much harder. Developing international offices is the preserve of the very largest firms.

Nevertheless, there are benefits to be obtained from developing links with firms overseas. We live in a world where clients regularly move around the world and having an international connection means that clients living abroad can have a local firm to deal with their tax matters and the firm can make use of their knowledge when undertaking tax planning for them. Connections may be particularly relevant where the firm regularly deals with clients from one particular country.

17.30 If the practice does not already have links with the targeted country, they should contact their professional body or join one of the marketing and networking organisations, many of which have international partners. Care must be exercised in developing links independently, as it may be difficult to vet firms without incurring considerable costs.

As an alternative, consider using an international firm when the need arises (see 21.2).

Selling a practice

17.31 The time may come when running a tax practice is no longer an attractive idea (see Chapter 1). In this case the firm may decide to sell out to another practice. No two sales are ever structured in the same way but generally the sale will either comprise the whole firm, including premises and staff, or simply a block of fees. Most firms do not sell goodwill.

17.32 Few tax practices are actually sold outright because funding the purchase would be too expensive and it is unusual for all partners to want to sell out at the same time. The route most practices take is to merge with another firm, with the majority of partners continuing in the new business (see 17.25).

17.33 Selling out to a consolidator could produce a cash payment but it is more likely to be structured as a merger. The partners in the merged firm will still have their capital tied up in the firm; they are unlikely to see a return of capital and may have to introduce further sums to finance the new business.

17.34 If the fees are more than about £450,000, they are difficult to sell. Selling smaller blocks of fees is much easier, particularly if they are in the range of £100,000 to £250,000. Saleable fees are recurring fees. One-off projects are usually excluded unless the firm can demonstrate a regular pattern of fees which will be unaffected by the sale. To justify the calculation of gross recurring fees it is vital to have maintained very good work in progress and billing records for several years.

17.35 The rates for purchasing fees vary and will depend on the quality of the clients and the purchaser's perception of their future value. The range rates will usually be between 0.5–1.5 of gross fees. For example, if the multiplier was 1.25 and the fees were £350,000, the practice would sell for £437,500. Of this sum, a certain percentage may be guaranteed, with the rest payable as a bonus if the clients stay with the practice. Payment will be made over an agreed period of time. All fees are subject to detailed negotiation.

17.36 To find a buyer for the firm, it is usual to place the practice with a practice sale agent or advertise it in the trade press. Many sale agents do not charge a fee to the vendor.

Managing the sale

17.37 Managing the sale and transfer is important for both the vendor and purchaser as both have a vested interest in making the deal work. This requires careful handling of clients and employees. The timing of the sale is also important. The ideal time to sell a predominantly personal tax practice is February and March before the start of the new tax year.

17.38 In most situations clients should not be told about the changes until the sale is complete because if it falls through they will be left feeling very uncertain about their future with the firm and may leave anyway. Once the sale has taken place all the clients should receive a letter straightaway telling them about the changes and what it will mean for them. The partners will need to be on hand to reassure clients about the arrangements by telephone and each client should be offered the chance to attend a 'hand-over' meeting where they can be introduced to the new firm. It is worthwhile putting in considerable effort at this stage because if the clients do not transfer to the new practice the vendor will not receive payment for them.

17.39 Staff should be told about the changes as soon as they are at an advanced stage of negotiation and before there are any leaks or rumours. Finding out in this way will cause immediate distrust. Early notification will also give the staff time to get used to the change and be involved in it. Some employees may be frightened of change and uncertain about working for a new firm. They will require a lot of reassurance about the practicalities of the change and their employment conditions (see 12.44). Make a special effort with those who are hostile or passively resistant to the change. Offer encouragement and outline the career or other benefits. Treat staff gently if morale is low during the change-over period. Where staff are told about the deal before the firm's clients it is vital that they do not discuss it with any client either deliberately or inadvertently.

17.40 Firms selling out must be prepared for the sale period to be stressful. Clients may feel shocked, abandoned and annoyed at the loss of a close, personal relationship. However, the advisor/client relationship is for the most part purely commercial and given time most clients will transfer to the new firm quite happily and remain with it. The clients most likely to leave are those who were already dissatisfied with the firm for another reason (see 6.11).

Retirement

17.41 Retirement issues affect all partnerships, not just those with partners aged over 60. Some partners will want to retire early or may be forced to retire unexpectedly through ill health, others may simply wish to leave the partnership to pursue other interests.

17.42 It is essential for tax partners to retire before they have had enough of being in practice and before they become jaded, out of date or out of touch. It is better for all concerned to retire at a high point with the clients still wanting more.

Succession planning

17.43 Tax practices should have formal succession plans because the retirement of a partner needs careful consideration, particularly if the partner concerned owns a majority of the firm's capital. Arrangements should be in place to buy out the partner's share in the practice. If not the firm may have to merge with another practice or sell fees in order to finance the retirement. All retirement issues and arrangements should be included in a retirement deed.

17.44 The retiring partner should consider the following issues as part of the retirement process.

- Setting a retirement date.
- Drawing up a timetable for completing outstanding work and handing over clients to another partner.
- How their current and capital accounts will be repaid (all at once or over a period of time).
- How goodwill (if any) will be valued.
- Whether they will receive an annuity.
- Whether there will be a consultancy agreement.
- Obtaining indemnities from the remaining partners with regard to work undertaken after their retirement.
- Providing an indemnity to the remaining partners with regard to the excess on the professional indemnity insurance policy in the event of there being a claim relating to their time as a partner.
- The need for ongoing professional indemnity insurance.
- Accounting issues to the date of retirement including the valuation of work in progress and the release of tax provisions.
- The right to receive information to complete their personal tax returns.
- Consent to notices informing the public about the retirement (for example, in the *London Gazette*).
- Post-retirement perks such as the right to keep property or to remain in the firm's group insurance policies.

17.45 If the partner is leaving the firm but not retiring from tax practice, the following additional issues should also be covered.

- The use of partnership names.
- Non-competition (geographic area and time scale).
- Details of any clients taken by the retiring partner with the consent of the firm.

- Warranties about not approaching the firm's clients to obtain work.
- Warranties about not inducing the firm's employees to leave the practice.
- Warranties about not using information, software or other data obtained from the firm.

The issues relating to an incoming partner are considered at 17.15.

Managing retirement

17.46 Many partners find it psychologically hard to retire. There are two ways of retiring: gradually and suddenly. Retiring gradually gives clients (and the partner) a chance to get used to the idea and to transfer existing client loyalties to colleagues. It can be achieved by reducing the number of days worked each week and by not taking on any new clients. After retirement it may be possible to continue with the firm as a part-time consultant.

Leaving suddenly is very difficult. Clients need time to say goodbye. Many will want to offer their personal thanks. There will be an element of bereavement on both sides of the relationship.

17.47 Many partners worry unduly that they are irreplaceable and that their clients will leave the firm after they retire. Some may but the vast majority will stay with the firm and adapt to the new partner. If the firm has operated on a team basis, retiring is often easier.

17.48 Retirement represents the end of an era. It is important to mark the occasion in a special way both within the firm (for example, by holding a party) and after retiring. Consider an extended trip abroad, learning a new skill, taking up a new hobby or voluntary activity.

17.49 It is also important to say 'no' to work after retirement (unless it is wanted). Former clients may request help with voluntary organisations, offer treasurerships and request ad hoc advice.

17.50 Firms should treasure their ex-partners and keep them involved with the practice, for example, by inviting them to events and providing them with a free tax return service. Ex-partners can be an excellent source of client referrals.

Compulsory retirement

17.51 The departure of a partner is not always a happy occasion. The partnership deed should contain provisions for the forced removal of partners in certain situations such as gross misconduct or permanent incapacity. The agreement should include:

- the reasons for dismissal;
- the notice period (on both sides);
- dismissal procedure (votes or management committee);
- restrictive covenants;
- the extraction of their capital.

Quick review

17.52

- If the advisor wants to work alone, he or she will be a sole practitioner. If they want to work with others, it will be necessary to form a partnership or limited company. Most tax practices operate as sole traders or partnerships.
- It is possible to operate as a limited liability partnership (LLP) under the *Limited Liability Partnerships Act*.
- All partnership changes should be reflected in deeds of admission or retirement. Legal advice may be necessary.
- All changes in the structure of a firm will require notification to the regulatory authorities.
- The firm should have a sound internal structure of inter-related departments.
- The firm should expand and develop at a controlled and managed rate.
- To succeed, a partnership requires a strategy and management.
- The management of the firm should encompass:
  - clear communication both with clients and internally (see Chapter 4);
  - motivation of partners and staff (see 12.23 and Chapter 19);
  - managing time and priorities (see 18.3);
  - having well-organised teams or departments (see 12.41).

Chapter 18

Cost and Financial Control

18.1 For a tax practice, spending time on the firm's finances can seem something of the proverbial 'busman's holiday'. Firms that do find that it pays handsome dividends. If the practice does not know which are its most profitable clients or fee earners it cannot reward staff and partners appropriately and is likely to make the wrong marketing decisions.

Chapter 17 considered some of the structural issues relevant to tax practices. This chapter looks at the financial aspects including:

- work in progress and time management;
- controlling debtors;
- banking issues;
- ways to monitor profitability.

The checklist in Appendix 18:1 will help the firm to identify the management issues which may require change. It can also be used for value-added client reviews.

Time management

18.2 Unless a firm undertakes value billing or charges fixed fees, essentially what tax practitioners sell is time. It is a precious resource and accordingly it requires management. All staff should know the cost to the firm of each minute of their time.

18.3 If time is properly managed not only will it improve productivity but it should also minimise the hours that everyone spends in the office. This in turn will reduce stress. Firms should avoid a culture which equates the hours worked with success. Exhausted staff and partners do not produce good work. Clients will be reluctant to request more work or recommend new clients to a practice that appears to be struggling to cope with its existing workload.

18.4 All staff and partners should be trained in time management skills. The training will last a lifetime and may revolutionise their work patterns. Time management skills include the following.

- Keep a 'to do' list but delete tasks which will never be done.
- Get the day off to a good start by tackling a routine task.
- Try to work at the right time of day. Everyone has individual preferences although most people have effective work peaks in the mid to late morning and the mid to late afternoon. This is the time to tackle important tasks. Many people experience a fall in productivity in the early and late afternoon.
- Be organised. Use an organiser or diary system to keep track of the tasks which need doing (see 15.22). Keep offices and desks tidy. Do not allow papers to accumulate in briefcases and in-trays.
- Review the priority of tasks daily. Do the first priority task first. Rank the priority of other work. Ask whether it is a return with an impending deadline, a planning exercise which, whilst important, is not urgent, or a small daily task such as routine correspondence.
- In assessing priorities, ask what would happen if the work was not done today.
- For each new task, decide whether it is urgent. Can it be delegated? Does the fee justify the work being treated as top priority?
- Do not start a task at the last possible moment.
- Aim to touch each piece of paper only once. Be decisive about each item of post; delegate it, deal with it, file it or bin it.
- When dealing with large cases or planning exercises break the task down into a series of manageable parts. Aim to chip away at the task each day.
- Communicate quickly and briefly; e-mail is ideal.
- Deal with telephone calls in a batch rather than scattering them throughout the day.
- Learn to delegate effectively (see 12.34). Read the *One Minute Manager* books by Kenneth Blanchard and Robert Lorber.
- Take a break from work at least once during the day.
- Partners and managers should allow themselves time each day to work without interruption. This means no telephone calls or staff interruptions. A period of concentrated effort can clear a lot of work.
- Do not produce internal information or implement systems that no one wants. Before doing so ask what it will achieve.
- At the end of the day tie up loose ends and organise the priorities for the next day.

18.5 Avoid time wasters such as the following.

- Losing things – be organised and tidy.
- Junk mail – ignore it.
- Meetings – are they necessary or do they overrun? Consider holding 'stand-up' meetings for quick decisions (see 17.19 and 18.6).
- Interruptions from colleagues – consider the office layout.
- Telephone calls – are they necessary or too long?
- Direct selling telephone calls – do not take them.
- Reverse delegation by staff – do not automatically take on the task but offer support and training to enable them to make further progress.
- Procrastination and perfectionism – take a balanced view of what is required and what the client will pay for.
- Crises and 'urgent' requests – is it really a crisis or even urgent?
- Travelling – use the time spent travelling on public transport to catch up with technical reading.

Meetings

18.6 No firm can function without meetings but they can take up a lot of time. Firms should appraise whether all meetings are worthwhile and whether the cost is justified by the benefit. To take a simple scenario: a five-partner firm holds a two-hour partners' meeting each month. Assuming that their charge-out rates average £125 an hour, each meeting costs £1,250 or £15,000 over the whole year. Firms should consider whether there is a less costly alternative that would achieve the same result. For example, could the meeting be held in half the time? Is time wasted because of interruptions, mobile phones, partners not concentrating because they are signing out their post, ineffective chairing, bickering or social chit-chat?

Work in progress

18.7 Setting charge-out rates and fee levels was considered at 3.13. This chapter considers how to monitor and control work in progress to best effect. Most practices still complete time sheets because they charge fees based on an hourly rate. When completing time sheets fee earners should account for time accurately and honestly. This means not loading time onto large fee jobs but equally not pre-judging fee recovery by failing to record time actually worked on a case. If the time is not recorded it will never be billed to the client. Inaccurate time records are useless for management and comparison purposes. If the firm has many cases where this occurs or partners who prefer to work in this way, it should charge fixed fees negotiated in advance with the client. In this case time sheets may be unnecessary unless the firm wants to use the information to help it set the fee levels.

18.8 The firm should consider carefully the time units it uses. The choice may depend on the work it undertakes. A firm with a few large clients may be happy with 15-minute or even 30-minute units. A practice with many smaller clients should consider 6 or 10-minute units. The danger with using too large a block of time is that there is a tendency to round down and time may not be charged at all for short telephone calls. The problem with small units can be keeping track of them.

18.9 If partners and staff find it difficult to account for all their time in the day, they should consider using time sheets with the hours and minutes pre-printed down one side. Even if such sheets are only completed for a short period of time, they may be instructive in helping the firm account for its time more profitably.

18.10 Make the time system easy to use. Have a time sheet template on the computer. This could be linked directly to the time recording system. Where time sheets are manually entered onto the time recording system care needs to be taken to ensure that sheets do not get missed out and a reconciliation will be necessary.

18.11 The reports generated by the work in progress system are vital to the way that time is managed. Instead of producing reports in alphabetical or client number order, the system should be designed to produce them in value order. The report could also show the client's ranking in the firm (either by work in progress generated or turnover) and the fee earner with the most hours or recoverable fees. This information will enable the firm to focus on key clients and to set staff targets.

18.12 Instead of each fee earner reviewing the work in progress report separately to decide which clients should be billed, the report could be discussed in a tax department meeting. This will allow for open discussion of write-offs, work difficulties and problem clients. If the reports are not discussed in a meeting, they should be reviewed at least monthly by the tax manager or partner and explanations sought for all large unbilled amounts, write-offs or unusual items.

Write-offs

18.13 Work in progress write-offs should always be carefully monitored as they provide useful management information. Regular large write-offs (15 per cent to 20 per cent or more of the time) may indicate that the charge-out rates are set too high and should be adjusted to a more realistic level. The advantage of setting them high is that in some cases a higher fee may be recovered than would otherwise be the case.

Setting rates on the high side may be a particularly good policy for:

- a tax consultancy where high fees may often be justified by large tax savings;
- efficient staff and partners.

18.14 Partner approval should be sought for all write-offs over a certain limit, for example, £50 or 5 per cent to 10 per cent of the work in progress value. Firms should be careful to ensure that all write-offs are examined critically and that they are not simply a habit.

18.15 Write-offs should be incorporated into the firm's work in progress report by fee earners so that they can be used to determine productivity bonuses (see 12.25).

18.16 Ways to avoid write-offs include the following.

- Set time budgets for non-routine jobs; these can be formal or informal.
- Review clients' records when they reach the firm and do not start work on a job until the information is complete (see 15.52 and Chapter 7).
- Aim to touch each piece of paper as few times as possible and do not keep picking up a job and putting it down.
- For small tax return cases do as much work as possible when the file is out. Do a planning and compliance review and complete all letters and claims and elections so that the job does not have to be revisited.
- Encourage staff to report problems early.
- Ensure that work is done to a good standard from the outset and that junior staff are well supervised.

Lock up

18.17 Many tax practices have a lot of working capital tied up in work in progress and debtors. This is partly due to the seasonal nature of some of the work. The amount locked up should be reviewed regularly in tax department meetings and if it starts to increase beyond acceptable limits action may need to be taken to reduce it. The amount of working capital involved will depend on the work that the practice undertakes. Routine compliance work may tie up working capital for longer periods. This should be considered when setting charge-out rates. Consultancy work usually lasts for a discrete period of time and can be billed upon completion or in stage payments.

A sole practitioner consultant may have as little as two to three months' work locked up. Partnerships may have four to six months. Above six months and the firm should consider remedial action.

Debt management

18.18 Once the tax services have been provided and the job is complete, the practice needs to invoice the client. Some of the fee recovery issues were considered at 3.25. This section considers how firms can improve their cash flow by good invoicing practice.

Invoicing

18.19 If a firm delays the bill for too long, clients will forget how much work has been done or how pleased they are with it. They are then much more likely to question the charge. Do not just send out bills once a month; it should be an ongoing process. Try the following.

- For straightforward tax return cases send a bill with the completed return or shortly after. This will usually bring in the money quickly.
- Some clients may prefer to be billed when the costs reach a certain level.
- Others prefer a monthly, quarterly or annual bill.
- Agree with clients at the outset of the engagement how frequently they would like to be billed.
- Invoice clients regularly to avoid the costs building up.
- Include the firm's credit terms in the engagement letter.

Settlement

18.20 Firms should also offer clients imaginative ways of paying for their tax services. Consider the following.

- Obtain monthly standing order payments on account of fees. Make sure that clients understand that these are payments on account. Send an invoice for the balance of the fees at the end of the year and do not let it run on indefinitely. If the client requests extra work, increase the standing order.
- If clients want work quickly or want to queue jump (particularly close to the filing deadline) consider obtaining payment up front or charging premium rates. Keep a record of very slow payers. If they require extra work, obtain money in advance.
- Offer discounts to encourage prompt payment. For example, add an extra one-ninth to the bill and then invite clients who pay within ten days to deduct one-tenth. For a bill of £300, this would increase it to £333. The discount would bring the bill back to the usual level for prompt payers. Slow payers would suffer a higher charge. This can

be justified to clients on the basis that prompt payers do not then subsidise the slow ones.

- Offer payment by credit or debit card and post-dated cheques. Make it as easy as possible for clients to pay. Credit card companies charge between 2 per cent and 4 per cent of the payment as a handling fee but this will be worthwhile if it brings in payment early. If the firm is offering Internet advice or helpline services, payment by credit and debit card is essential.
- Charging interest on overdue accounts is another option but most people simply ignore the charge.

Debt collection

18.21 However much care the firm puts into invoicing and in spite of offering a variety of means of payment, there will always be clients who are slow to pay.

18.22 Tax practices are usually generous with their credit terms. Many firms offer 30 days' credit and then only seriously chase the debt after four or five months. Research by Experian has shown in a survey of 150,000 companies that the average payment period is 59 days plus. Consider reducing credit terms to 10 days or 'payment on demand' and following up with a statement after 30 days. However, make sure that clients know about the changes in credit terms.

18.23 Partners and fee earning staff do not like chasing clients for payment. Delegate this task to the office administrator or, if the firm is large enough, to a credit controller. Some clients do not respond well to written statements or payment demands. In these cases telephone or use fax or e-mail to chase payment.

18.24 If a client has not paid within the stipulated credit terms:

- send a statement;
- telephone the client; and
- stop work.

If payment is still not forthcoming place the matter with a solicitor or a collection agency. Make sure that clients know that you are serious about collection. Many practices are concerned that they will upset clients by chasing them for payment. Remember, those clients who do not pay are not worth having as clients.

Bad debts

18.25 Avoiding frequent or large bad debt involves a two-track approach: distinguishing the clients who cannot pay from those who will not pay. Working with clients who cannot pay to resolve financial difficulties is often the best solution and promotes loyalty. For those who will not pay there is only one answer; be tough, even if it means losing the client.

18.26 Procedures to adopt to avoid bad debts include the following.

- Initial credit checks before taking on a client. The February 2000 edition of *Accountancy*, page 39, includes a list of useful Internet sites and software packages to assist with this.
- When in doubt ask for payment in advance or by standing order.
- Make sure clients can afford the work before undertaking it.
- Invoice them as soon as practical after starting work to see how they react to the first bill.
- State credit terms clearly.
- Send prompt statements and follow them up with a telephone call.
- If payment is not forthcoming from a client who can afford to pay, take swift, decisive action.

Bank facilities and financing

18.27 Banking is now much more competitive. Tax practices should ensure that their banking arrangements are cost effective. If they have not been reviewed for several years this could be another way to reduce costs. Consider the following.

- Electronic banking (if it is not already being used).
- Alternative bankers.
- Are the bank charges and interest in line with the agreement with the bank?
- Have they ever been checked?
- Ask the bank how their charges can be reduced.
- Does the firm have set-off arrangements between accounts to minimise interest charges?
- Does the bank regularly make mistakes?
- What security (if any) does the bank hold?
- Are cars and computers financed in the most cost effective way?
- Are the partners financing the firm? Would they prefer to withdraw their capital and replace it with bank loans?
- Are the partners likely to face capital calls in the near future?
- Review the terms of commercial mortgages and consider the options.

Payments

18.28 Most tax practices have little scope for improving practice profitability by more efficient purchasing because the majority of their costs are staff salaries, interest and rent. Payment for these items is required monthly and the terms are unlikely to be negotiable. Many other costs, such as subscriptions and fees, require payment in advance.

18.29 One cost effective way of reviewing overheads is to review them for significant variances at the end of the year. Comparison should be made against the budget and with the previous year's expense. The practice manager should then be given the task of finding out why the variance occurred and how the costs can be reduced. Their bonus could be linked to such savings.

18.30 Firms should also consider the following.

- Pay within the permitted credit terms but only just.
- Agree favourable credit terms when negotiating contracts (see 14.52).
- Review contracts regularly and ensure that the firm is not dependent on only one supplier.
- Weigh up the extra cost of paying insurance and other costs monthly (where this is possible) compared to annually in advance.
- The timing of staff bonuses.
- The *Late Payment of Commercial Debts (Interest) Act 1998,* which permits interest to be charged on the late payment of invoices.

Accounting systems

18.31 When firms are choosing accounting systems, they should take into account the extent to which it is integrated with other practice management functions, for example, time recording, billing, credit control, payroll, budgeting and reporting. The greater the degree of integration the more efficient the system is likely to be for the practice. Accounting systems should be reviewed to ascertain how well they handle the points highlighted in this chapter, in particular the ease and flexibility with which management reports can be generated.

18.32 However good the accounting system the firm will need to set up standard accounting adjustments to produce reliable management accounts, for example, accruals, prepayments and depreciation. Standard adjustments should be reviewed regularly to ensure that they are still valid, otherwise by the year-end the accounts could be inaccurate.

18.33 The requirement to produce year-end accounts which show a true and fair view means that the accounts must be prepared on an accruals basis with an appropriate value for work in progress. Firms will have to decide whether they produce management accounts with work in progress at full value and adjust it to an appropriate value at the year-end or make the adjustments more regularly. However, if firms use the reporting criteria detailed below it is unlikely to be important which method they adopt.

Monitoring profitability

18.34 Tax practices often claim to be too busy to manage their practices in the same way as they would consider appropriate for their clients. If they only prepare accounts for tax purposes at the end of the year, this is likely to be too little, too late.

18.35 Firms should develop simple reporting criteria to enable them to monitor profitability at least quarterly and preferably on a monthly basis. The appropriate criteria will depend on the size of practice and the extent to which costs and overheads are fixed. Since it is unlikely that monitoring overheads will yield significant additional profits, the emphasis should be placed on income and staff costs.

18.36 To know whether it is on target, a practice will require a budget; in particular one for chargeable hours for each fee earner. Firms should not just monitor financial data; non-financial indicators can be just as important. Suggestions of key indicators to review are as follows.

Monthly

- Total practice profit compared to budget.
- Total chargeable hours compared to budgeted hours.
- Work in progress by fee earner compared to budget.
- Administration and non-chargeable hours.
- Work in progress write-offs and write-ons.
- Average credit period taken by clients.
- Credit period taken by the firm from its suppliers.
- Clients gained (numbers and fee value) and clients lost (numbers and fee value).
- Marketing advances.
- Computer problems.
- Website hits.
- Tax returns submitted.

Annually

The annual review should be against the previous year's data (if it is available) and the budget.

- Revenue and profit per partner.
- Revenue and profit per fee earner.
- Revenue and profit per staff member.
- Borrowings compared to partners' capital accounts.
- Salaries to revenue.
- Premises' costs to revenue.
- Other overheads to revenue.
- Expenditure variances.
- The most profitable clients.
- The least profitable clients.
- Persistently bad payers.

18.37 Summaries of the above data should be discussed, circulated to staff or put on the firm's notice board to keep staff informed and motivated. The use of graphs and charts will communicate the data more effectively.

Quick review

18.38

- The number of chargeable hours produced by each partner can have a dramatic effect on practice productivity.
- Time sheets for some staff may eventually become a thing of the past. Software can now monitor the time spent processing a particular case. This automated system is currently most suitable for bulk tax return processing in call centres but it will eventually have wider use.
- Good work in progress records are vital if the firm wants to sell up or merge with another practice.
- Treat the practice as if it were an important client. Spend an appropriate amount of time on both accounting and tax planning.
- The Institute of Chartered Accountants in England and Wales operates an inter-firm comparison. In the May 2000 edition of *Accountancy*, Alan Taylor provides key statistics from the exercise including fees and profits per partner.

- For most tax practices, profitability depends on:
  - setting the right charge-out rate (see 3.13);
  - having an appropriate staff:partner ratio (see 12.17);
  - recording work in progress correctly (see 18.7);
  - productivity (see 12.21);
  - fee recoverability (see 18.13, 18.18 and 3.25).

Appendix 18:1

Practice Management Checklist

Question	Action required
Structure	
Is there a signed partnership agreement?	
Are regular partners' meetings held?	
Does the firm have committees relevant to its needs run by both staff and partners?	
Do partners have clear responsibilities, for example, for financial information, personnel etc.?	
Does the firm have a strategy for the next year/five years?	
Does the practice have plans for the retirement/admission of partners?	
Does the practice have clear direction or are partners too involved in client work or administration to manage the firm?	
Accounts and budgets	
Is there a practice budget and is it monitored?	
Are management accounts produced at least quarterly? Are they compared to the budget and the key ratios and trends identified?	
Are all fee earners given financial targets?	
Fees and debt recovery	
When were charge-out rates last reviewed (apart from being increased for inflation)?	
Does the firm know which are its least profitable/most profitable clients?	
How good are the time records? Are write-offs/write-ons monitored and action taken?	
How often does the firm bill its clients?	
How long do clients take to pay? Does the firm offer incentives to clients to pay quickly?	

Question	Action required
Cash management	
When did the firm last review its banking arrangements?	
Does the firm have significant borrowings? Are they monitored and the terms reviewed?	
Payments	
What credit does the firm take from its suppliers?	
How much money is tied up in prepayments?	
Are contracts for goods and services regularly reviewed?	
Staff	
How does the firm motivate its staff?	
Does the practice pay overtime and bonuses?	
How does it monitor peaks and troughs in its workload?	
Are partners appraised by their peers?	
Has the practice considered the structure of its teams/departments to ensure that they comprise the correct partner/staff ratios?	
Do partners and staff undertake management and personal development training?	

Chapter 19

Partner Reward

19.1 Tax partners can only receive drawings and not the interesting remuneration packages, share options and bonuses of employed practitioners. However, partners' rewards do not have to be dull. There are a number of creative ways in which profits can be divided and non-financial incentives should not be overlooked. This chapter reviews some of the possible options.

What do partners want?

19.2 Many tax practices have never assessed what motivates their partners. This means that they are not necessarily getting the most out of them. Partners, like any member of staff, need to feel appreciated and valued. Unmotivated partners may have a detrimental effect on the morale of their team, lose clients and suffer stress. Ultimately profits will suffer and this has an impact on all the partners.

19.3 What motivates one partner will not be as important for another. Financial reward is usually the most important but other factors should not be overlooked. Key motivators include:

- financial success;
- security;
- career progression;
- status;
- flexible working.

A profitable firm

19.4 If financial reward is a partner's main motivation, the practice will only be able to pay out high levels of drawings if it is profitable and has good systems of financial control and cash management. If profits and, in consequence, drawings are low or if too much working capital is tied up in work in progress and debtors thereby restricting the partners' drawings, the practice needs to address these issues before considering how the profits are divided up (see 18.17).

Profit shares

19.5 Firms need to think creatively about how profits are shared. By doing so they can reward:

- responsibility, such as being the managing partner;
- particular duties, such as being the financial services compliance partner or being responsible for staff training;
- partner profitability;
- team/department profitability;
- partners who have invested the most capital in the firm.

The special responsibility and duty payments are necessary to balance the payment of productivity bonuses. Partners with large numbers of administrative duties are unlikely to achieve high productivity payments.

19.6 A fixed profit share for one year only can be used as a form of 'golden hello' to entice a partner with particular expertise from another firm.

19.7 The firm can also restrict the profit share of junior partners by paying a fixed profit share and no 'super' profits.

19.8 Partnership profits may, therefore, need to be divided in the following way:

- interest on capital;
- fixed salaries;
- special responsibility and duty payments;
- pension contributions (see 19.27);
- inducements;
- bonuses for productivity and performance;
- profit sharing ratio.

19.9 The firm's methods of profit allocation should be recorded in the partnership deed which should be regularly reviewed and updated.

Productivity 'bonuses'

19.10 It is only right that partners who choose to work longer hours or who achieve high fees are rewarded fairly for their effort. Bonuses should be based both on personal and team performance. This ensures that partners who undertake routine compliance work (dependent more on the work of others) and specialist tax planning have an equal chance to earn bonuses.

19.11 The bonuses should be based on fees recovered after allowing for write-offs of work in progress and bad debts (see 18.13 and 18.25). Other variations, such as an allowance for clients introduced (or lost), could also be incorporated. Negative bonuses should be possible and should be deducted from the profit share where productivity is below expectation. The firm will require accounting systems to monitor fees per partner and for each team (see 18.34).

19.12 In order to determine the bonuses, the firm needs to set targets and budgets. If they are exceeded a bonus could be paid, for example, 25 per cent of any excess over the target. Alternatively, the firm could pay the partners a percentage of fees recovered. For example, if a firm has a turnover of £1 million and a profit of £350,000, it could consider paying a bonus of 10 per cent of fees recovered (£100,000) as a first slice of the profits, the remainder being divided in the firm's profit sharing ratio.

19.13 The profit sharing ratio should also be regularly reviewed. It should reflect the length of time partners have been involved in the firm, clients introduced, hours worked and the partner's standing within the firm. Under the prior year basis of assessment it used to be more complicated to change profit sharing ratios because they were applied to the profits of a tax year and not an accounting period. Now that all firms are taxed on a current year basis, this is no longer a problem.

Fee basis

19.14 Some firms share their profits based on the fees earned from each partner's own clients. This can lead to the firm effectively being a collection of individuals with no responsibility for the partnership as a whole. It can also cause problems with the allocation of new clients that do not come recommended to one particular partner, expansion and the allocation of staff and overheads. Whilst such an allocation may rightly form part of the profit sharing calculations, to rely on it as the sole basis may cause partnership problems.

Salaried partners

19.15 Salaried partners are different from those on a fixed profit share (or salary). Effectively they are senior employees who do not share in the firm's equity. Their salaries are taxable under Schedule E and liable to employer's National Insurance. Benefits in kind are liable to Class 1A contributions. Salaried partners should always request indemnities from the firm's equity partners in the event that they are held out as partners and sued for negligence. In light of this limitation and the high cost of employer's National Insurance, firms should review their arrangements for salaried partners. A fixed profit share could achieve the same result at a much lower cost. Indemnities from the existing equity partners and professional indemnity insurance will cover the risk of being sued.

19.16 Under the prior year basis it was sometimes easier to appoint a salaried partner where the firm was unsure how long they would remain with the partnership because of the inconvenience of continuation elections and the potential mis-match between profits and tax. Under the current year basis each partner is taxed individually as if he or she had started (or left) their own self-employment. Accordingly, having partners joining or leaving the partnership on a frequent basis is no longer as complicated as it once was, particularly if the firm has a 5 April year-end.

'Perks'

19.17 Whilst there is really no such thing as a perk for a partner, all such payments being an appropriation of profit, it is possible to provide partners with benefits which:

- are cheaper because of the collective buying power of the partnership;
- minimise interest paid by making funds available to the partners;
- make life administratively easier.

Group policies

19.18 The collective buying power of the partnership can be used to good effect to buy group policies for permanent health insurance, private medical insurance, life and 'key man' insurance, motor policies and car leasing, to name a few. Even a small practice can negotiate savings. Arranging the policies for the partnership as a whole is also administratively convenient.

Services

19.19 Firms with investment business advisors should ensure that partners have access to financial advice. Firms could also offer the partner and his or her family tax compliance and planning services. A free or highly subsidised service should also be offered to partners on retirement.

Paying out current accounts

19.20 Partnerships should maintain separate capital and current accounts. The partnership agreement should stipulate that the capital accounts are fixed and cannot be drawn but that the balance on the partner's current account should be paid out periodically. This will enable the partners to meet their personal financial obligations in a tax-efficient way given that there is no tax relief on personal overdrafts, credit card debts or mortgages. Even if the firm requires a higher overdraft to achieve this, the rate of interest charged net of tax relief is likely to be lower than the interest rate paid by the partners personally.

Cars

19.21 Cars may be owned by the partnership but are more usually owned by the individual partners. If they are owned by the partnership, the partners should agree a budget for the amount that they can spend on purchasing the car outright or under a leasing agreement. Group discounts may be available if several cars are involved. The partnership should also agree who will settle the car running costs and how adjustments for private use of the cars are to be made.

19.22 If the vehicles are owned personally, the firm should consider paying out the balance on the current accounts to make financing the purchase as convenient and cost effective as possible.

19.23 Capital allowances on personally-owned vehicles have to be claimed in the partnership return. Individual partners can no longer make separate claims. This may result in inequality between the partners since it is more likely that if partners purchase their own cars, some will have more expensive cars than others or will replace them more frequently. When dividing the profits between the partners these differences may need to be taken into account. A similar treatment will apply to any other assets owned personally.

For example, Orla and Penny run a mixed tax practice. They share profits equally and own their cars personally. Orla owns an expensive car which she uses 70 per cent of the time for work purposes (capital allowances are £3,000 × 70 per cent = £2,100). Penny is entitled to capital allowances of £2,750 on a car she uses 35 per cent of the time for work purposes (£2,750 × 35 per cent = £963). The profits after partnership capital allowances are £80,000 less Orla's capital allowances of £2,100 less Penny's capital allowances of £963 = £76,937. The profits will be allocated as follows.

	Total	Orla	Penny
	£	£	£
Partnership profits	76,937		
Add back:			
Orla's capital allowances	2,100		
Penny's capital allowances	963		
Adjusted profit (shared 50:50)	80,000	40,000	40,000
Less:			
Capital allowances	3,063	2,100	963
Taxable profit	76,937	37,900	39,037

If the adjustment had not been made the profit of £76,937 would have been shared equally, giving each partner profits of £38,468.

19.24 As an alternative course of action the partnership could decide that the above adjustment is unnecessary on the basis that Orla has a greater need for an expensive car than Penny because she drives more business miles.

Expense claims

19.25 The partnership should agree what expenses will be reimbursed to the partners. Where these differ widely the partnership may make an adjustment similar to that shown above to maintain equality. Expenses paid personally may include motor and travel expenses incurred for business journeys or an allowance for working from home. Wherever possible expenses should be paid for directly by the partnership.

Tax reserves

19.26 Life can be made administratively easier for partners by maintaining a partnership tax reserve. This should be separately designated for each partner within the firm's accounts. Even though there are no longer joint partnership assessments, tax reserves are not obsolete. No one likes to pay tax and if it is dealt with at the partnership level it removes this burden as well as preventing an embarrassing situation arising if one partner is unable to pay his or her tax liabilities. Tax reserves also maintain equity between the partners when dealing with the catching up charge arising on the withdrawal of the cash basis of accounting, on cessation and changes in the composition of the partnership.

Pensions

19.27 There are several possibilities for partners to enhance their pensions in a cost effective way.

- The partnership can make funds available to partners to enable them to pay maximum contributions. The earnings cap for personal pensions will affect many partners. However, this is academic where partners cannot afford to or do not have the cash flow to make maximum contributions.
- The partnership could decide that partners should pay a certain level of pensions (not necessarily the maximum available) and allocate an initial profit share and drawings to facilitate this.
- The carry-forward of unused pension relief from the previous six years is abolished for personal pensions from 2001/2002 (*Finance Act 2000*). This means that tax practices should consider a one-off

payment from current or capital accounts to pay maximum contributions to utilise this relief. This could be achieved by improving cash management or increasing the firm's overdraft. Care must be taken that the partners' current and capital accounts do not become overdrawn such that tax relief on the interest is restricted.

- Annual withdrawals from the capital account (if one is maintained) should also be considered for partners approaching retirement to enable them to make maximum contributions.
- Some pension policies permit loans (either secured or unsecured) to those with sufficiently large accumulated funds. Interest is usually paid annually (and is generally not eligible for tax relief) but the capital repayments may be taken from the tax-free lump sum on retirement. This type of pension will enable the partner to fund the pension to the maximum extent if they cannot afford to do so otherwise. Borrowing from the pension may also enable a partner to contribute to a capital call if the partnership requires more funds. In this case the loan interest would be eligible for tax relief.
- Partners could consider self-invested pension schemes. These allow a group of partners (or two or more partnerships) to pool their resources and direct where some or all of the funds are held. Contribution limits, tax relief and benefits are governed by the rules for self-employed pensions. There are three types of scheme: self-investing personal pensions, private funds and friendly societies. All schemes are subject to tight rules and specialist advice will be required before a scheme is set up. One of the main problems with self-invested schemes is that a minimum level of initial and ongoing premiums is usually required. Administrative charges and fees for investment advice can also be high.

  The members of self-invested schemes must not be able to benefit from the investment prior to retirement and transactions with members and connected persons are prohibited. This precludes the purchase of property already owned by the partnership. However, the pension scheme may purchase an office and subsequently let it to the partnership on commercial terms. Problems can also arise when partners retire or leave the scheme, as the existing partners have to find funds to pay pensions or transfers. If the membership of the scheme falls, there may also be funding difficulties.
- Where partners want to contribute more than the earnings cap, they should consider the use of Individual Savings Accounts (ISAs) if these are not being funded to the maximum extent.

Drawings

19.28 Drawings should be based on the budgeted profit shares and kept under regular review as the year progresses to avoid significantly over or underpaying the partners. Asking partners to repay drawings is never good news. If the partnership maintains a tax reserve for the partners this will need to be deducted from the drawings, as will a contingency factor to allow for variations in the profits. If capital accounts are not maintained sufficient funds should also be retained to cover the firm's working capital requirements.

19.29 It is not necessary to pay the drawings in twelve equal instalments. Everyone, partners included, likes to get a 'bonus'. Accordingly, keeping back, say, 10 per cent of the drawings to pay a 'bonus' (for example, at Christmas) engenders goodwill. If the practice pays out its current accounts, further payments may be due once the partnership accounts have been agreed.

Non-financial incentives

19.30 Non-financial factors, in particular flexible working and career progression, can be motivational. Firms should be open to a wide range of options but care must be taken to ensure that the arrangements are fair between the partners.

Holidays

19.31 Some partners want more holidays than others. The firm should offer partners a choice of taking between four and six weeks' leave each year. If the partnership also pays bonuses based on fees generated, all the partners will be fairly treated. Those who want to take more holidays receive a lower profit share.

19.32 It is important that all partners take a minimum level of holidays, otherwise they may become overworked. An alternative course of action is to value each day of holiday taken above the minimum at a cost per day and deduct it from the partner's profit share.

Part-time work

19.33 A similar arrangement could be applied to partners who do not want to work full time by deducting a set amount per day not worked from their profit share. The partner trades time for money. When calculating such a figure care must be taken with the allocation of fixed overheads such as office space. If a partner is not generating as many fees as a colleague but still has an office, the costs will be absorbed over fewer hours or lower fees. This means that the deduction for days not worked will need to be proportionately higher. Partners who want such arrangements will need to be flexible about sharing desks. A 'hot desk' arrangement may work best.

Job-sharing

19.34 Firms should explore partnership job-sharing. Two partners with similar skills could pool a portfolio of clients. This provides continual cover since holidays can be staggered. If partners have complementary skills, the clients may obtain an enhanced service. The partners would be rewarded by sharing the profit allocation. This has an advantage over part-time work since office resources will not be wasted.

Flexible working

19.35 Communications technology makes it possible for partners to work from home at least some of the time. Those undertaking specialist tax planning are better placed to do this than those running a compliance team. Tax practices should avoid a culture of long hours and promote efficient working instead. This means that as long as the work gets done and the results are achieved, it does not matter where the work is performed. It is likely to be more cost effective for a partner to spend a morning working on a tricky problem at home than to be distracted in the office.

19.36 The same principle applies to the hours worked. Some partners may prefer to be in the office at 7am to have two quiet hours before their staff arrive. In this case no partner should frown upon a colleague leaving the office in the mid-afternoon. Similarly, there will be those who prefer to work in the evening or at weekends but arrive at work later than their colleagues.

Sabbatical

19.37 Many partners (not just those with children) would enjoy and benefit from a career break. Partnerships should consider this option for partners with, say, ten years' service. The partnership will benefit from a revitalised colleague. If the sabbatical is timed for a quiet time of year (including February and March for those doing personal tax compliance) it will cause minimum disruption to the firm. The firm should ensure that a suitable adjustment is made to the profit allocation to ensure that the arrangements remain fair between the partners.

Parental leave

19.38 The partnership agreement should make suitable provision for maternity and paternity leave. A partnership that values its partners will ensure that this at least mirrors employee rights (see 12.44). Similar principles should apply to sick leave.

Career development

19.39 Some partners are motivated by career progression. This means that partnerships should be open to the opportunity to second staff to clients, government bodies or third parties. This allows tax practices to develop a wider range of experience.

19.40 Practices should encourage and assist partners taking up honorary or public appointments and providing voluntary services by allowing them time off to do so, preferably without suffering a loss of profit. Such services may include working for an organisation such as TaxAid, serving on the committee of a professional body, serving as a JP or working for a charity.

19.41 Some partners enjoy training and may be incentivised by obtaining more tax qualifications or studying (for example, for an MBA). Firms should be open to expanding their partners' knowledge. All proposals, including those for non-tax related training, should be considered favourably and without penalty to the partner concerned. For further information about training see 12.28.

Flexible package

19.42 Firms should be prepared to offer a flexible reward package to their partners in much the same way as 'menu' driven remuneration might be provided for employees.

First, at the profit sharing level, there could be an option to trade time off for a lower profit share and special rewards for productivity and responsibility. Secondly, having divided the profits equitably, the partner has a further choice about how he or she will draw the profits. The drawings package may include pensions, private medical insurance, the purchase of a car and a tax reserve combined with regular monthly drawings. Alternatively, the partner could take higher drawings and none of the extras.

Quick review

19.43

- The formula for sharing profits can be as complicated or straightforward as the firm chooses.
- For further details about bonus payments and productivity see 12.21.
- Partnership agreements are central to partners' reward packages. The terms should be reviewed periodically. Some rewards should be mandatory, for example, permanent health insurance and a minimum level of pension contributions to absolve fellow partners of further responsibility for sickness or annuities on retirement.

19.43 *Partner Reward*

- Partners may consider that setting up the arrangements mentioned in this chapter will be administratively expensive. Whilst they undoubtedly have a cost, keeping partners happy and motivated is essential and well worth a small amount of extra administration.

Chapter 20

Regulation

20.1 Tax practices have to comply with a myriad of regulations ranging from professional rules to the criminal law. Although complying with the regulations is an administrative burden, advisors who are familiar with the regulatory details can put this knowledge to good use in providing value-added service to their clients particularly in new business start-up situations. The checklist at Appendix 20:1 can be used for tax practices to ensure that their own notifications are not overlooked and to provide additional services to clients.

This chapter considers the main regulated areas affecting tax practices including:

- professional ethics;
- the *Financial Services Act*, money laundering and client money regulations;
- the *Data Protection Act*;
- Consumer credit;
- tax authorities.

Many of the issues dealt with in this chapter, particularly with regard to the *Financial Services Act*, are extremely complex. This chapter is intended for general guidance only and reference should always be made to the legislation and the advisor's professional body when considering issues relevant to a specific practice.

Professional ethics

20.2 Most tax practices are subject to the rules of one of the professional bodies. A detailed consideration of the rules and regulations of each of the professional bodies is beyond the scope of this book but all tax practitioners should know what their organisation expects of them in order to avoid falling foul of its rules and regulations. Professional bodies have the power to discipline members by fining them or excluding them from membership for breaching their codes of conduct.

20.3 *Regulation*

20.3 Regardless of which professional body the practice and its personnel belong to, operating ethically is vital to good client relationships as well as to avoid bringing the practitioner, the firm and tax practitioners generally into disrepute. Ethical behaviour for tax practitioners is accepted as including the following tenets.

- Advisors should act with integrity in all professional and business relationships. This includes honesty, fair dealing and truthfulness. For example, advisors should not recommend work to clients that they do not need and the cost/benefit of each piece of work or advice should always be considered. They should keep promises and not make ones that they cannot keep.
- Practitioners should strive for objectivity in all professional and business judgements. Areas of risk include family relationships, close business involvement, loans and hospitality.
- They should be alert for issues of independence or conflicts of interest. These may arise because of a conflict between a firm's interest and that of the client, between different clients or as a result of the receipt of commission or other benefits from a third party. One area of particular concern is between a private company and its shareholders. Where there is a conflict of interest, or a potential one, it is safest to obtain consent to act from all parties. If it is not forthcoming the firm must consider whether it can continue to act.
- Advisors should not accept or perform work which is not within their capabilities and qualifications unless they obtain suitable advice and assistance.
- They should carry out their professional work with due care, skill and diligence and with proper regard for the technical and professional standards expected of them.
- Practitioners should conduct themselves with courtesy and consideration towards all whom they come into contact with during the course of performing their work.
- Information confidential to a client acquired in the course of professional work should not be disclosed except where their consent has been obtained or there is a legal right or duty to disclose it.
- Advisors should make full disclosure of all relevant matters to the tax authorities and clients.
- They must operate within the law.
- Confidential information obtained during the course of professional work should not be used for the advantage of the advisor or a third party.

20.4 In addition to the general ethical considerations noted above, tax practitioners must also comply with the guidance laid down in 'Professional Conduct in Relation to Taxation'. These guidelines have been agreed between the main professional bodies and reviewed by the Inland Revenue and Customs and Excise. They were updated for self-assessment in March 2000 and cover the following subjects.

- Client relationships, including engagement letters (see 2.24), termination of the engagement (see Chapter 6) and making and retaining notes of meetings and telephone calls (see 15.18).
- Changes of appointment (see 2.15).
- The distinction between tax avoidance and evasion (see Chapter 8).
- Disclosure to the Revenue (see Chapter 7).
- Revenue discovery powers (see Chapter 8).
- Files and working papers (see Chapter 7 and 15.28).
- Legal professional privilege (see 15.44).
- Irregularities and errors by taxpayers (see Chapters 6 and 7).
- Tax authority errors (see Chapters 6 and 7).
- Materiality and the true and fair view.
- Money laundering (see 20.46).
- Investigation of tax accountants.

The guidance also includes a summary of the:

- notification and chargeability provisions;
- civil interest and penalties sections;
- criminal offences; and
- tax authority information powers.

20.5 Firms not only need to know about the relevant ethical considerations but they must apply them in practice. Setting a good example must come from the top. Staff should be trained to identify ethical problems. If they arise they should be discussed between the partners and the outcome communicated to personnel at a tax department meeting. Examples of contentious ethical issues include:

- fee manipulation (see 3.34);
- back-dating documentation, for example, dividend documentation to clear overdrawn directors' loan accounts;
- providing incorrect information about a child's residence for the purposes of claiming the Children's Tax Credit.

20.6 Advisors must ensure that they do not provide misleading information to the Revenue out of a misplaced desire to keep the client happy and to do their best for them. All practitioners should be aware of the provisions of

TMA 1970, s 99, which imposes penalties of up to £3,000 for assisting in the preparation of an incorrect tax return. Documents relating not only to the client in question but to all the firm's clients could be seized (see 9.39).

Financial services

20.7 It is an offence to give investment advice without authorisation under the *Financial Services Act 1986*. It is unlikely that any tax practice can avoid being registered since the definition of investment business is wide ranging. It not only includes specific advice to clients about investments and pensions but such diverse topics as commenting on the advice of an independent financial advisor and advising clients about the purchase of shares in a private company. Although generic advice is not investment business, this is not defined either in statute or the regulations and if the firm is not authorised it is easy to stray into the provision of investment business without being fully aware of it. Even if the practice is aware of the boundaries, it may frequently have to decline to comment, thereby failing to provide the full range of services expected of a tax practice.

20.8 Most tax practices are regulated for financial services by their professional body, namely the three Institutes of Chartered Accountants, The Chartered Association of Certified Accountants and the Law Society. The professional bodies have delegated power from the Securities and Investments Board (SIB) to authorise firms to carry on investment business and they may impose their rules.

20.9 Some tax practices will find that the regulatory regime laid down by their professional body is too restrictive. If so, they will usually form a separate company regulated by the Personal Investment Authority (PIA). A consideration of the requirements of the PIA is beyond the scope of this book.

20.10 The regulatory structure for financial services is currently being reorganised. In the future, registration for firms undertaking 'mainstream' investment business will be dealt with by the Financial Services Authority rather than the professional bodies. No date has yet been set for the introduction of the new system but it is expected to be before 30 June 2001.

Categories of authorisation

20.11 Tax practices should consider carefully the type of work the firm wants to undertake in deciding which category to be registered under. They must ensure that it is wide enough to meet their needs fully. For example, using the authorisation categories of the three Institutes of Chartered Accountants, those firms wanting to provide a full range of services will need to be registered under category C or D (see 10.18). Being authorised to provide advice under these categories involves demonstrating competence in financial services by passing exams. Some staff or partners may, however, be interested in doing so as a means of career progression. Category A is likely to be too restricted for the majority of firms, leaving most to be registered under category B. This is the most common category for tax practices which provide general advice to their clients as an integral part of their tax service.

20.12 All partners and staff should know the firm's registration category and what it means in practice for the day-to-day advice they can give. For example, under category B, the firm can comment on the pensions advice given by an independent financial advisor but it could not give alternative advice.

Using an independent financial advisor

20.13 Those tax practices that do not want to provide detailed financial advice in-house usually develop a relationship with one or more firms of independent financial advisors (IFAs). The best way to choose an IFA is by recommendation, for example, from another practitioner, solicitor, or client. Alternatively, the firm could use another tax practice with the appropriate authorisation. Most full-time advisors are authorised by the PIA and many are members of networks or groups which provide them with up-to-date information and compliance systems.

20.14 The practice should interview a shortlist of suitable firms and ensure that they meet the firm's requirements. The following points should be considered when making a choice.

- How long has the firm been in business?
- What qualifications do the principals hold, for example, the Advanced Financial Planning Certificate?
- How experienced are the advisors?
- Is there a rapport with them?
- How do they communicate with clients?
- Do they have an Internet site?
- Do they cover the full range of services a client is likely to need, for example, pensions, investments, mortgages, insurances?
- Do they have other useful contacts, for example, with stockbrokers?
- How do they charge clients – fees or commission?
- What rate of commission will they pay the practice?

20.15 Having decided that the IFA is suitable, the practice must have a written agreement with them, setting out:

- how the relationship is to be conducted, for example, how referrals are to be made;
- the commission sharing arrangements;
- confirming that the IFA takes full responsibility for the investment advice given to the client.

This is best done by means of an engagement letter. Suitable wordings for such letters are available from the regulators and in the *Investment Business Regulations and Guidance* published by the three Institutes of Chartered Accountants. The IFA should sign the letter and return it to the firm. The IFA is responsible for issuing each client recommended to it with an investment business engagement letter.

For further details about relationships with other professionals see 21.32.

Engagement letters

20.16 The fact that the IFA has issued the client referred to them with an engagement letter does not mean that the tax practice has no concerns about *Financial Services Act* engagement letters.

20.17 If the firm is not registered for investment business, the engagement letter should make this clear to clients.

20.18 If the firm is registered under the *Financial Services Act* and provides general investment business advice as part of its tax services but detailed advice through an IFA, the engagement letter should make this clear. It should also state that the practice may receive commission from the arrangement.

20.19 If the firm provides a full investment business service, it should issue its investment business clients with suitable engagement letters. Suitable wordings are available from the regulators and in the *Investment Business Regulations and Guidance* produced by the three Institutes of Chartered Accountants.

20.20 The engagement letter should be signed by the client and returned to the firm. For general comments on engagement letters see 2.24. Many firms find it easiest to include an investment business paragraph in their standard engagement letter rather than to issue one each time a client becomes an investment business client. This makes it less likely that relevant matters will be overlooked.

Fees versus commission

20.21 Many IFAs now prefer to charge clients a fee negotiated in advance rather than to work on a commission basis. If this is the case commission sharing arrangements will not apply. If the amount of commission received is likely to be small, accounting for it to clients may be administratively inconvenient. In this event it may be preferable to negotiate a lower charge-out rate for clients of the tax practice.

20.22 A fee basis will work better for many clients because often IFAs' charges are lower than the commission. The commission that would have been paid is then reinvested in the policy, thereby giving the client a better investment.

20.23 The only person that does not benefit from this arrangement is the tax practice. Although the connection enables the firm to offer a full range of services to its clients, the only fees it will earn are for making the introduction, attending meetings and calculating net relevant earnings. The only way round this is to bring the provision of investment business services in-house by employing suitably qualified staff and registering under a higher authorisation category or with the PIA (see 10.19).

Commission

20.24 Clients should be told about the payment of commission in the firm's engagement letter and reminded about commission and charging arrangements when discussing investment business or being referred to an IFA. When the commission is received for investment advice, it must be notified to the client and paid to them unless:

- the firm's engagement letter allows the firm to keep the commission;
- the client's contract with an associate allows the associate to keep it;
- the client agrees, after being fully informed of the amount and nature of the commission, that the firm or associate can keep it.

20.25 The practice must also inform the client of the amount of commission received as soon as possible after receipt. There are additional rules for renewal commission and commission paid to an associate.

20.26 Commission may also be received in situations other than in connection with investment business. In this case the practice must comply with the regulations laid down by its professional body. It has several choices about what to do, including to:

- account to the client for the commission (or other benefit) less its fees;
- obtain the client's consent in advance to keeping the commission;
- obtain the client's general consent in a letter of engagement –

however, before retaining the commission, the client must be given specific examples of the likely amounts involved;

- obtain the client's subsequent and express consent – this option is least acceptable because of the potential conflict of interest.

A practice will also be able to retain commission if a client, having been given full information about the commission arrangements, impliedly consents to the firm keeping it, for example, by proceeding with the transaction knowing that commission will be paid to the firm.

Clients' money regulations

20.27 In choosing its authorisation category, a tax practice must consider whether it needs to hold clients' money for investment business. If so, the firm must be authorised to hold clients' funds for investment business and comply with the regulations relating to the operation of clients' accounts.

If a firm that is not authorised to hold investment business clients' money actually does so, the money must be received and held in accordance with the regulations.

20.28 Where firms hold client investment money, they should check with their regulatory body as to the upper limit of funds that can be held. For example, the Institute of Chartered Accountants in England and Wales impose a limit of £50,000 for any one client at any one time. If the firm needs to hold more than this, it may protect the excess by purchasing a bond.

20.29 Practices must also comply with the regulations laid down by their professional body for the handling of *non-investment business* clients' money. In this situation clients' money includes fees paid in advance of the work being undertaken and clients' tax refunds paid directly to the firm (see 3.39).

20.30 For both investment business and non-investment business client money the firm should comply with the regulations relating to:

- the opening of client bank accounts and instructing the bank;
- the circumstances when funds should be paid (or transferred) into a client account;
- the circumstances when a specifically designated client account must be used;
- withdrawals from the account;
- the payment of interest;
- record keeping and reconciliations;

- the requirement for a report by an independent accountant (investment business money only).

Staff (including administration staff) and partners need to be trained in all the issues concerned with the operation of clients' accounts to avoid mistakes occurring.

Investment business services

20.31 A detailed consideration of the provision of investment business services is beyond the scope of this book but broadly firms should aim to:

- put the clients' best interests first;
- act within the professional competence of the firm;
- hold clients' assets separately from those of the firm;
- record and document all relevant transactions.

Firms should be familiar with the ten principles laid down by the SIB. These are set out in Appendix 20:2.

20.32 The specific objectives laid down in *Investment Business Regulations and Guidance*, published by the three Institutes of Chartered Accountants, are also worthy of consideration as they provide a framework for firms to follow. They cover:

- general requirements (the status and identity of the client and the firm's authorisation);
- advertising and marketing;
- using authorised third parties;
- engagement letters and fees;
- independence and conflicts of interest;
- suitability and advising clients;
- dealing for clients;
- clients' assets;
- information to clients;
- insider dealing;
- cessation of investment business.

20.33 A brief agenda for use when transacting investment business is included in Appendix 20:3.

Corporate finance

20.34 Where a client can be treated as a corporate finance client, the investment business regulations are modified. Partners and staff should be able to identify corporate finance activities and clients.

A corporate finance client is any client, whether a company, unincorporated entity or an individual, for whom the firm performs corporate finance activities. Corporate finance activities include assistance to a business or its associates in connection with the valuation of businesses or assets, raising finance, management buy-outs or buy-ins, restructuring and general corporate finance advice.

20.35 Where a firm provides investment business services to a corporate finance client a suitable engagement letter must be agreed with the client. It must include a prominent warning that the client will be treated as a corporate finance client and that, therefore, the firm does not consider it necessary to give the client the greater protection given to ordinary clients.

20.36 The following investment business provisions still apply to dealings with corporate finance clients:

- business letters;
- trustee clients;
- investment advertisements;
- independence;
- material interests and conflicts of interest;
- benefits in kind;
- best execution;
- clients' assets;
- requirement to keep records;
- insider dealing;
- cessation of investment business.

Compliance

20.37 Each firm must appoint an investment business compliance officer who is responsible for monitoring compliance with the investment business regulations. Sole practitioners are personally responsible. The compliance officer should have a good understanding of the rules and develop internal controls and procedures and ensure that they are adhered to. These must be set out in writing except where the firm is a sole practice with only one office and less than five employees.

20.38 The procedures required include the following:

- investment business training for partners and staff;
- ensuring that all partners and staff are aware of what is expected of them;
- recruiting and disciplining staff;
- maintaining personnel records to identify which principals and staff are competent in investment business and their areas of expertise;
- handling complaints – standards are laid down in the guidance;
- ensuring that partners, staff and the firm are fit and proper persons to conduct investment business.

20.39 A firm must review its compliance procedures at least once every twelve months. This should include a review of client files and the firm's books and records. A written record of the review should be retained for six years.

20.40 The practice must complete an annual return reporting the firm's investment business income and commissions, and make declarations about compliance with the investment business rules. An annual fee is payable depending on the size of the practice and its authorisation category, including an annual levy to fund a compensation scheme for investors. Firms must have professional indemnity insurance (see 16.12).

20.41 Periodically, usually assessed on the basis of risk, the firm may be inspected to ensure compliance with the rules.

Partnership changes

20.42 Where an authorised tax practice makes any changes, such as merging, dissolving or changing its name, the authorising body must be notified. A new registration may be required.

20.43 The authorising body must also be advised of changes in resources which could affect registration, any matter which calls into question the firm's fit and proper status, changes of compliance officer or failure to comply with the competence requirements.

Sole practitioners

20.44 Sole practitioner tax practices must appoint an alternate to deal with investment matters in the event of their death (see 17.6). The details of the alternate must be provided in its engagement letter.

Trustee investment business

20.45 There are specific provisions governing investment business services to trusts or estates. A consideration of these is beyond the scope of this book. For further details refer to the firm's authorising body.

Money laundering

20.46 Tax practices need procedures to deal with money laundering issues. Money laundering is the process by which criminals try to conceal the true origin and ownership of the funds derived from criminal activities (often drug trafficking) so that 'dirty' funds become 'clean'. Tax practices, along with other providers of financial services, are vulnerable to money launderers. It should be noted that tax evasion can also amount to criminal conduct and may also give rise to money laundering offences.

20.47 A tax practitioner who assists a client to obtain, conceal or retain assets which are the proceeds of criminal conduct is committing a criminal offence if they know or suspect (or in the event of terrorist funding should have known or suspected) that the client is engaged in criminal conduct. Such assistance can be liable to a fine or up to 14 years' imprisonment. It is a defence if the practitioner did not know that the arrangement related to the proceeds of criminal conduct or if they reported the suspicion to the law enforcement agencies.

20.48 A more likely scenario facing tax practices is failing to report knowledge or a *suspicion* of money laundering (from drug trafficking or terrorist activities) acquired during the course of professional work. This offence is liable to a fine or up to five years' imprisonment, as is tipping off a client or third party so as to prejudice a money laundering investigation.

20.49 All tax practices, and not just those involved in financial services, should have procedures to guard against being used by money launderers and to ensure that partners and staff are trained in the scope of the legislation and the duty to report. The duty to report may be included in general terms in the firm's letter of engagement.

20.50 In particular, the practice should ensure that when taking on a new client they see and retain a photocopy of evidence proving the client's identity and address. Ideally, they should also check their date of birth. For companies, enquiries must be made to ensure that the entity exists for a legitimate economic reason. A company search should also be carried out. The firm should draw up a list of acceptable documents for verifying both identity and address. The practice should also keep transaction records in respect of relevant financial business. All records should be kept for at least five years after the end of the firm's relationship with the client or the last transaction was completed.

20.51 The firm must appoint a Money Laundering Reporting Officer (MLRO) who decides whether to report to the authorities. For employees, simply making a report to the MLRO is sufficient to relieve them of further responsibility. Partners, however, need to ask the MLRO to confirm that a report has been made to the enforcement agencies. If it has not then, unless the suspicion is groundless, the partner may have a duty to report the knowledge or suspicion directly. Large practices may require an assistant MLRO.

20.52 If a firm is considering a report to the enforcement agencies, it may need to take legal advice. Whilst there is a defence of 'reasonable excuse' for failing to report knowledge or suspicion of money laundering, this is unlikely to extend to a threat or fear of physical violence.

20.53 Money laundering reports should be made to the Economic Crime Unit of the National Criminal Intelligence Service (NCIS), which is staffed jointly by Customs and Excise and the police. The NCIS recommend the use of a standard report form but this is not obligatory. Details of tax-related crime will be passed on to the Inland Revenue's Special Compliance Office.

20.54 The source of the information supplied to the NCIS is protected as far as the disclosure of evidence rules permit and the NCIS consider that maintaining confidentiality is of paramount importance in maintaining trust between firms and themselves. Some feedback may be given as the case progresses.

20.55 The NCIS can be contacted at the following address: PO Box 8000, Spring Gardens, Tinworth Street, London, SE11 5EN, telephone 020 7238 8607, fax 020 7238 8286.

20.56 The NCIS will usually authorise the reported transaction to continue. Such authorisation is a defence to a money laundering charge. Care should be taken when terminating an engagement under investigation that this does not 'tip off' the client concerned.

20.57 Indicators of potential money laundering include:

- transactions which have no commercial substance or appear irrational;
- transactions which are inconsistent with the client's usual activities;
- changes in the pattern of transactions;
- international transactions when the client has no obvious links with the country concerned;
- complex webs of companies and trusts.

Data protection

20.58 The *Data Protection Act 1984* requires computer users who record, use and process personal information by computer to register with the Data Protection Registrar (now the Data Protection Commissioner). The *Data Protection Act 1998* came into force on 1 March 2000 and extends the original Act to comply with EU Directives. The main change is that personal data held in structured manual filing systems is now covered by the *1998 Act*.

20.59 The application for registration is made to the Data Protection Commissioner who will take down initial details over the telephone and send out an application form tailored to the needs of the tax practice. The form should be checked to ensure that it covers all the firm's work. Once the application has been made the practice is deemed to be registered and data can be held from the date of application. The application form will then be processed and the registration confirmed.

20.60 The Data Protection Register shows what a data controller is registered to do. It can be inspected in person or searched via the Internet on www.open.gov.uk/dpr/dprhome.htm

20.61 Each registration shows the following.

- Those about whom personal data is held.
- The items of data.
- The purposes for holding it.
- The sources from which the information may be obtained.
- Those to whom it may be disclosed.
- Overseas countries to which it may be transferred.

20.62 The Data Protection Commissioner has set out a series of standard 'purposes' for which data may be held. Each purpose has a general description together with examples of typical activities which fall within the category. Those most likely to apply to a tax practice are:

- P001 – Personnel/employee administration;
- P008 – Purchaser/supplier administration;
- P013 – Customer/client administration;
- P036 – Accounting and related services (including tax);
- P038 – Other financial services;
- P039 – Legal services.

20.63 Within each purpose are a series of standard data classes. These include identification data, personal characteristics, family and social circumstances, education and skills, employment and financial details, business information and health details.

20.64 The application lasts for three years. Currently a fee of £75 is charged. Those registered under the *1984 Act* will automatically be registered under the *1998 Act* without the payment of a further fee.

20.65 The Data Protection Commissioner can be contacted at the following address: Wycliffe House, Water Lane, Wilmslow, Cheshire, SK9 5AF, telephone 01625 545740, e-mail data@wycliffe.demon.co.uk

20.66 Firms must notify the Commissioner of any changes, including mergers and changes, of address and ensure that their entry is kept up to date.

20.67 In processing data, firms must comply with eight data protection principles.

1. Personal data shall be processed fairly and lawfully.
2. It shall be obtained for one or more specific legal purposes.
3. It shall be adequate, relevant and not excessive.
4. It shall be accurate and up to date.
5. It must not be retained longer than necessary.
6. The subject of the data shall have rights of access to it and they can prevent the use of information for direct marketing and data processing if damage to them is likely to result.
7. The data shall be kept securely.
8. Data cannot be transferred to a non-EEC area unless there is adequate protection for the personal data in that country.

20.68 Individuals about whom the information is held can request a copy of the data held (for a fee of up to £10 per register entry), they can apply for it to be corrected and claim compensation for inaccurate data or unauthorised disclosure or destruction of data.

20.69 Firms must reply to a request for data within 40 days. If the data contains any codes or references these must be explained.

20.70 Failing to register or operating outside the terms of the registration is a criminal offence. The penalty can be up to £5,000 on conviction in a Magistrates' or Sheriff Court or an unlimited fine in the Crown or Sheriff Court.

Consumer credit

20.71 Tax practices are required to have a consumer credit licence under the *Consumer Credit Act 1974* if they carry on the business of consumer credit, credit brokerage, debt adjusting and counselling. Practices authorised by some professional bodies, for example, the Institute of Chartered Accountants in England and Wales or Chartered Association of Certified Accountants, are covered by a group licence as part of their membership subscription.

20.72 Some clients may have difficulty obtaining credit because of data held about them. They have a right to see their credit reference details under the *Consumer Credit Act 1974, s 158(1)*. A leaflet explaining how to check the details is available from the Office of Fair Trading (telephone 0870 606 0321). Alternatively, the two main credit reference agencies will supply an individual with his or her credit file for a £2 fee. (Call Experian on 0115 976 8747 or Equifax on 0990 143700.)

The tax authorities

20.73 The tax authorities must be notified when a new firm is set up and must also be notified of all changes to it.

Inland Revenue

20.74 Both tax practitioners and partnerships must notify the Inland Revenue of the new entity on Form CWF1. This should be done as soon as possible. If the principal or partner does not usually receive a tax return, they must notify the Inland Revenue by 5 October following the end of the tax year in which the liability arises of their need to receive one.

20.75 Partners are individually responsible for the tax due on their share of the partnership profits. The taxable profit is computed on the partnership return and transferred to the partner's personal tax return for the purposes of calculating the tax liability. New and merged practices should provide the Inland Revenue with sufficient information to understand the work it does, the way it operates or the effect of the merger. Doing so may prevent an enquiry.

20.76 The tax practice and the individual partners must keep accounting and tax records for five years ten months from the end of the tax year to which the records relate.

National Insurance

20.77 All self-employed principals and partners must pay Class 2 National Insurance unless they qualify for deferment or small earnings exception. New partners must complete the Form CWF1 to arrange payment. Payment is usually made monthly by direct debit but contributions can be paid quarterly in arrears by cheque.

VAT

20.78 Most tax practices will be either compulsorily or voluntarily VAT registered. The admission and retirement of partners does not affect the registration but changes should be notified to Customs within 30 days.

20.79 Where a sole-trader tax advisor admits a partner, this amounts to a change in the business for VAT purposes. The change must be notified to Customs within 30 days. The VAT registration can be cancelled and a new registration started but usually the registration will be transferred. In this case Form VAT 68 should be completed.

20.80 Where a merger between two firms occurs, one firm's VAT registration will usually be retained. Customs should be notified within 30 days of the merger of any change in the partnership name or address as well as being provided with details of new and retiring partners. The merging of the partnership assets will usually be treated as the transfer of a going concern and will not have any VAT consequences. The firm whose registration is cancelled must notify Customs of the merger within 30 days and submit a final VAT return.

20.81 Partners are jointly and severally liable for VAT. New partners are not liable for VAT prior to becoming partners and retiring partners are not liable after their retirement is notified to Customs.

PAYE

20.82 Practices employing staff must be registered with the Inland Revenue and have a PAYE scheme in order to deduct PAYE and National Insurance from their staff. Tax practices are required to administer the collection of student loans and make payment of the Working Families Tax Credit. Records of benefits in kind provided to staff will also need to be kept.

Quick review

20.83

- A detailed knowledge of the guidance in 'Professional Conduct in Relation to Taxation' is essential to the management of ethical issues within a tax practice. It should appear on every advisor's bookcase.

- Firms should ensure that they meet the requirements laid down by their regulatory body as to the permitted percentage of investment business fees to total fees.
- Each time a client is recommended to an IFA, the firm should retain a copy letter, e-mail or fax making it clear who is responsible for providing the investment business services.
- Firms authorised under the *Financial Services Act* must include a statement to this effect on their letterhead and on any other document issued in connection with investment business.
- If the client has given the firm permission to keep the commission and the firm agrees to offset it against the client's fees, VAT is charged on the fee net of the commission. If the client has not given the firm such permission, VAT is charged on the gross fee.
- Regulation affects all areas of a firm's work. Care should be taken to ensure that the practice does not inadvertently breach any rules or laws particularly when commencing in business or making changes to the firm.

Appendix 20:1

Checklist of Registrations and Notifications

This checklist can be used as an aide-memoire when setting up a tax practice or making partnership changes, such as admissions, retirements or mergers, thereby ensuring that no registration, notification or ethical issue is overlooked.

Chapter reference	*Action*	*Done (initials/date)*
20.2 ff	*Professional body*	
	Notify changes in partners' names and addresses	
	Ensure that the firm's procedures comply with the ethical requirements of its professional body	
7	*Tax procedures*	
	Ensure that the firm's tax procedures comply with the guidance in 'Professional Conduct in Relation to Taxation'	
20.7 ff	*Financial Services Act*	
20.8	Register	
20.11	Check that the registration covers the work undertaken by the firm	
	Notify changes in partners' names and addresses	
20.27	Ensure compliance with the client money regulations (both investment business and non-investment business)	
20.24	Ensure that the receipt of commission is dealt with properly (both investment business and non-investment business)	
20.46	Ensure that the firm has procedures to prevent money laundering	
20.39	Undertake an annual compliance review	
20.58 ff and 13	*Data Protection Act*	
20.59	Register	
20.62	Check that the registration covers all the work undertaken by the practice	
20.71	Ensure that the firm's procedures comply with the requirements of the Act. Keep the registration under review to ensure continuing compliance	

Chapter reference	*Action*	*Done (initials/date)*
20.71	*Consumer credit*	
	Ensure that the firm has a consumer credit licence or is deemed to have one by virtue of its membership of a relevant professional body	
20.73 ff	*Tax authorities*	
20.74	Notify the Inland Revenue about the new practice	
20.78	Register for VAT	
	Notify the tax authorities of changes in partners, names and addresses	
20.77	Register to pay Class 2 National Insurance	
	Employees	
20.82	Set up a PAYE scheme	
12.44	Ensure that employment contracts and practices comply with employment law	
13	*Computers*	
13.26	Ensure that all software is licensed	
14	*Office*	
14.48	Ensure compliance with health and safety legislation	
16	*Insurance*	
16.12	Obtain professional indemnity cover	
16.2	Obtain public and employee liability cover	
	Assess and obtain other insurance cover as required	
	Notify insurance companies and brokers of changes in the firm	
	Accounting and financial	
	Notify bankers, financiers and suppliers of changes in the firm	
	Clients	
	Notify clients of changes in the firm's structure	

Appendix 20:2

The SIB Principles

'1 Integrity

A firm should observe high standards of integrity and fair dealing.

2 Skill, care and diligence

A firm should act with due skill, care and diligence.

3 Market practice

A firm should observe high standards of market conduct. It should also, to the extent endorsed for the purposes of this principle, comply with any code or standard as in force from time to time and as it applies to the firm either according to its terms or by rulings made under it.

4 Information about customers

A firm should seek from customers it advises or for whom it exercises discretion any information about their circumstances and investment objectives which might reasonably be expected to be relevant in enabling it to fulfil its responsibilities to them.

5 Information for customers

A firm should take reasonable steps to give a customer it advises, in a comprehensible and timely way, any information needed to enable him to make a balanced and informed decision. A firm should similarly be ready to provide a customer with a full and fair account of the fulfilment of its responsibilities to him.

6 Conflicts of interest

A firm should either avoid any conflict of interest arising or, where conflicts arise, should ensure fair treatment to all its customers by disclosure, internal rules of confidentiality, declining to act or otherwise.

A firm should not unfairly place its interests above those of its customers and, where a properly informed customer would reasonably expect that the firm would place his interests above its own, the firm should live up to that expectation.

7 Customer assets

Where a firm has control of or is otherwise responsible for assets belonging to a customer which it is required to safeguard, it should arrange proper protection for them, by way of segregation and identification of those assets or otherwise, in accordance with the responsibility it has accepted.

8 Financial resources

A firm should ensure that it maintains adequate financial resources to meet its investment business commitments and to withstand the risks to which its business is subject.

9 Internal organisation

A firm should organise and control its internal affairs in a responsible manner, keeping proper records, and where the firm employs staff or is responsible for the conduct of investment business by others, should have adequate arrangements to ensure that they are suitable, adequately trained and properly supervised and that it has well-defined compliance procedures.

10 Relations with regulators

A firm should deal with its regulators in an open and co-operative manner and keep the regulators promptly informed of anything concerning the firm which might reasonably be expected to be disclosed to them.'

Appendix 20:3

Agenda for Providing Investment Business Services

The following checklist provides an aide-memoire to ensure that no relevant issues are overlooked when providing investment business services to clients.

- Obtain and record information about the client's personal and financial situation (consider using the checklist in Appendix 2:4).
- Find out and record the client's investment objectives and their attitude to risk.
- Send them an engagement letter and obtain their written agreement to it.
- Discuss commission (or fee) arrangements and obtain the client's agreement to them.
- Give advice and risk warnings. Record it. Disclose any commission payable.
- Record the client's instructions and pass them on to brokers.
- Advise the client of the transactions carried out.
- Record the handling of title documents.

Chapter 21

Other Professionals

21.1 From time to time every practitioner will be faced with a case beyond his or her capabilities. When this happens it is important to know who to contact. The first part of the chapter considers the use of experts and counsel.

Firms may also be approached by clients who are unsuitable for them either because their affairs are too complex or large, or because they are too small and cannot afford the firm's fees. This chapter considers the options available to firms.

Finally, the chapter considers the firm's relationship with the tax authorities, government departments and other professionals such as solicitors, bankers, stockbrokers, independent financial advisors, computer consultants and surveyors.

Experts

21.2 Firms must only offer advice within the limits of their competence but the increasingly complex tax system makes it unlikely that, with the exception of very large firms, they will be able to deal with every situation that arises or answer every question that clients pose. It is therefore important for them to have a list of experts to call on.

Before using a particular expert, the practice needs to ensure that they are suitable for both the client and firm's needs. The firm should also have a procedure so that all consultations are made through a partner or with the knowledge of the head of the tax function (depending on the size of the firm).

21.3 Experts can be found in a variety of ways including the following.

- Seeking a recommendation from another professional.
- Using the expert services offered by training and marketing groups (there are several of these).
- Contacting the practitioner's professional body. For example, the Tax Faculty of the ICAEW offers its members a 'hotline' referral system. For a nominal fee of £20 plus VAT an approved consultant

will offer 15 minutes of advice. If the problem cannot be resolved within this period, further services will be subject to the advisor's normal commercial terms.

The firm may require a number of different contacts to cover a variety of specialist areas, in particular VAT and investigations.

21.4 Where the expert is used simply to check or confirm the practice's view, and where no confidential information about the client is disclosed, there is no need to tell the client and the firm assumes full responsibility for the advice. In this case the firm should ensure that it keeps detailed notes of the telephone conversation with the specialist.

21.5 Where an expert is consulted either at the client's request or where the problem is beyond the firm's experience, it should seek the client's approval to disclose confidential information to a third party. This consent could be included in the firm's engagement letter. The client should also be advised of the reason for contacting a specialist and the cost, including the cost of the firm's time in liaising with the expert. The practice should make it clear to the client who is responsible for the advice by having suitably worded engagement letters with both the client and the expert and by checking the wording of reports.

21.6 Where the situation goes beyond a firm's expertise but the client refuses to seek an expert opinion, the firm must consider whether it can continue to act for the client (see 6.20). If it does continue to act, the firm must emphasise the limitations of its advice and include strong disclaimers if necessary.

Counsel

21.7 Sometimes the most suitable expert will be a tax barrister. The tax Bar now operates more flexibly and in a wider range of circumstances than just advocacy. For example, many chambers will allow a telephone discussion of a short point if pre-arranged with the Clerk to the Chambers. In this case the advisor should enquire whether there will be a written summary of Counsel's opinion. Full written opinions tend to be expensive.

21.8 The Tax Faculty of the Institute of Chartered Accountants in England and Wales (ICAEW) operates a joint advisory scheme whereby its members can obtain telephone or fax advice from the Revenue Bar Association for a fixed fee. The scheme is most suitable for a discussion of short points capable of explanation over the telephone. A fax containing not more than one side of A4 paper can be sent in advance and a call can be made to the Clerk of the Chambers to arrange a mutually convenient time for the discussion. The cost of this service is £75 per hour plus VAT, subject to a minimum of £30 plus VAT. The charge will include the time spent on the telephone and to make a note of the call which will be signed and sent to the member. Therefore, it is likely that a half-hour telephone call will be charged as one hour. If the case is too complicated to be handled in this way, the Clerk will provide an estimate of the likely fee.

21.9 If the client's problem involves more than the discussion of a short point, the firm may need to brief Counsel formally. Many tax sets offer advisors a preliminary discussion to establish whether there is a problem or not before formal instructions are submitted. Fixed fee and success fee arrangements can also be discussed. Most members of the tax Bar are happy to advise on all areas of tax. The Clerk may suggest who would be most helpful to the case in hand.

21.10 For a tax practitioner to brief Counsel directly there are three conditions which must be met:

- the advisor must be a member of a recognised body;
- he or she must brief Counsel personally and not in the name of the firm;
- the brief must be confined to areas of the advisor's expertise, for example, a tax matter and not a personal injury case.

21.11 When formally briefing Counsel, the advisor should:

- expressly state what questions Counsel is to advise on, or whether they are to consider the matter generally;
- indicate what form their response should take, for example, in writing, by fax or in conference;
- include a list of the documents sent;
- make it clear who is the party concerned;
- specify any dates set for appearance at the Commissioners or VAT tribunal;
- summarise the issues and facts concisely;
- give details of any relevant cases or statute.

21.12 The Tax Faculty of the ICAEW and the Chartered Institute of Taxation operate a special advocacy scheme to enable their members to secure the services of members of the Revenue Bar Association (RBA) to represent them in straightforward cases at the General and Special Commissioners and at VAT tribunals. It should be noted that there is nothing to stop a tax practitioner appearing for his or her client at the General Commissioners or even in some situations before the Special Commissioners. The most suitable cases for the special advocacy scheme are:

- those which involve a short legal or technical point – cases lasting more than one day are unsuitable;
- those where the tax at stake is under £40,000;
- small back duty and penalty cases;
- surcharge and serious mis-declaration cases.

To use the scheme the initial contact should be made to the Clerk to the Chambers. The Clerk should be advised that the member wishes to use the scheme, the member's name, location, date and time of the case and key details about it.

The RBA member will read the case papers and decide if it is appropriate to be dealt with under the scheme. They will give advice as to what needs to be done to prepare for the case, attend the hearing and represent the taxpayer.

Under the scheme they will charge a standard fee of £500 plus VAT. If the case does not proceed they will charge £350 plus VAT. In some cases additional fees or expenses will be negotiated.

21.13 *Taxation* magazine regularly publishes lists of tax Counsel. For further information about using Counsel, including details of their websites, see *Taxation*, vol. 144, no. 3735, 2 December 1999, page 211 and *Taxation*, vol. 144, no. 3743, 10 February 2000, page 413.

Other tax advisors

21.14 If a firm has thought carefully about the type of clients it wants and has a new business strategy, it will know whether a potential new client is right for the firm. If the firm does not want to accept a new client for reasons of size, expertise or economics, it is professional and courteous to have other firms to recommend instead. Such an arrangement can benefit both the firm and the other practice if both parties recommend clients to each other.

It is useful to cultivate links with a range of different firms, according to the practice's needs. These might include a large firm, international practice, smaller firm, sole practitioner and a niche or specialist practice. See 21.2 and 6.27 for further details about developing links with suitable firms.

Voluntary agencies

21.15 The situation may occasionally arise where the tax practice is unable to help an existing or prospective client because they cannot afford the firm's (or any other tax practice's) fees. Some firms will accept a small amount of low fee or 'pro-bono' work but where this is not possible the firm should know who to refer the client to.

21.16 In making the referral, the firm must first assess the client's problem. In straightforward situations directing the taxpayer to an Inland Revenue tax enquiry centre may be the right course of action (see 21.21). Where the matter is too complex, it may be appropriate to recommend the client to TaxAid. Other advice agencies, Citizens Advice Bureaux and charities often refer cases to TaxAid where they can not help, so rather than refer clients to these organisations, a direct referral to TaxAid may be preferable.

TaxAid

21.17 TaxAid is a charity which provides free, confidential tax advice and assistance to persons in financial need and promotes public education in tax matters. It is staffed by volunteer qualified tax professionals. All meetings are by appointment only.

TaxAid can offer advice on most tax problems, including tax demands, arrears, self-employed accounts, tax codes, allowances, tax returns, refunds, investigations and Revenue maladministration.

21.18 TaxAid operates as follows.

- First they ask the caller questions to confirm that they lack the financial means to pay for help.
- Then they enquire about the problem and try to offer advice over the telephone wherever possible. Many straightforward problems can be solved this way.
- If the problem is complicated, the caller will be offered an appointment at the charity's London offices where they will be seen by a qualified tax advisor.
- The organisation's approach is to encourage and support self-help. The advisor will discuss the problem with the client and then advise them about their situation and what action they can take. A follow-up visit or telephone calls may be necessary.
- If the problem is too complex, the advisor may enter into negotiations with the tax authorities on the client's behalf.

TaxAid have considerable experience in tax debt and offer support to tax practices who are providing free help to clients with tax arrears.

21.19 TaxAid can be contacted at the following address: Linburn House, 342 Kilburn High Road, London, NW6 2QJ, telephone (advice) 020 7624 3768 between 10am and 12 midday Monday–Thursday, telephone (administration) 020 7624 5216, fax 020 7624 5248, e-mail: mail@taxaid.org.uk

It should be noted that TaxAid could not operate without considerable financial support from the tax profession, including donations of time and money.

Citizens Advice Bureaux

21.20 Citizens Advice Bureaux offer free, independent advice on a wide range of issues. All advisors have some tax training and may be able to help with entitlement to allowances, benefits, form completion and correspondence. Some offices may have more experienced volunteers; others will refer the taxpayer to an appropriate third party for help, for example, to TaxAid.

Inland Revenue

21.21 Sometimes the best advice to clients or prospective clients is to refer them directly to the Revenue. For example, where:

- the client cannot afford to pay for professional advice;
- the client wants to keep their costs down and they are capable of handling the matter themselves;
- the firm has an arrangement with the client to help them to help themselves rather than doing everything for them.

The best way to make referrals to the tax authorities is to direct clients to the helplines or to a tax enquiry centre.

Helplines

21.22 The tax authorities operate a number of helplines covering a variety of issues. In particular they are useful for new businesses and employers dealing with the increasingly complex PAYE regime. The helpline numbers are included in Appendix 21:1.

Inland Revenue Enquiry Centres

21.23 The Inland Revenue began reorganising its offices in 1993 and aims to have converted all offices by 2002. Under the new structure:

- Taxpayer Services Offices (TSO) combine personal self-assessment with preliminary collection;
- Tax District Offices (TDO) handle corporation tax, in-depth accounts examination, local recovery and fully-trained Inspector work;
- Integrated Offices (IO) cover the work of both a TSO and TDO.

All TSO, TDO and IO offices have an Inland Revenue Enquiry Centre.

The addresses for these are available in *Tolley's Tax Office Directory 2000*.

21.24 Enquiry centres can help taxpayers in the following ways:

- answering enquiries and providing help over the telephone or face to face;
- providing specialist help;
- supplying leaflets and forms;
- accepting payment where a taxpayer needs to pay locally.

21.25 Great care should be taken when referring clients to Inland Revenue Enquiry Centres because they cannot, by definition, be independent or help taxpayers to plan their affairs in a tax efficient way.

Tax authorities

21.26 The firm will also have to deal with the Revenue on behalf of its clients. It is essential to maintain a professional and courteous relationship with the tax authorities. This will be done by:

- submitting clients' returns on time;
- producing accurate returns;
- handling enquiries and appeals correctly;
- dealing with correspondence quickly and in full or providing an explanation if there is to be a delay;
- not providing misleading or incorrect information;
- by being polite both in correspondence and on the telephone.

21.27 The relationship with the Inland Revenue is subject to the rules of the advisor's professional body and in particular to the guidance set out in 'Professional Conduct in Relation to Taxation' (see 20.4).

Maintaining a professional relationship does not mean that the firm cannot be robust in its handling of enquiries (see Chapter 9).

If the Revenue is dissatisfied with the quality of a tax advisor's work and where there are persistent mistakes, they will raise the matter with the firm and may request a meeting. If matters do not improve, they will refer the matter to the advisor's professional body.

21.28 Many firms will have few dealings with the General or Special Commissioners under self-assessment. Cases will now relate to specific facts or technical issues rather than 'delay' hearings and specialist advice from an expert or Counsel may be required (see 21.7).

Occasionally firms may have dealings with the Special Compliance Office (see 9.36) or other specialist departments, such as the Share Valuations Division. If the firm is unfamiliar with the workings of the department concerned, specialist help may be needed.

Revenue Adjudicator

21.29 From time to time the standards of the tax authorities will fall short of those outlined in their codes of practice. If a complaint is justified it should be made to the officer concerned or to his or her superior if the outcome of the complaint is unsatisfactory. If the firm and/or taxpayer are still unhappy, a complaint should be made to the Revenue Adjudicator. Care must be taken to raise only genuine grievances.

21.30 The work of the Adjudicator's office covers complaints about the Inland Revenue, National Insurance Contributions Office, Customs and Excise, and the Valuation Office Agency. The Adjudicator acts as an impartial referee in cases involving delays, poor or misleading advice, mistakes and the exercise of Revenue discretion. Both sides of the complaint are heard and if it is justified the Adjudicator may make recommendations about putting matters right. The remedies available include issuing an apology, compensation, consolatory payments and forgone tax and interest. Their recommendations are independent and free.

For further information, see *Taxation*, vol. 145, no. 3762, 22 June 2000.

21.31 The Adjudicator can be contacted at the following address: Haymarket House, 28 Haymarket, London, SW1Y 4SP, telephone 020 7930 2292, fax 020 7930 2298.

Other professionals

21.32 Clients expect their tax advisor to have a variety of contacts with other professionals, such as solicitors, banks and independent financial advisors. Cultivating such relationships is essential to providing clients with a full service and the relationship may work both ways, with the other professionals recommending work to the firm.

Contacts with other professionals can be made in a variety of ways including recommendations by other tax practices and meetings at Chambers of Commerce and clubs.

21.33 Before making referrals it is important to find out the type of work or clients that the other professional is seeking so that their time is not wasted by inappropriate recommendations. This works both ways. If they are likely to refer clients to the firm, it is important to clarify what work the firm wants and any areas of expertise. It is a good idea to have a meeting at the other professional's offices to discuss formally their services, charges and ways of working and to obtain supplies of their leaflets and brochures.

21.34 The firm should establish procedures for making recommendations tailored to the specific relationship. They can be informal where occasional recommendations are made to a surveyor or computer consultant but will need to be formalised where investment business is involved (see 20.15).

21.35 The practice should always remain professional and impartial in making a recommendation and it should certainly not feel under any obligation to do so. All referrals should be made on the basis of merit and because the firm believes that the other professional can provide a cost effective and efficient service to their client.

21.36 In all cases the firm should make it clear to the client that it is simply effecting an introduction and it is up to the client to decide whether or not they want to use their services. Care should be taken not to introduce problem clients, as this may be very poor PR for the firm.

21.37 Tax advisors will also be required to liaise with a client's other advisors in the course of handling their affairs. For the most part such interaction is unlikely to cause complications but the following points should be borne in mind.

- Do not provide confidential information without the client's prior consent.
- If the contact is being made for the first time, confirm with the client that the firm may discuss matters with the other professional.
- Make sure that all parties understand who is responsible for the work.
- Do not exceed the remit of a tax practice by undertaking work done by another professional. For example, the *Solicitors Act 1974* makes it illegal for certain documents to be drawn up by persons who are not solicitors, although they could be drafted by someone else and sent to the solicitor for approval and completion.

Other regulatory bodies

21.38 Tax practices can be a useful source of information for clients. The firm should assess its clients' needs and refer them, where necessary, to appropriate organisations. The firm should maintain an up-to-date contact list (including websites and e-mail addresses) of regulatory bodies, agencies and other business contacts. Details of many organisations are available in publications such as *Butterworths Tax Compliance Manual*. Large practices may produce their own contact lists and these can be made available to all personnel on the computer system. The information could also be provided to clients on the firm's website, including relevant links to other sites.

21.39 The information categories to include on such a list are:

- Companies House;
- professional organisations, for example, the Law Society;
- trade associations, for example, the National Federation of Builders;
- national business associations, for example, the CBI, Institute of Directors, Federation of Small Businesses;
- local business associations, for example, Chambers of Commerce, Business Links;
- government departments, for example, the DTI, Legal Aid Board;
- employee relations, for example, ACAS, employment tribunals;
- charities and Housing Associations, for example, the Charity Commission;
- consumer issues, for example, the Office of Fair Trading, public utility regulators;
- standards regulators, for example, British Standards Institution, Patents Office;
- computer issues, for example, the Data Protection Commissioner, National Computing Centre.

Quick review

21.40

- Practitioners should learn to judge when they need help on a case and know the limit of their abilities.
- There is no disgrace in consulting others for an opinion. Start with fellow partners and, if they cannot help, seek the view of an expert.
- Consider using the readers' questions pages in tax magazines but take care not to rely solely on the advice.
- Maintain high ethical standards when dealing with other professionals (see 20.2).

Appendix 21:1

Tax Authority Helplines

	Telephone
Inland Revenue, Customs and Excise and National Insurance	
Joint helpline for employers, including Working Families Tax Credit and VAT registration (Monday–Friday 8.30am–5pm)	0345 143143
Electronic Business Unit	
Helpdesk for electronic services – PAYE, self-assessment and the construction industry (e-mail helpdesk@ir-efile.gov.uk)	0845 60 55 999
Inland Revenue	
Enterprise Support Initiative (Weekdays 8am–8pm, Sunday 10am–4pm)	0845 6070143
Self-assessment helpline (Monday–Sunday 8am–10pm)	0645 000444
Employers Construction Industry Scheme	0345 335588
National Minimum Wage	0845 845 0360
National Insurance	
Class 1A	06451 55176
Contracted-out Employment Group	06451 50150
Self-employment/Class 2	06451 54655
International Services	06451 54811

Chapter 22

Conclusion: The Future

22.1 Over the last six years tax practitioners have had to deal with many changes, including self-assessment, increased computerisation, the impact of the Internet and a tax system which is more complex than ever before. This chapter suggests ten challenges which the tax profession may face in the future. It also demonstrates how firms can use the ideas in this book to meet them and to survive into the twenty-second century.

Internet services

22.2 The Internet is probably the single most important challenge. No aspect of tax practice is likely to change as significantly over the next few years.

Some firms already have websites but most are still using them as a shop window or as an alternative means of advertising. They can and must become fee generators and service providers in the brave new world of the future.

22.3 As soon as Filing By Internet (FBI) encompasses agents and allows for the digital signing of returns, a full tax compliance service can be provided on the Internet. Consider how it could operate.

Clients will be alerted by e-mail of the need to complete a tax return. They will be able to log-on to the firm's website to find out what information they need to complete the form and then enter it onto their own secure page. The advisor will work on the information and finalise the return. It can then be viewed by the client, approved and digitally signed. Once the advisor is happy that the return is complete, it will be sent to the Revenue by e-mail. Clients and advisors will be able to view the statement of account on an ongoing basis.

22.4 The Revenue needs to iron out the FBI teething problems and overcome consumer mistrust of encryption technology before Internet tax compliance services will be fully viable. Internet banking has already taken off and tax services seem set to follow in the very near future. In spite of the Revenue's assurances to the contrary, manual returns will eventually be abolished; the only issue is how long it will take.

22.5 Bureau services are already operated over the Internet and this will eventually become the norm, with the firm, client and possibly even the Revenue having access to the firm's payroll and accounting systems. Shared tax service centres may become more common. Bureaux and tax compliance centres will be increasingly operated abroad in countries where salaries are lower.

22.6 Corporate reporting will take place via a company's website and firms will play a vital role in the quality assurance of the financial information disseminated over the Internet.

22.7 Many more websites will provide 'pay for use' interactive software. This could be used by firms in a variety of ways including the following.

- To provide answers to the common questions such as 'do I have to charge VAT on international services?' and 'will I get tax relief on a certain expense?'.
- To perform comparative calculations. For example, comparing the cost of leasing or buying a car, reviewing the consequences of changing a business's year-end or to compare the different options in a remuneration package.
- To aid decision-making and choice management by outlining the financial and tax consequences of a course of action, for example, with regard to investments and business or lifestyle options.
- To register a client for VAT or with the Inland Revenue. For example, a client considering VAT registration could enter information about their last twelve months' income to check whether they need to register. They would then complete the application form on-line and download an appropriate accounting system to help them keep accurate records and complete their VAT returns, which will, of course, also be completed and submitted via the Internet.

22.8 Internet filing of returns and interactive software is already here. The Inland Revenue has already used interactive software in a limited way on their website. In future clients may not call the firm for advice in the first instance but instead access the firm's website and pay by credit card for using it to solve their problems. They will only e-mail or call the practice if they cannot find the answer.

Simply supplying information is no longer the preserve of the expert but applying it is. If clients want cost effective help delivered electronically, firms must address how they can provide that service before another practice does.

22.9 Wider use of the Internet will allow radical change in the provision of tax services. For many taxpayers, seeing their tax advisor is on a par with a visit to the dentist. Firms must work hard to overcome this barrier. Making clients feel more at ease when dealing with their tax affairs will encourage them to spend longer at the firm, during which time they can be sold additional products and services.

22.10 Consider running a tax practice from a cyber-café. It could offer a range of services from helping taxpayers to complete their own returns via the practice's website (complete with targeted advertising) to a full tax compliance service provided 'while you wait' for those who want or need it. Charges would be menu driven.

Such an operation offers ample scope to sell clients additional services whilst the return is completed and the tax café could become a centre for other people to offer complementary services. This could be done either by charging them rent or by setting up a series of franchises. They could be related to the firm's client base and examples of possible services include:

- business counselling;
- Internet-based training;
- a bookshop selling business and self-help books;
- a computer shop selling equipment and software;
- a coffee shop/restaurant;
- gallery/exhibition space;
- alternative practitioners offering relaxing treatments such as massage or reflexology.

For further information about the Internet see Chapter 13. See Chapter 10 for a consideration of the alternative services that a tax practice could offer its clients. See Chapter 14 about creating a conducive office environment.

Changes in work patterns

22.11 The second challenge is intrinsically linked to the first. Society has partly changed because of the Internet but the Internet has developed because of those changes. Its widespread use will fundamentally affect work patterns and the way in which firms offer their services.

22.12 We increasingly live in a 24-hour society. The Internet facilitates this and many services are now available round the clock. The Inland Revenue is already offering weekend and evening helplines (see Appendix 21:1). Firms need to adapt to client demand by developing their websites and providing services in the evening and at weekends. Doing so does not have to be the burden it sounds. This way of working will suit many partners and members of staff who want to have a greater choice of the hours they work and to get away from the nine to five routine.

22.13 Offering a 24-hour service does not mean that it has to be provided from the firm's offices. E-mail and telephone help can be provided by personnel working from home on a rota basis. This could offer practitioners greater flexibility in combining their work and domestic lives and may reduce the stress that the current long-houred, office-based culture engenders.

22.14 If the firm provides the Internet services envisaged above, there is little reason for practitioners to work from the firm's offices. Many 'meetings' could take place over the Internet by using web-cameras and, in time, virtual reality headsets. Firms will be able to pay for this equipment by having smaller offices since they will only be used for meetings not conducted by other means.

22.15 Practitioners based from home will save time and money on commuting. For those who want the social connections that the workplace offers, there could be neighbourhood offices set up to provide desk-space and computer facilities for personnel from many different companies. Work will no longer be a place; it will be an activity.

For further information about flexible working see Chapters 12 and 19. For a consideration of working from home see Chapter 14.

Competition

22.16 Competition is the third challenge. It has yet to materialise in the way that was advocated following the introduction of self-assessment. At that time it was predicted that the market would be flooded by cheap tax shops and large tax return providers such as American Express and the banks. However, it would be wrong to be complacent.

- Franchise-based tax shops are still being set up and promoted on the basis that simply being numerate and a good communicator are the only skills required.
- It would appear that the larger providers have not entered the market because tax return completion in the UK is not universal, Internet filing by agents is not mandatory and because of the high proportion of self-employed taxpayers. These constraints could change.
- The current trend for the consolidation of mid-tier firms may bring competition from another source.

22.17 Firms can best defend their position by offering an integrated tax service and excellent client care. This may require changes in their internal structure, for example, a move to an 'account manager' approach where one person in the firm is responsible for the client's affairs.

22.18 Partners would initially appear to be obvious 'account managers' but to do this job well they will have little time to undertake actual client work or to manage the practice. Some partners' skills are technical or administrative, and firms will benefit from exploiting their partners' skills rather than expecting them to be good at everything.

22.19 Tax practices should consider appointing 'account managers' who are not necessarily partners. This will enable smaller firms to offer a more structured career progression to their senior employees. The account manager would co-ordinate with the other team members to deliver the required services and bring in and manage fees. In order to maximise the fees from clients and to service their needs, the person appointed requires the ability and time to think creatively. Using an account manager will make the firm client focused, which in turn should maximise the fees generated from them.

For further information about client care refer to the chapters in Part I.

Joining forces with others

22.20 Internal change alone may not be enough to enable small practices to remain competitive and match the larger firms on expertise and breadth of service. Developing Internet and new services is costly and may only be achieved by joining forces with other firms in a similar position. The future will inevitably see tax practitioners working in bigger firms but more flexibly. Working with others is the fourth challenge. It can be achieved not only by merging with other firms but in a variety of other ways.

Multi-disciplinary practices

22.21 Multi-disciplinary practices incorporate practitioners from other professions, primarily lawyers and independent financial advisors, so that the firm becomes a one-stop business advisor able to handle all aspects of a client's affairs. The larger firms have already taken on legal teams with mixed results. Such arrangements are fraught with difficulties, not least regulation and potential conflicts of interest.

'Chambers'

22.22 A better alternative would be to work as barristers do, in 'chambers' of complementary advisors. This would suit many small firms and sole practitioners. It would provide a means of sharing office space and allows for communal facilities such as meeting rooms and administrative support. Clients and firms would have access to a range of advisors, cases could be referred between them on normal commercial terms and independence would not be an issue.

Networks

22.23 Membership of a network gives a firm access to the resources that are available internally to larger practices without sacrificing their independence. The benefits of joining an existing network, or setting up a new one, include:

- it will have the resources to develop new and innovative services;
- it has access to industry and technical expertise;
- it will give the firm national and international links.

Consolidators

22.24 As tax and the business world becomes ever more complex and clients more demanding, some firms may find their resources stretched too far. One way round this is to join a consolidator. Their attraction is:

- strong management;
- shared administration;
- the possible chance for partners to realise their investment in the practice (but not if it is a merger of firms);
- better staff recruitment and retention;
- wider skills base;
- the potential for capital growth.

It would seem that the consolidators are only interested in firms with a turnover of several million pounds, high partner profitability and growth potential. Even if the practice meets those criteria joining a consolidator is fraught with problems. Until the firm knows who else will be involved, it may be highly risky to sell out to such an organisation and then be tied into it. It is unlikely to be an exit route. The consolidator will want the firm's ongoing skills and there is no guarantee of a sufficient or better return.

For further information see Chapters 14, 17, 20 and 21.

Stability and sustainability

22.25 Partners, staff and clients find the current culture of reorganisation stressful. Firms are constantly reorganising to stay on top. Many are in the process of one, thinking about one or getting over it. The fifth challenge is how to achieve long-term stability without the need for frequent change.

Sustainability can be achieved through good management, designing a strategy and developing the right client relationships.

Firms need strong, trained management as well as good tax practitioners. These are two separate jobs and few people do both well. The firm may need to bring in outside managers who are not necessarily tax practitioners.

22.26 The firm must also set a strategy that encompasses short and long-term goals. As long as the firm is achieving its goals and aims, it matters little what work the firm does or how large it is. Each firm will ultimately find the level it wants to be at. Those firms in most danger are those that are unfocused.

22.27 Managing client relationships is a two-way process. Clients are demanding and increasingly so, but if they receive an excellent service and client care, they will keep coming back for more. The firm should concentrate on obtaining and retaining those clients who want advice and an ongoing relationship, not just a pure compliance service. The challenge is to move beyond preparing tax returns efficiently. Soft skills and good communication have never been more important in the management of a practice. Firms should put clients at the centre of their practice, not the tax system or office administration. If advisors can understand something of their clients' psychology and develop a rapport with them they will instinctively know what tax planning and general business advice an individual client needs and how best to present it.

For further information about practice structure see Chapter 17. For information about client care refer to the chapters in Part I.

Fees

22.28 The sixth challenge is to make firms more profitable. They can only adapt to change and invest in IT, new services and training if they can increase their fees. Many firms have so far failed to benefit financially from self-assessment or their expenditure on computers and software.

Practices should not be afraid to charge for good service. All firms should consider increasing their charge-out rates significantly. Even if 20 per cent of the clients leave, the firm will still be better off. It will have more time to service those clients and be available to take on new and better paying work in the future.

For further information see Chapters 3, 18 and 19.

A thirst for knowledge

22.29 Embracing life-long learning is the seventh challenge. A detailed technical knowledge of tax is only one aspect of being a tax practitioner. The most successful advisors will be those who keep up with latest thinking and abreast of technology, both from the point of view of managing the practice and advising clients. Those with specialist knowledge will be particularly well placed. Knowledge and experience of all aspects of life and business practice can help advisors provide a better service to their clients. Consider the following.

- Joining a special interest group through a professional body or network, for example, farming, entertainment, solicitors and the medical profession.
- Training for a related qualification, for example, investment advisor or counsellor.
- Studying for an MBA or undertaking other management training.
- Applying for the ICAEW advanced diplomas.
- Taking the ATII exams.
- Improving computer skills.
- Identifying personal weaknesses and learning relevant skills such as note-taking, speed-reading and presentation.

For further information see Chapter 12.

A simpler tax system

22.30 The eighth challenge is to develop alternative services to offer to clients in the event that the tax system is simplified.

The current tax system is highly complex with numerous different tax rates, complicated rules on expenses, the distinction between being employed and self-employed, taper relief and an intricate VAT regime, to name but a few. It may not always be so. The system is already creaking dangerously and although it would be a brave and bold move, the system could be subject to wholesale reorganisation.

22.31 In some ways the process has already started with The Tax Law Rewrite Project and although it has so far been slow to deliver, it may eventually provide simpler tax law. Clients will then expect a cheaper and more certain response from their advisors.

IR35 has seen the introduction of a flat 5 per cent tax deduction into the system and this could be extended to other situations.

For further information see Chapters 7, 8 and 10.

Self-assessment

22.32 Self-assessment for both individuals and companies is now implemented and largely under control but its full impact is yet to be felt, particularly with regard to enquiries. Managing these is the ninth challenge.

The Inland Revenue is putting increasing resources into enquiry work and this will have an impact on all practices. In the future discovery and disclosure will be major issues, as will the consequences for professional indemnity insurance claims. Firms need to manage the risk that this issue presents.

For further information see Chapters 7, 9 and 16.

Regulation

22.33 The tenth challenge is regulation. Regulation of the tax profession seems almost inevitable following the increase in the audit threshold and the consequent need to find alternative services, combined with increased competition from unqualified advisors. Regulation by the professional bodies will ensure consistent standards and denote the mark of a quality tax practice. The fact that the Inland Revenue is, on a trial basis, reporting firms whose tax work is unacceptable to the professional bodies may be the first stage in the process. Adopting the practices recommended in this book will help firms to satisfy the regulators' requirements.

For information about quality control, refer to Chapter 11. See Chapters 7 and 15 for information about tax and office procedures.

22.34 The challenges outlined in this chapter are far from fanciful. Many of them are already here, albeit only in part. The tax profession, together with the work and business environment generally, will continue to change significantly throughout the twenty-first century. The tax profession has already proved how adaptable it can be. The ultimate challenge will be to turn future change to its advantage.

Index